A. E. HOUSMAN
A REASSESSMENT

A. E. Housman

A Reassessment

Edited by

Alan W. Holden

and

J. Roy Birch

First published in Great Britain 2000 by
MACMILLAN PRESS LTD
Houndmills, Basingstoke, Hampshire RG21 6XS and London
Companies and representatives throughout the world

A catalogue record for this book is available from the British Library.

ISBN 0–333–65803–5

First published in the United States of America 2000 by
ST. MARTIN'S PRESS, INC.,
Scholarly and Reference Division,
175 Fifth Avenue, New York, N.Y. 10010

ISBN 0–312–22318–8

Library of Congress Cataloging-in-Publication Data
A.E. Housman : a reassessment / edited by Alan W. Holden and J. Roy
Birch.
p. cm.
Includes bibliographical references and index.
ISBN 0–312–22318–8 (cloth)
1. Housman, A. E. (Alfred Edward), 1859–1936—Criticism and
interpretation. I. Holden, Alan W., 1926– . II. Birch, J. Roy.
PR4809.H15A849 1999
821'.912—dc21   99–12180
                                                              CIP

This book is printed on paper suitable for recycling and made from fully managed and
sustained forest sources.

10   9   8   7   6   5   4   3
09 08 07 06 05 04 03 02 01

Printed and bound in Great Britain by
Antony Rowe Ltd, Chippenham, Wiltshire

Contents

Acknowledgements

Grateful acknowledgements for copyright permissions in the UK are due to:

- the Society of Authors as the literary representative of the Estate of A. E. Housman;
- Random House UK Limited for the use of the poem 'A worm fed on the heart of Corinth', by Isaac Rosenberg (from *The Collected Poems of Isaac Rosenberg*, eds Bottomley and Harding, Chatto & Windus, 1937, re-issued 1979, ed. I. Parsons);
- the poem 'A. E. H.' (Copyright © 1979 Kingsley Amis) is reprinted by kind permission of Jonathan Clowes Ltd, London, on behalf of the Kingsley Amis Literary Estate.

For copyright permission in the USA:

- From: THE COLLECTED POEMS OF A. E. HOUSMAN by A. E. Housman, Copyright 1939, 1940, © 1965 by Henry Holt and Company, Inc., © 1967 by Robert E. Symons. Reprinted by permission of Henry Holt and Company, Inc.

Grateful thanks are also due to Jeremy Crow, at the Society of Authors, for his help and courtesy throughout, and to Charmian Hearne and Julian Honer, at Macmillan, for their help and patience. Many thanks also to Elnora Ferguson for compiling the index, and Cathy Scoffield for typing the text.

Notes on the Contributors

John Bayley was Warton Professor of English Literature at Oxford University from 1973 to 1992, and is now Emeritus Professor. His books include *The Characters of Love* (1960), *Tolstoy and the Novel* (1966) and *Housman's Poems* (1992), as well as studies of Shakespeare, Pushkin and Hardy. His novels are *In Another Country* (1953) and a trilogy, *Alice* (1994), *The Queer Captain* (1995), and *George's Lair* (1996).

Archie Burnett is the editor of the Oxford English Texts volume, *The Poems of A. E. Housman* (OUP, 1997). It contains all of Housman's verse and a comprehensive textual apparatus and commentary. Previously a Research Fellow of St John's College, Oxford, Dr Burnett teaches English at Oxford Brookes University. He plans a full edition of Housman's correspondence.

Carol Efrati, an American who has resided for many years in Israel, received her doctoral degree from the Hebrew University in Jerusalem for a dissertation on the role of friendship, love and passion in Housman's poetry. Her work on Housman has appeared in *Victorian Poetry* and she is a regular contributor to the *Housman Society Journal.* She teaches English composition and literature at the Achva Teachers' College in Jerusalem.

Benjamin F. Fisher, Professor of English at the University of Mississippi, has been bibliographer and American vice-president of the Housman Society for many years. He is an internationally recognized specialist in American and Victorian studies, with particular interests in Poe, the Housmans, the Gothic and bibliographic studies. He serves on the Advisory Boards of *Victorian Poetry, English Literature in Transition* and *Poe Studies.* He is currently working on several projects concerning Ella D'Arcy, best known for her connection with *The Yellow Book.*

George P. Goold retired as Lampson Professor of Latin from Yale University in 1992 and is now Professor Emeritus. He held professional appointments at various universities from 1955, including the Chair of Latin at University College, London, 1973–78 (the chair earlier held by Housman). He is General Editor of the Loeb Classical Library. Besides many reviews and articles on Latin and Greek subjects, he has edited and translated Manilius, Catullus, Propertius and Chariton, and is currently revising the Loeb Virgil.

Geoffrey Hill, the distinguished poet, was born in 1938 but a few minutes walk from the birthplace of Housman. Hill attended the County High School in Bromsgrove and Keble College, Oxford, where he is an Honorary Fellow. He has taught at Leeds University and later at Cambridge where he is Honorary Fellow of Emmanuel College. Since 1988 Geoffrey Hill has been a member of the University Professors Programme at Boston University, USA. He is the author of six books of poetry, his latest being *Canaan* (Penguin, 1997), who also publish Hill's *Collected Poems*).

Trevor Hold was born in 1939 and studied music at Nottingham University. He has held teaching posts at the Universities of Aberystwyth, Liverpool and Leicester, but now works as a freelance composer, lecturer and writer. His compositions, many of which have been broadcast, include orchestral, choral and chamber music, song cycles and piano music. He is also a poet and, as well as supplying the libretti for his own song cycles and operas, has published three collections of poetry. He has written on twentieth-century English songwriters, including articles on Warlock and Gurney and a study of Quilter's songs, *The Walled-in Garden*, which has recently been republished.

Keith Jebb was born in Shropshire. His book *A. E. Housman* was published in 1992 by Seren Books. A widely published poet and reviewer, he is currently working on the project to revise the complete *Oxford English Dictionary*.

P. G. Naiditch is the Publications Editor of the Department of Special Collections, and the Classics Bibliographer for the Charles E. Young Research Library, University of California, Los Angeles. He is the author of *A. E. Housman at University College, London: the Election of 1892* (1988) and *Problems in the Life and Writings of A. E. Housman* (1995). He is currently engaged on a reconstruction of Housman's library and a bibliography of his works.

Takeshi Obata is Professor of the English Literature course at Shirayuri College, Tokyo, and is Chairman of the Housman Society in Japan. He is also one of the Vice-Presidents of the Eighteen-Nineties Society. He is the author of *A Study of A. E. Housman* and of a Japanese version of *The Name and Nature of Poetry*, the latter in collaboration with some members of the Housman Society. He has written articles, in various scholarly periodicals, on A. E. Housman, Christina Rossetti, Ernest Dowson, Edward Thomas and Iris Murdoch.

Norman Page is Emeritus Professor of Modern English at the University of Nottingham and Emeritus Professor of English at the University of Alberta. His numerous books on nineteenth-century and twentieth-century literature include *A. E. Housman: A Critical Biography* (Macmillan, 1983; reissued 1996). Among his other biographies are *Tennyson: an Illustrated Life* (1992) and *Auden and Isherwood: the Berlin Years* (Macmillan, 1998).

Kenneth Womack recently completed his dissertation, *The Heavy Industry of the Mind: Ethical Criticism and the Academic Novel*, in the Department of English at Northern Illinois University. He works as a Correspondent for the *World Shakespeare Bibliography* and serves as Associate Editor of the *George Eliot–George Henry Lewes Studies*. In addition to co-authoring *Recent Work in Critical Theory, 1989–1995: an Annotated Bibliography* (1996), he has published articles in such journals as the *Yearbook of Comparative and General Literature*, *Biography* and *The Library Chronicle*. He has recently been appointed Assistant Professor of English at Penn State Altoona.

Introduction

That the body of work which constitutes A. E. Housman's poetic output is small has often been remarked on. The two books of verse published in his lifetime, *A Shropshire Lad* and *Last Poems,* contain 105 poems. Laurence Housman printed 72 after his brother's death in *More Poems* and *Additional Poems.* There are also a few translations and the light verse. Moreover, these poems are nearly all short or very short. The longest, 'Hell Gate' (*LP* XXXI), is 104 lines, and the two longest other poems are 'Terence, this is stupid stuff' (*ASL* LXII) at 76 lines and 'The Merry Guide' (*ASL* XLII) at 60 lines. In the work published in Housman's lifetime, about five-eighths of the poems are 20 lines or fewer in length. And yet this small body of work has aroused intense interest from 1896 to the present day.

The volume edited by Philip Gardner (*A. E. Housman: the Critical Heritage*, London and New York: Routledge, 1992) is of great value in showing that there was lively and widespread critical attention paid to *ASL* from the beginning, in both the UK and the USA. The American reviewers were rather more grudging in their response, but, as P. G. Naiditch pointed out in a review of Gardner's book,[1] there were numerous reviews not reproduced by Gardner, a caveat underlined in some measure by Ben Fisher in the article reproduced in this volume (Chapter 2). Critical interest seems to have outrun general appreciation; it is well known that the first edition (of 500 copies) took about two years to sell out. Grant Richards, who had been much impressed by the book on its appearance and had written a review for the *Review of Reviews*, became a publisher shortly after, and took over the publication of *ASL* for its second and subsequent editions, as well as publishing *LP* and some of Housman's classical work. The 1898 *ASL* was also extensively noticed in the press; some of these articles were long and detailed, and, again, were mostly favourable. But even though Richards was an enthusiastic promoter of *ASL*, this second edition (also of 500 copies) sold slowly, so that, by the end of 1902, after two further editions, under 1500 copies had been sold in the UK. From then on, however, the story is of steady growth in public appreciation, aided by numerous cheap editions (partly made possible by Housman's refusal, for many years, to take any royalties) and song-settings by many English composers. The 1914–18 war undoubtedly had the effect of increasing the popularity of the poems. It followed naturally that *Last Poems* would sell in large numbers from the day of publication in 1922. Richards was very cautious in printing only 4000 copies (against Housman's suggestion of 10 000). By the end of the year (the book was published in October), a further 17 000 had been printed.

Again, most reviewers of *LP*, in both the UK and the USA, were high in its praise. Some used the occasion for an extended consideration of Housman's poetry; these writers included J. B. Priestley, H. W. Garrod and J. F. M. MacDonald. Reviews of the posthumous work and the *Collected Poems* of 1939, as well as of the lecture *The Name and Nature of Poetry* (1933), were also generally favourable.

It is worth noticing the main thrusts of these commentaries from 1896 on. Many writers believed that the poet was a new voice in the world of the 1890s (one remembers A. E. H.'s protests, when, in later years, an editor wished to include some of the poems from *ASL* in an anthology of 1890s poetry – on which see Ben Fisher's essay in Chapter 2). A number drew attention to the narrow limits of the poetry, in both style and content, but stressed the consummate skill within these limits. There was considerable reference to the artlessness of the verse (the 'perfect simplicity' of Hubert Bland, the 'sancta simplicitas' of Louise Guiney); but as many critics wrote of the art which conceals art and of a hard-earned surface simplicity (and indeed, this balance between the simple-seeming surface and the linguistic and metric artifice is a feature which may exercise critics in our own day). Local colour ('fresh country pictures', for instance) was sometimes remarked on, or on occasions denied.

Influences or supposed influences upon the poetry were also noted from an early date. The work of Heine was referred to more than once, as were Burns, Robert Louis Stevenson, the ballads, Blake and others, though some reviewers thought the poet in no one else's debt. Rather curiously, for an age much more familiar than our own with the Bible, Housman's biblical allusions do not seem to have aroused much comment from early commentators.

Gardner, in his long and useful introduction to his *Critical Heritage* volume, notes that it was not until after Housman's death that 'a significant number of critics began to express dissatisfaction with his work', and P. G. Naiditch, in the article referred to above, refines this, making the point that it was the later critics, such as Raymond Mortimer, Orwell and Lawrence Leighton, who drew specific and unfavourable attention to what they took to be Housman's self-pity and the 'adolescent' qualities of the verse, terms apparently not used by the early critics at all. Cyril Connolly's piece in the *New Statesman* of May 1936, an obituary, which evoked replies from F. L. Lucas, Martin Cooper, L. P. Wilkinson and John Sparrow, spoke of triteness of technique, banality of thought and the 'metrically morbid experiments in the five-line stanza' (a puzzling phrase, then and now; Connolly was clearly not aware of the quite common use of the five-line stanza, with varying rhyme-schemes, by such Victorian poets as George Meredith, D. G. Rossetti and Arthur Symons). Connolly also loftily dismissed Housman's claim to be a classical poet – a claim, as one of the correspondents pointed out, never made by Housman himself.

Now came the time for the biographers and the writers of memoirs. One of the earliest books was the Bromsgrove Memorial Supplement, *Alfred Edward Housman: Recollections*, with contributions by, among others, Katharine Symonds, A. E. H.'s sister, Laurence Housman, R. W. Chambers, and A. S. F. Gow. Laurence Housman's *A. E. H.* (published in the USA as *My Brother, A. E. Housman*) followed in 1937. This contained a memoir, a number of letters (most of them previously unpublished), poems (the *Additional Poems*), and light verse and parodies. In quick succession followed *A Buried Life* by Percy Withers (1940) – Withers had known A. E. H. from 1917 – and, of great importance and entertainment value, Grant Richards's *Housman: 1897–1936* (1941). Richards had of course known Housman for a long time and had gradually established a friendship with him (such that they sometimes went on holiday together). His book contained numerous letters. The biographies proper began to appear after the Second World War: George L. Watson's *A. E. Housman* in 1957, and Maude M. Hawkins's *A. E. Housman: Man Behind a Mask* and Norman Marlow's *A. E. Housman: Scholar and Poet* both in 1958.

When Christopher Ricks edited the volume *A. E. Housman: a Collection of Critical Essays* in 1968, he stated in the introduction that 'the quality of Housman's poetry . . . is no longer assured of recognition'; though even so, he acknowledged that the poems 'disrupt all the normal allegiances', since among Housman's admirers were to be counted William Empson and (represented in the volume) Cleanth Brooks, F. W. Bateson and Randall Jarrell. Hugh Kenner and F. R. Leavis were noted as adverse critics. Ricks printed poems by Auden, Pound and Kingsley Amis to underline the close attention paid to A. E. H. by modern poets.

The essays chosen by Ricks were almost exclusively reprinted from elsewhere. A number offer close readings of particular poems, Randall Jarrell's and Cleanth Brooks's contributions being the most noteworthy in this respect. Brooks, in one of his general comments, makes comparisons with the work of William Faulkner and Ernest Hemingway – courage and stoic endurance are presented for our consideration and approval by all three writers. John Wain sees as a fault what the earlier reviewers of *Last Poems* saw largely as a virtue, namely that there is no development discernible between 1896 and 1922. There is some attention paid to relationships (or lack of them) between the poetry and the life, and between the scholarship and the poetry. J. P. Sullivan's essay is concerned with defining what he takes to be Housman's limitations as a model for contemporary classical scholarship, and in the only article written especially for the volume, F. W. Bateson stresses (though not in great detail) the importance of considering Housman's sexual orientation in any approach to the poetry.

The years since Ricks's volume have seen a further increase in the amount of attention paid to Housman, as man, poet and classical scholar. The Housman Society was founded in 1973 in Bromsgrove, Housman's birthplace. Its purpose is to foster interest in the Housman family, including Laurence and Clemence, brother and sister of A. E. H., both of them writers and artists, but inevitably most of the material in the Journal (published annually since 1974, except for a gap in 1976) is concerned with A. E. H. Several worthwhile books have been published in the critical, biographical and bibliographical fields: John Pugh's *Bromsgrove and the Housmans* (1974), Richard Perceval Graves's *A. E. Housman* (1979), Norman Page's *A. E. Housman: a Critical Biography* (1983, reprinted 1996), John Bayley's *Housman's Poems* (1992), Keith Jebb's *A. E. Housman* (1992), *A. E. Housman: a Bibliography* (John Carter and John Sparrow, revised edition by William White, 1982) and P. G. Naiditch's *Problems in the Life and Writings of A. E. Housman* (1995).

The 1996 celebrations marking the centenary of the publication of *A Shropshire Lad*, with academic lectures, poetry readings and music, in venues as varied as Ludlow, Oxford, London and Bromsgrove (the list is by no means exhaustive), were well attended and enthusiastically received; the current appeal of Housman is not simply to the scholarly.

The present volume, which was conceived as part of the centenary celebrations, shows that academic interest in A. E. H. is still strong and widespread: contributions from the UK, the USA, Israel and Japan are included. As to the variety of focus, that is clearly apparent. Here are, for instance, close readings, historical and bibliographical studies, and comparisons with other writers – indeed, with another culture. Housman is seen as poet, man, classicist, and source of inspiration for song-writers. Some might challenge Keith Jebb's assertion '[w]hat *ASL* is about... is not Housman's homosexuality, but the inexpressibility of homosexuality as such, of a homosexual community,' but the challenge would need to explore the linguistic parameters in the close detail evident in his essay. Perhaps a bibliographer with much time at his disposal could take up either – or both – of the challenges offered by Ben Fisher and Paul Naiditch: to present the totality of the initial responses in the press to the publication of *ASL* (as Professor Fisher remarks, there were, in 1896, 70-odd daily newspapers in London alone), and to determine exactly how many copies of *ASL* were printed, and sold, by Grant Richards.[2] Geoffrey Hill, one of the most highly regarded of contemporary poets, has provided us with a challenge to examine the tension in Housman's poetry between form and content and to reconsider whether the simple delight and pleasure commonly held to be derivable from the poetry is so simple. And Carol Efrati's suggestion that it is possible that Housman knew some Hebrew could surely bear some further investigation.

This introduction began with a restatement of the familiar paradox that Housman's poetry, though limited in scale and apparently in scope, has nonetheless evoked much attention since the first publication of *ASL*. John Bayley confesses that his earlier statement, that 'we always know where we are with Housman', needs considerable qualification: 'his personality is both extremely definite and remarkably evasive' – and, as he and other critics point out, the same simultaneous clarity and evasiveness present one of the most intriguing aspects of the verse, perhaps still to be completely

assessed. But, equally intriguingly, there are other areas of
A. E. H.'s works which have not been fully explored. Housman
always had a great interest in metrics; in *The Name and Nature of
Poetry*, he tells us that he had first thought of taking the 'Artifice
of Versification' as his subject for the lecture, and claims that he
could have added a few useful pages to the 'few pages of Coventry
Patmore and a few of Frederic Myers [which] contain all, so far
as I know, or all of value, which has been written on such matters'
– a coat-trailing assertion when one remembers the audience for
the lecture (a footnote mentions some of the topics he might have
touched on). But has there been a full treatment of Housman's
practices in matters of rhythm, rhyme and verse-form? A re-exam-
ination of Housman's Notebooks, now in the Library of Congress,
is part of Dr Archie Burnett's complete re-edition of the poems
(see Select Bibliography), and will no doubt establish whether,
as has been suggested, Tom Burns Haber's book[3] has quite
substantial omissions. Housman's prose has not been fully or
adequately discussed, though Norman Page has some excellent
paragraphs on the subject.[4] More peripherally, perhaps, little
attention has been paid to the comic verse, or to Housman's
influence on other poets.

It is of course of little use to look forward even twenty or thirty
years, to try to guess in what ways Housman's poetry will be
read, if at all. Perhaps during the next century his wry view of
pastoralism will become impossibly remote for the general reader
and an exhausted, or pointless, topic for the literary critic (supposing such continue to exist). We cannot know. But then, few
reviewers or readers in 1896 could have predicted that the new
slim volume, of so little consequence to any publisher that the
poet had to pay the costs of publication himself, would remain
constantly in print for the next one hundred years.

Notes

1. *Housman Society Journal*, vol. 20 (1994) 79–103.
2. As Naiditch writes: '[D]espite sixty years of bibliographical investigation, no one at present knows how many editions and reprints of
   ASL have appeared; none, how many copies of all these printings
   were issued. Of copies printed and bound, none can say how many
   were sold.'

3. *The Manuscript Poems of A. E. Housman* (London: OUP, 1955).
4. *A. E. Housman: A Critical Biography* (London: Macmillan, 1983, repr. 1996) pp. 139–47.

Throughout this volume, the accepted convention for referring to Housman's poems has been generally followed: *ASL* (for *A Shropshire Lad*); *LP* (for *Last Poems*); *MP* (for *More Poems*); *AP* (for *Additional Poems*); *CP* (*Collected Poems*).

1

A. E. Housman's 'Level Tones'

Archie Burnett

A. E. Housman was the favourite poet of the late Kingsley Amis,[1] who paid apt tribute in a poem:

> *A. E. H.*
> Flame the westward skies adorning
> Leaves no like on holt or hill;
> Sounds of battle joined at morning
> Wane and wander and are still.
>
> Past the standards rent and muddied,
> Past the careless heaps of slain,
> Stalks a redcoat who, unbloodied,
> Weeps with fury, not from pain.
>
> Wounded lads, when to renew them
> Death and surgeons cross the shade,
> Still their cries, hug darkness to them;
> All at last in sleep are laid.
>
> All save one, who nightlong curses
> Wounds imagined more than seen,
> Who in level tones rehearses
> What the fact of wounds must mean.[2]

Amis's poem is an admiring imitation, not a parody; but it objectifies and defamiliarizes as parody does, and provides an insight into the workings of the poetry it imitates. Most tellingly, it adopts the 'level tones' of the so-called 'Laura Matilda' stanza. Housman may have used the stanza in only four poems and the metre in one more,[3] but he thought it 'the most beautiful and

1

the most difficult in English',[4] and excluded 'Atys' ('Lydians, lords of Hermus river') from *Last Poems* because, as he told Laurence Housman, 'it was written in a metre he was so fond of, that he always doubted the merit of any poem in which he had succumbed to its attraction'.[5] The metre in Amis's poem, complemented by parallelism and sound patterns, intimates a composure undisturbed by disturbing events: the aftermath of battle, with 'standards rent and muddied' and 'surgeons', causes the redcoat to curse and to weep with fury; but the impact of such emotion does not register in the verse. A strict formality is observed that favours declaration over dramatic enactment: a curb on expression serves to curb overt expressiveness. The cries of the wounded are stilled neither by surgeons nor by death: with dignified control, the wounded 'still their cries, hug darkness to them'. 'Hug darkness to them' contains an echo of *Measure for Measure* III. i. 81–3: 'If I must die, / I will encounter darkness as a bride, / And hug it in mine arms.' The allusion, discreetly made like many an allusion in Housman, makes the poignant suggestion that only darkness is there to be hugged; yet the embrace before sleep remains unsensational, and, just as quietly, 'all at last in sleep are laid'. Throughout Amis's poem, the 'level tones' are symptomatic of a verse form and phraseology that do not give way to emotion but (in more senses than one) contain it.

Such writing observes a principle of classical rhetoric, with precedents in Horace, Longinus and Quintilian. Pope stated it in *An Essay on Criticism*:

> 'Tis more to *guide* than *spur* the Muse's Steed;
> Restrain his Fury, than provoke his Speed;
> The winged Courser, like a gen'rous Horse,
> Shows most true Mettle when you *check* his Course.[6]

Housman well knew that a judicious classical restraint in form and phrase could work both psychologically and aesthetically, sublimating emotion and making it sublime. Consider, for example, the 'level tones' at the close of *Last Poems* VII:

> The lover and his lass
>   Beneath the hawthorn lying
> Have heard the soldiers pass,
>   And both are sighing.

And down the distance they
　With dying note and swelling
Walk the resounding way
　To the still dwelling.

How gentle they go into that goodnight! Syntactic linkages and
line divisions coincide, structures are smoothly coordinate ('And
both are sighing ... And down the distance'), and sounds are
harmonious in alliteration, echo and rhyme. However, the 'level
tones' preserve a superficial simplicity that contains deeper
complexities, producing, as Housman often does, an Empsonian
version of pastoral.[7] 'The lover and his lass' invokes the innocent pastoral of *As You Like It* V. iii. 15 ('It was a lover and his
lass') in a context that intimates its demise, and the 'sighing' of
the lovers is laden with the sadness of mortality. The words 'Pass',
'dying' in 'dying note' and 'still' in 'the still dwelling' may be
ominous; 'swelling' and 'resounding' may be exultant; and 'dying'
and 'swelling' and 'resounding' and 'still' may be disturbingly
paradoxical; but ominousness, exultation and disturbance are alike
levelled by a consistency of tone and mood. In the notebook drafts,
'And down the distance they' replaced three other versions: 'And
you with colours gay', 'And deep in distance they', 'And ever
onward they'. Gaiety would obtrude, 'ever onward' would be
too earnestly resolute; and 'deep in distance' would sacrifice both
the foreboding of 'down the distance' and the surface unremark-
ableness of walking down to the dwelling. 'With dying note and
swelling' replaced 'And martial music swelling', 'The quickstep
faintly swelling', and 'With fainter music swelling': the literalism
of 'martial' and 'fainter', and the intrusive liveliness of 'quickstep', were alike rejected for 'dying note and swelling', which is
portentous, but not pompous: beneath the sombre overtones is
the flatter statement that the military music alternates dying and
swelling notes, crescendo and diminuendo. In a context where
surface innocence blends with darker experience, the everyday
insouciance of 'Walk' takes on uncommon dignity – 'Run' or 'Stroll',
say, would be unthinkable, and in the second notebook draft
Housman cancelled 'Pace' and 'Tread'. 'Level tones' preserve that
dignity until the soldiers, and by suggestion the lovers, reach
the finally (and finely) placed 'still dwelling'. The whole poem,
and the ending in particular, fulfils the function of poetry that
Housman once expounded in a letter to his sister:

The essential business of poetry, as it has been said, is to harmonise the sadness of the universe; and it is somehow more sustaining and healing than prose.[8]

Such a statement suggests strongly that Housman in his poetry is concerned not merely with honouring classical precedent or with achieving correctness and polish, but rather with the handling of emotion, which in turn means finding an appropriate tone. Tone in Housman's poetry has attracted considerable attention, notably from Cleanth Brooks, Christopher Ricks, Brian Rosebury and John Bayley.[9] 'Level tones' are of particular significance, however, and for the reason that they give expression to an emotional life that is often far from level. Though Housman's poetry contains a considerable range of tone, the power and distinction of many of the poems seem to me to derive from intense personal feeling presented with formal public decorum.

A *Shropshire Lad* XXXI is a notable manifestation:

> On Wenlock Edge the wood's in trouble;
> 　His forest fleece the Wrekin heaves;
> The gale, it plies the saplings double,
> 　And thick on Severn snow the leaves.
>
> 'Twould blow like this through holt and hanger
> 　When Uricon the city stood:
> 'Tis the old wind in the old anger,
> 　But then it threshed another wood.
>
> Then, 'twas before my time, the Roman
> 　At yonder heaving hill would stare:
> The blood that warms an English yeoman,
> 　The thoughts that hurt him, they were there.
>
> There, like the wind through woods in riot,
> 　Through him the gale of life blew high;
> The tree of man was never quiet:
> 　Then 'twas the Roman, now 'tis I.
>
> The gale, it plies the saplings double,
> 　It blows so hard, 'twill soon be gone:
> To-day the Roman and his trouble
> 　Are ashes under Uricon.

The violence of the gale is emphasized. Nature is relentlessly, hectically active: the Wrekin heaves the forest fleece, the gale plies the saplings double, the leaves snow thick on Severn, the wind in anger threshes the wood, the hill heaves, the wind riots. Verbs are starkly monosyllabic ('heaves', 'plies', 'snow', 'threshed') and tremors surge through the poem's pervasive alliteration and assonance: 'On Wenlock Edge the wood's in trouble; / His forest fleece the Wrekin heaves'. No doubt it was such turbulence that prompted Vaughan Williams to create an uninhibitedly violent musical setting. Housman's poem, however, is not a turbulent one. The stanza stays regular, and balanced structures further establish a controlled steadiness, in simple coordinations:

> The gale, it plies the saplings double,
>   And thick on Severn snow the leaves.
>
> 'Tis the old wind in the old anger,
>   But then it threshed another wood

or in the syntax and rhythm of individual lines: ''Tis the old wind in the old anger', 'Then 'twas the Roman, now 'tis I', 'It blows so hard, 'twill soon be gone'. Repetitions abound: 'the wood's in trouble' is echoed by 'the Roman and his trouble', 'the Wrekin heaves' reverberates in 'yonder heaving hill', and two lines are identical: 'The gale, it plies the saplings double'. Single words also recur – 'Roman', 'Uricon', 'wood(s)', 'gale' – and further accentuate the contrast between past and present that underlies the poem's theme: 'where Uricon the city stood' becomes 'ashes under Uricon', 'then' becomes 'now', and the present tenses of the first and last verses alternate with the past tenses of the others.

It is possible to read the poem as protest or as elegy: such is its capacity to resolve its internal conflict between passion and resignation into a single complex attitude. The speaker can say 'The tree of man was never quiet', and say it quietly; or remark 'It blows so hard, 'twill soon be gone' in the same breath. Throughout, repetitions can seem soothing or aggressively insistent. The speaker does not sound world-weary: the poem harnesses too much energy for that. But neither is he clamorous or distraught: it is too composed for that. Emotion is recollected in tranquillity, but the emotion recollected is not tranquil: the poem achieves equanimity, not by denying the forces of disturbance, but by containing them. Its art, as Christopher Ricks once said of Milton's,

'is in its way external, but it is not unexperiencing'.[10] And in such
art one can see what T. S. Eliot meant when he said: 'Poetry is
not a turning loose of emotion, but an escape from emotion; it is
not the expression of personality, but an escape from personality. But, of course, only those who have personality and emotions
know what it means to want to escape from these things.'[11]

In its handling of emotion Housman's poetry often provides a
forceful reminder of what Tennyson said in *In Memoriam* v. 5–6:
'for the unquiet heart and brain, / A use in measured language
lies'. In the same context (v. 1–4) Tennyson, measuring his
language, confessed:

> I sometimes hold it half a sin
>   To put in words the grief I feel;
>   For words, like Nature, half reveal
> And half conceal the Soul within.

It was of particular importance for Housman that poetry could
offer the means to achieve a measure of equanimity and to 'half
reveal / And half conceal the Soul within': at the heart of his
emotional life lay unrequited love for Moses Jackson, a love that
dared not speak its name, and about which it was impossible to
stay silent. Housman's poems, John Bayley observes, 'have an
instinct both for revelation and for concealment'.[12] The revelation could never be open: the relatively outspoken 'Because I
liked you better / Than suits a man to say', and the protest poem
about the trial and imprisonment of Oscar Wilde ('Oh who is
that young sinner with the handcuffs on his wrists?'), were
published posthumously. But even in the posthumous poems,
the exact nature of 'unlucky love' (*MP* XII. 5), the reason why
the speaker can only spend the night alone striking his fist upon
the stone (*MP* XIX. 11–12), or the identity of the person to whom
it is said 'Shake hands, we shall never be friends . . . I only vex
you the more I try' (*MP* XXX. 1–2), are all undisclosed. The fantasy of 'he and I together' is codified in terms of 'Shipmates on
the fleeted main' and of 'Locking hands and taking leave, / Low
upon the trampled heather / In the battle lost at eve' (*AP* II. 1,
6–8). But 'level tones' can at once disclose and conceal:

> Ask me no more, for fear I should reply;
>   Others have held their tongues, and so can I;

Hundreds have died, and told no tale before:
   Ask me no more, for fear I should reply –

How one was true and one was clean of stain
   And one was braver than the heavens are high,
And one was fond of me: and all are slain.
   Ask me no more, for fear I should reply.

(Additional Poems VI)

Stanza and rhythm match the tense regularity of the refrain, holding in what is disclosed, holding back a more complete disclosure. The poem's vagueness prompts questions – Ask what? Reply what? Held their tongues about what? Told no tale about what? – but questions are not invited: 'Ask me no more'. The poem is as much about not saying what cannot be said as it is about saying what can be said. The second verse does give something of a reply, but the reply remains a veiled one. The balanced coordinations and even rhythm establish a cool equipollency between being true and being clean of stain, and between bravery and love. Within the series of coordinations, and following the over-statement 'And one was braver than the heavens are high', 'And one was fond of me' should be a climax; and so it may be, but in the form of a shy, understated admission: 'fond of me'. In this case, one can look to allusions for less reticence: 'Ask me no more' echoes not only Thomas Carew's idealistic tribute to a lover,[13] but a passage in Tennyson that links death with the overwhelming power of love:[14]

   Ask me no more: what answer should I give?
    I love not hollow cheek or faded eye:
    Yet, O my friend, I will not have thee die!
   Ask me no more, lest I should bid thee live;
     Ask me no more.

   Ask me no more: thy fate and mine are sealed:
    I strove against the stream and all in vain:
    Let the great river take me to the main:
   No more, dear love, for at a touch I yield;
     Ask me no more.

Another echo, of a passage in *Endymion* which Housman marked in his copy of Keats,[15] reveals a similar context, but, tellingly, a marked difference of manner:

> Ah, bitter strife!
> I may not be thy love: I am forbidden –
> Indeed I am – thwarted, affrighted, chidden,
> By things I trembled at, and gorgon wrath.
> Twice hast thou ask'd whither I went: henceforth
> Ask me no more! I may not utter it,
> Nor may I be thy love. We might commit
> Ourselves at once to vengeance; we might die;
> We might embrace and die: voluptuous thought!
> Enlarge not to my hunger, or I'm caught
> In trammels of perverse deliciousness.
> No, no, that shall not be: thee will I bless,
> And bid a long adieu.[16]

Where Keats is all passionate agitation, struggling to repress a fully acknowledged warmth of desire, yet managing to state candidly 'I may not be thy love', Housman's 'level tones', as though by force of will, declare but do not overtly express emotion – 'And one was fond of me: and all are slain' – before shutting out further disclosure: 'Ask me no more, for fear I should reply'. Housman well knew what he could not say: in his copy of *Apocrypha*,[17] *Ecclesiasticus* 20:6 is marked in pencil: 'Some man holdeth his tongue, because he hath not to answer: and some keepeth silence, knowing his time.' His grief, like Tennyson's in *In Memoriam* (v. 12), could be 'given in outline and no more'.

In real life, Housman was a master of level tone. A. S. F. Gow remembers in Housman's Cambridge lectures 'the level, impassive voice setting out, without enthusiasm but with an athletic spareness and precision of phrase, just so much commentary as was necessary for the interpretation of the passage under discussion'.[18] F. L. Lucas vividly recalls the 'quiet, immaculate figure, setting straight, with even-voiced, passionless, unresting minuteness the jots and tittles of a fifth-rate ancient',[19] and Gundred Savory, in a reminiscence of Housman at University College London about the turn of the century, testifies to 'his calm judicial pronouncements' and 'unmoved dignity'.[20] He was, however, fundamentally and unmistakably, a deeply passionate man. The phrase in which

T. S. Eliot characterized Tennyson can apply equally to Housman: 'the most instinctive rebel against the society in which he was the most perfect conformist'.[21] In Housman's classical scholarship, the celebrated rhetoric of invective, however entertaining, glows with a moral fervour that reduces mere convention and prejudice to absurdity:

> Most men are rather stupid, and most of those who are not stupid are, consequently, rather vain; and it is hardly possible to step aside from the pursuit of truth without falling a victim either to your stupidity or else to your vanity. Stupidity will then attach you to received opinions, and you will stick in the mud; or vanity will set you hunting for novelty, and you will find mare's nests. Added to these snares and hindrances there are the various forms of partisanship: sectarianism, which handcuffs you to your own school and teachers and associates, and patriotism which handcuffs you to your own country. Patriotism has a great name as a virtue, and in civic matters, at the present stage of the world's history, it possibly still does more good than harm; but in the sphere of intellect it is an unmitigated nuisance. I do not know which cuts the worse figure: a German scholar encouraging his countrymen to believe that 'wir Deutsche' have nothing to learn from foreigners, or an Englishman demonstrating the unity of Homer by sneers at 'Teutonic professors,' who are supposed by his audience to have goggle eyes behind large spectacles, and ragged moustaches saturated in lager beer, and consequently to be incapable of forming literary judgments.[22]

In personal life, his composure, usually intact and well guarded, could be shaken. Percy Withers recalls Housman telling him of a lady recently dead: 'and in the telling his voice faltered and a look of unutterable sadness suffused his face'.[23] Notably, poetic composition had extraordinary power to discompose. Enoch Powell recalls that in his Cambridge lectures Housman 'could indeed at times scarcely master his emotion sufficiently to read aloud the verses of Horace or Propertius, Catullus or Virgil, upon which he was about to comment'.[24] Mrs T. W. Pym tells of a specific incident:

> One morning in May, 1914, when the trees in Cambridge were covered with blossom, he reached in his lecture Ode 7 in Horace's Fourth Book, 'Diffugere nives, redeunt iam gramina

campis'. This ode he dissected with the usual display of brillance, wit, and sarcasm. Then for the first time in two years he looked up at us, and in a quite different voice said: 'I should like to spend the last few minutes considering this ode simply as poetry'. Our previous experience of Professor Housman would have made us sure that he would regard such a proceeding as beneath contempt. He read the ode aloud with deep emotion, first in Latin and then in an English translation of his own.[25] 'That,' he said hurriedly, almost like a man betraying a secret, 'I regard as the most beautiful poem in ancient literature', and walked quickly out of the room. A scholar of Trinity (since killed in the War), who walked with me to our next lecture, expressed in undergraduate style our feeling that we had seen something not really meant for us. 'I felt quite uncomfortable,' he said. 'I was afraid the old fellow was going to cry.'[26]

This was the Housman who in *The Name and Nature of Poetry* (1933) confessed:

as for the seventh verse of the forty-ninth Psalm in the Book of Common Prayer, 'But no man may deliver his brother, nor make agreement unto God for him', that is to me poetry so moving that I can hardly keep my voice steady in reading it.[27]

and who knew tears could well up at six words from Milton's *Arcades* (l. 96): 'Nymphs and shepherds, dance no more'.[28] R. D. Bloomfield, who attended the lecture, reports that:

When he came to passages about himself, which in effect were rather moving, he spoke with restraint, and it was evident that he was curbing the emotion which he was describing.[29]

In poetry, speaking with restraint was a necessity for Housman, for reasons at once aesthetic, emotional and social. He was never one to write without control, in prose or in poetry, and the fastidiousness he brought to classical scholarship can be seen also in the extensive drafting and redrafting of poems in his notebooks. Sometimes, however, emotion breaks through, threatening the 'level tones':

Shot? so quick, so clean an ending?
   Oh that was right, lad, that was brave:
Yours was not an ill for mending,
   'Twas best to take it to the grave.

Oh you had forethought, you could reason,
   And saw your road and where it led,
And early wise and brave in season
   Put the pistol to your head.

Oh soon, and better so than later
   After long disgrace and scorn,
You shot dead the household traitor,
   The soul that should not have been born.

Right you guessed the rising morrow
   And scorned to tread the mire you must:
Dust's your wages, son of sorrow,
   But men may come to worse than dust.

Souls undone, undoing others, –
   Long time since the tale began.
You would not live to wrong your brothers:
   Oh lad, you died as fits a man.

Now to your grave shall friend and stranger
   With ruth and some with envy come:
Undishonoured, clear of danger,
   Clean of guilt, pass hence and home.

Turn safe to rest, no dreams, no waking;
   And here, man, here's the wreath I've made:
'Tis not a gift that's worth the taking,
   But wear it and it will not fade.

The poem is probably the nearest Housman came in his lifetime to speaking out about homosexuality. It relates to the suicide on 6 August 1895 at the age of 19 of Henry Clarkson Maclean, a gentleman Cadet at the Royal Military Academy, Woolwich. In his copy of *A Shropshire Lad*, at poem XLIV, Housman kept a press cutting of the coroner's inquest into the suicide,[30] and the source of the cutting was independently identified by William White as *The Standard* of 10 August 1895.[31] The poem was written between 10 August and 30 September 1895, and relates very closely to the event. Maclean in fact shot himself in the head with a revolver; the second draft of the poem in Housman's notebooks begins with his age, 'Nineteen!' (cancelled); and in the period of October to December 1895 Housman considered the alternatives 'Today?' and 'Last night?'. Maclean in his suicide note speaks of his action as 'better than a long series of sorrows and disgraces'; Housman's poem, of 'long disgrace and scorn' (l. 10). Also in the note, Maclean thanked God that he had not 'as yet, so far as I know, . . . morally injured – or "offended," as it is called in the Bible – any one else', but was certain that he could not live another five years without doing so. J. M. Nosworthy justly concludes that Housman attributed Maclean's depression to 'a recognition of irresistible homosexual tendencies'.[32]

The opening question, 'Shot?', makes an explosive impact, and, like the three occurrences of 'Oh' in the first 12 lines ('Oh that was right . . . Oh you had forethought . . . Oh soon'), it announces a tone far from level. What sounds like callously hectoring sarcasm in the opening verse is sustained in the first three. Then, in the next two, it is moderated into what sounds more like unequivocal praise. In the last two verses, the 'level tones' of elegiac tribute restore public decorum. The poem is the means of achieving composure. The opening verses are markedly unstable in tone and in attitude, and represent Housman's jibing mockery of conventional public complacency and piety. A similar tone and attitude underlie 'If it chance your eye offend you, / Pluck it out, lad, and be sound' (*ASL* XLV), 'Think no more, lad; laugh, be jolly: / Why should men make haste to die?' (*ASL* XLIX), and the poem on Wilde (*AP* XVIII):

> 'Tis a shame to human nature, such a head of hair as his;
> In the good old time 'twas hanging for the colour that it is;
> Though hanging isn't bad enough and flaying would be fair
> For the nameless and abominable colour of his hair.

(ll. 5–8)

Such tone, unsettled, or nettled, is a just counter-response to unsettling social attitudes.

Uniform tone holds its surprises and can release powerful incongruities. When, for instance, Housman says

> My heart and soul and senses,
> World without end, are drowned.

(ASL XIV. 7–8)

he is in fact invoking, among biblical contexts, Browning's *Saul*, ix. 11–12:

> How good is man's life, the mere living! how fit to employ
> All the heart and the soul and the senses, for ever in joy!

As often in his allusions, Housman begs to differ; but any romantic assertion of individuality – '*My* heart and soul and senses, / World without end, are drowned' – is registered only, and discreetly, in the allusion: the surface classical discipline suppresses special pleading. Again, when Housman says

> Now, and I muse for why and never find the reason,
>   I pace the earth, and drink the air, and feel the sun.
> Be still, be still, my soul; it is but for a season:
>   Let us endure an hour and see injustice done.

(ASL XLVIII. 9–12)

or

> So here are things to think on
>   That ought to make me brave,
> As I strap on for fighting
>   My sword that will not save.

(LP II. 13–16)

the calm tone is what might be expected in a statement of the unremarkable opposite – see justice done, sword that will save; and it is just this flat refusal to add self-conscious stress – '*in*justice', '*not* save' – that stiffens and validates the disillusioned stance. The calm release of unsettling incongruities is often seen also in Housman's comic verse:

> When Adam day by day
>   Awoke in paradise
> He always used to say
>   "Oh, this is very nice."
>
> But Eve from scenes of bliss
>   Transported him for life.
> The more I think of this
>   The more I beat my wife.

That sudden revelation of wife-beating astonishes because it is so coolly, so rationally, automatic, and so consistent with the unshockingly banal lines that come before. A similar principle underlies a still more shocking poem, 'A Ballad of a Widower', whose scurrility is moderated by its being a parody of John Davidson's poem 'A Ballad of Heaven', published in 1894. In Davidson's poem the wife and children of an aspiring but unsuccessful composer starve to death. He meets them again in heaven, where God tells him: 'Nothing is lost that's wrought with tears: / The music that you made below / Is now the music of the spheres', an outcome and sentiment that Housman, predictably, could not accept. In his parody, a writer whose fiction proves unsuccessful because too domestic murders his wife and children to enjoy success. The macabre humour belittles emotion through a verse form and rationality that remain as unruffled as each other:

> He seized her wrist: "Oh, don't! it hurts;"
>   She cried; "suppose you break the joint,
> Who do you think will mend your shirts?"
>   He said, "You wander from the point."
>
> Forthwith upon her back he plied
>   The poker till she ceased to stir:
> The woman ultimately died;
>   The man was then a widower.
>
> The children met a wretched fate;
>   Their father burnt them all alive
> To ashes in the kitchen grate;
>   Wherefore they none of them survive.

> After a time his buttons came
> Off one by one till all were gone:
> His wife, whom it were hard to blame,
> Was in no state to sew them on.

He meets his wife and children in heaven:

> The children whom he lately cooked
> Flew to his arms on eager wing;
> His wife was also there: they looked
> Extremely well, considering.

What is on display is a form of nonchalance or indifference, an attitude commonly found in the stoical stance of the serious poetry,[33] though there it is never simply one of indifference, and Housman would be the lesser poet if it were: as Christopher Ricks has said, Housman's poems 'again and again show the continuance of emotions which should in all reason have been quenched'.[34]

The capacity to absorb disturbance into decorum can be seen in the 'Epitaph on an Army of Mercenaries', where it is a measure of Housman's poetic power that he can rebuke indifference or smugness or contempt without raising his voice:

> These, in the day when heaven was falling,
> The hour when earth's foundations fled,
> Followed their mercenary calling
> And took their wages and are dead.
>
> Their shoulders held the sky suspended;
> They stood, and earth's foundations stay;
> What God abandoned, these defended,
> And saved the sum of things for pay.

It is a very public poem, first printed, signed, in *The Times* on 31 October 1917 beneath a leading article entitled 'The Anniversary of Ypres'. It commemorates, in the tradition of military epitaph, the achievement of the British professional army that as part of the Allied force repelled three German attacks in the first battle of Ypres, at a cost of over 50 000 British lives. On the term 'mercenaries', Housman commented that 'it was not the German Emperor but the German people which called ours a mercenary army, as

in fact it was and is,'[35] and E. L. Woodward notes that the term
was used throughout Germany in the Boer War.[36] In the phrase
'mercenary calling', however, Housman issues a challenging paradox: it may indicate a professional vocation, or admit the suggestion
that the soldiers do their job out of self-interest or love of money;[37]
and in the context of 'wages', 'sum' and 'pay', the challenge is
put unflinchingly. 'And took their wages and are dead' may
benignly echo the dirge from *Cymbeline* (IV. ii. 262), a favourite
of Housman's:[38] 'Home art gone and ta'en thy wages'. Or, it may
judgementally echo Romans 6:23: 'the wages of sin is death'.[39]
'And saved the sum of things for pay' may indicate preservation
of the highest public good, or of the whole universe, the *summa
rerum* which is usually the responsibility of a deity or a divine
figure: 'What God abandoned, these defended'.[40] In that case 'for
pay' is climactically heroic: they did all that, and . . . for pay. Or,
they are paid wages to do what they do, and that's that: the
meaning 'sum of money' in 'sum' is activated by 'mercenary',
'wages', 'saved' and 'pay'.[41]

Richard Wilbur detects the 'clink of money', but needlessly
dismisses it from interpretation:[42] needlessly, because it is a funda-
mental strategy of Housman's poem to absorb favourable and
unfavourable attitudes to the soldiers. Virgil's *caelique ruina* (*Aeneid*
i. 129), Milton's 'heaven ruining from heaven' (*Paradise Lost* vi.
868), the biblical 'foundations of the earth'[43] and 'the earth and
the heaven fled away',[44] and the image of Hercules relieving Atlas
of the burden of the heavens are all invoked to affirm that the
soldiers avert nothing less than cosmic catastrophe. But, equally,
or equably, the poem also affirms that they are merely paid soldiers
who take their wages 'and are dead'. The power of the poem
lies in its 'level tones', which are achieved by steady rhythm
accentuated by parallelism and sound patterning, and, emphatically, by coordinations that resist differentiation: 'Followed their
mercenary calling / And took their wages and are dead', 'They
stood, and earth's foundations stay', 'What God abandoned, these
defended, / And saved the sum of things for pay'. If the poem
persuades, it does so by not seeming overtly persuasive: its starkly
uncompromising challenge rejects all adjectives but 'mercenary',
and there are no adverbs. Is there not a pressure to stress 'What
God abandoned, these defended' as though it were a heroic climax?
Yes, but the poem both resists and absorbs that pressure, calmly
insisting on the balanced weightiness of plain statement: 'What

God abandoned, these defended'. The emphasis on the pronouns 'These . . . their mercenary calling . . . their wages . . . Their shoulders . . . They . . . these' is unmistakably there, but it is not, as Richard Wilbur suggests, the result of special rhythmic stress. When he also thinks to read the poem in a flat voice,[45] he himself seems to sense, but not fully to acknowledge, that the poem again absorbs such potential emphasis in plain statements that are not so much unemphatic as wholly emphatic. The imperturbably assured manner constitutes the poem's chief rhetorical and moral force, and prompts us to reassess apparent overstatements and understatements: is 'And took their wages and are dead' not a climax? Is 'mercenary calling' perhaps in reality unparadoxical? Is the echo of Romans ironic, and are the soldiers saviours, not sinners? Nowhere in the eight lapidary lines is a potential change in attitude signalled by a change in tone: the poem asks us to accept its statements as neutrally true. It is a triumph of tonelessness, and prompts the reflection that what Enoch Powell said of Housman's textual scholarship can be applied to many of the poems:

> The severity of Housman's presentation was the severity not of passionlessness but of suppressed passion, passion for true poetry and passion for truthfulness.[46]

Notes

1. Kingsley Amis, *Memoirs* (London: Hutchinson, 1991) pp. 28, 58.
2. Kingsley Amis, *Collected Poems 1944–1979* (London: Hutchinson, 1979) p. 98.
3. *ASL* IV, XXXV, *LP* VIII, *AP* I. He used the metre in *MP* XLVI.
4. To J. W. Mackail, 25 July 1922: *The Letters of A. E. Housman*, ed. Henry Maas (London: Rupert Hart-Davis, 1971) p. 200. In a letter of 18 December 1925 to Robert Bridges, he expressed pleasure at Bridges using 'the old and beautiful stanza, now unjustly despised because so often ill managed . . . which ought not to be left to Laura Matilda': *Letters*, p. 231. 'Laura Matilda' was the pseudonym of Horace and James Smith when they used the stanza for 'Drury's Dirge' in their *Rejected Addresses* (1812). For further information on 'Laura Matilda', see D. M. Low and George De Fraine, *Notes and Queries* 197 (1952) 547–8, and R. L. Moreton, *ibid.*, p. 569.
5. Laurence Housman, *A. E. H.* (London: Jonathan Cape, 1937) p. 212.
6. *Alexander Pope: Pastoral Poetry and An Essay on Criticism*, eds E. Audra

and Aubrey Williams (London and New Haven: Methuen and Yale U.P., 1961) pp. 248–9, where a note cites classical precedents.

7. See William Empson, *Some Versions of Pastoral* (London: Chatto & Windus, 1935; rptd 1986) pp. 22, 53.

8. *Letters*, ed. Maas, p. 141.

9. For Brooks and Ricks, see *A. E. Housman: A Collection of Critical Essays*, ed. Ricks (Englewood Cliffs, NJ: Prentice-Hall, 1968) pp. 62–84, 106–22. Brian Rosebury's 'The Three Disciplines of A. E. Housman's Poetry' is in *Victorian Poetry* 21.3 (Autumn 1983) 217–28, and John Bayley's *Housman's Poems* was published in 1992 (Oxford: Clarendon Press).

10. 'John Milton: Sound and Sense in *Paradise Lost*' (1974), rptd in Ricks's *The Force of Poetry* (Oxford: Clarendon Press, 1984) p. 68.

11. 'Tradition and the Individual Talent' (1919) in *Selected Prose of T. S. Eliot*, ed. Frank Kermode (London: Faber & Faber, 1975) p. 43.

12. *Housman's Poems* (1992) p. 76.

13. *'Aske me no more where* love *bestowes':* *The Poems of Thomas Carew*, ed. Rhodes and Dunlap (Oxford: OUP, 1949; corrected reprint, 1970) pp. 102–3. Noted in Norman Marlow, *A. E. Housman: Scholar and Poet* (London: Routledge & Kegan Paul, 1958) p. 123. The poem is marked in pencil on p. 297 of Housman's copy of *The Oxford Book of English Verse 1250–1900*, ed. A. T. Quiller-Couch (Oxford: Clarendon Press, 1900), which is now at Bryn Mawr College, Pennsylvania.

14. Sts 2 and 3 of 'Ask me no more', added to *The Princess* in 1850: *The Poems of Tennyson*, ed. Christopher Ricks (Harlow: Longman, 1969) p. 829. Laurence Housman notes the parallel: *A. E. H.* (1937) p. 212.

15. Now at Bryn Mawr College, Pennsylvania.

16. *Endymion* iv. 751–63.

17. Now in St John's College Library, Oxford.

18. *A. E. Housman: A Sketch* (Cambridge: University Press, corrected reprint, 1936) p. 43.

19. 'Few, but Roses', *New Statesman and Nation* 23 (20 October 1923) rptd in *A. E. Housman: The Critical Heritage*, ed. Philip Gardner (London and New York: Routledge, 1992) p. 180.

20. *Birmingham Post*, 22 June 1937, quoted in Grant Richards, *Housman 1897–1936* (OUP London: Humphrey Milford, second impression, 1942) pp. 330–1.

21. *'In Memoriam'* (1936): *Selected Prose of T. S. Eliot*, ed. Frank Kermode (1975) p. 246.

22. *The Application of Thought to Textual Criticism*, in *A. E. Housman: Collected Poetry and Selected Prose*, ed. Christopher Ricks (London: Allen Lane, The Penguin Press, 1988) p. 328.

23. *A Buried Life: Personal Recollections of A. E. Housman* (London: Jonathan Cape, 1940) p. 14.

24. *The Independent Magazine*, 27 January 1990, 46, rptd in *Housman Society Journal* 16 (1990) 48.

25. See *More Poems* V.

26. Letter to *The Times*, 5 May 1936, quoted in Grant Richards, *Housman 1897–1936* (second impression, 1942) p. 289.

27. *A. E. Housman: Collected Poetry and Selected Prose,* ed. Christopher Ricks (1988) p. 364.
28. *The Name and Nature of Poetry:* Ricks (1988) p. 369.
29. *Housman Society Journal* 21 (1995) 6.
30. Laurence Housman, *A. E. H.* (1937) pp. 103–5.
31. *The American Book Collector* 10.2 (1959) 25–6.
32. *Notes and Queries* NS 17 (1970) 352.
33. See John Bayley in *Housman's Poems* (1992) pp. 186, 187.
34. 'The Nature of Housman's Poetry' (1964), rptd in *A. E. Housman: A Collection of Critical Essays,* ed. Ricks (1968) p. 114.
35. To The Richards Press, 14 November 1927: *Letters,* ed. Maas, p. 255.
36. 'Les Lauriers Sont Coupés' (1936): *A. E. Housman: The Critical Heritage,* ed. Philip Gardner (1992) p. 275.
37. *OED,* mercenary, *adj.* 1., 1.b., 2.
38. It appears in Housman's Commonplace Book (now at Southern Illinois University), and he praised it in *The Name and Nature of Poetry:* see Ricks (1988) p. 366. His poetry contains several echoes: *ASL* XLIII. 30–1, XLIV. 15–16, LIV. 2, *LP* II. 6, *The Manuscript Poems of A. E. Housman,* ed. Tom Burns Haber (Minneapolis: University of Minnesota Press, 1955) p. 59, l. 5.
39. Richard Wilbur, 'Round About a Poem of Housman's' (1962), rptd in *A. E. Housman: A Collection of Critical Essays,* ed. Christopher Ricks (1968) p. 93, notes only the echo of Romans.
40. See *OED,* sum, *sb.* 13.b., summa, 5; H. A. Mason, 'The Sum of Things', *Notes and Queries* NS 22 (1975) 309–10.
41. Cp. Wilbur, op. cit., p. 90.
42. Wilbur, op. cit., p. 96.
43. Psalms 82:5. See Vincent Freimarck, *Modern Language Notes* 67 (1952) 550.
44. Revelation 20:11. Contrast Psalms 104:5: 'Who laid the foundations of the earth, that it should not be removed for ever.'
45. Wilbur, op. cit., pp. 89–90.
46. *Housman Society Journal* 1 (1974) 28.

2

The Critical Reception of
A Shropshire Lad

Benjamin F. Fisher

In these times of our own *fin de siècle*, when detective novels such as Colin Dexter's *Daughters of Cain* or Andrew Taylor's *An Air That Kills* (replete with epigraphs from *A Shropshire Lad*) remind us of the continuing attention drawn to A. E. Housman's first book of poems, we might find our literary awareness expanded by a backward glance. The reception of this now long-familiar little book has never been exhaustively evaluated, and thus what follows, itself by no means exhaustive, may recall much to thoroughgoing Housmanians and offer additional or new perspectives for many others.[1] What with so many literary periodicals circulating at that time, plus the seventy-odd daily newspapers in London alone during the era when *A Shropshire Lad* was new literary fare, a team effort and much time might be essential to ferret out all early notices of Housman's first book of verse. From my assessment of the reviews, I hope to offer sensible conclusions in regard to the impression made by Housman's poems. My work includes substantial quotation from now century-old periodicals because, even with current methods of access retrieval, along with the panoply of contemporaneous notices reprinted by Philip Gardner, certain commentary might not readily attract investigators.

When *A Shropshire Lad* first appeared in February–March of 1896, published by Kegan Paul, followed by John Lane's American distribution in 1897, and when it reappeared under the imprint of Grant Richards in September of 1898, reviewers were quick to point out that a new poetic voice sounded here, although part of that newness consisted of Housman's descent from earlier British, as well as Greek and Latin classical poets. Herrick, Burns, Hood might be discerned in Housman's background, as might the *Greek Anthology*, said the press. Such antecedents had been lost sight of, we are to infer, because of nineteenth-century trends in foregrounding form at the expense of content in English poetry. A member of no current 'school', Housman created verse, so most reviewers thought, that stood apart from much else during the 1890s. In fact, Housman himself was to take his own firm position years later in regard to being too casually placed as an 1890s writer. Refusing permission for selections from *A Shropshire Lad* to be included in *A Book of Nineties Verse*, edited by A. J. A. Symons, Housman wrote to Grant Richards, his own publisher, on 9 October 1928, that 'to include me in an anthology of the Nineties would be just as technically correct, and just as essentially inappropriate, as to include Lot in a book on Sodomites; in saying which I am not saying a word against sodomy, nor implying that intoxication and incest are in any way preferable.'[2] Despite this customary astringent wit from its creator, *A Shropshire Lad* did coalesce significantly with currents that coursed through the 1890s' cultural milieu, as we shall see. Interestingly, those very characteristics were what reviewers were prone to touch upon, even though they did not specifically link Housman's themes or techniques with those that were deemed common literary fare.

Part of what was thought to distinguish *A Shropshire Lad* from much else on the current poetic scene was the simplicity pervading the poems. That element would have been sure to gain attention during the age of art for art's sake. Housman himself on two occasions endorsed the notice given by Hubert Bland, in the *New Age* for 16 April 1896, which opens:

> Here at last is a note that has for long been lacking in English poetry – simplicity, to wit. This our time is rife with poets and poetasters, and the most carping critic is compelled to confess that very much of their work is on a very fair level of excellence. But there is so much of it, and it is all so much alike . . .

He lamented that the poetry of the day was likewise too recognizably derivative: 'One catches echoes everywhere, and the echoes of Tennyson are thunderous.' Housman's book, by way of contrast, contained 'essentially and distinctively new poetry. The individual voice rings out true and clear.' If it is not wholly joyful, it 'says and sings things that have not been sung or said before, and this with a power and directness, and with a heart-penetrating quality for which one may seek in vain through the work of any contemporary lyrist, Mr Henley perhaps excepted'. Bland bolstered his argument by quoting 'Loveliest of trees' as exemplary of the 'perfect simplicity' that was wanted, and that Housman gave 'with the swift, unfaltering touch of a master's hand'. The 'direct expression of elemental emotions, of heart-thoughts, is the dominant note of all Mr Housman's work, as it was of Heine's alone among modern singers', so direct that many accustomed to contemporary poetry will find it 'bald', lacking in art. To Bland, Housman's 'artistic range is limited – it lies within narrow limits, even – but within those limits it is little short of consummate'.

Bland's wife, E.[dith] Nesbit, also stated, somewhat later, in the *National Observer*, that

> the dominant characteristic of Mr Housman's work is dignified simplicity, not necessarily simplicity of thought, but simplicity of expression. Here we have no elaborate confectionery, no artificial flowers wreathing the crook of Daphnis and Chloe, no laboured jewel-work, even. We have instead the perfect directness that marks the master, a reticence that is not baldness, a simplicity pregnant with thought and meaning. Here is no struggle for effect; only achievement without apparent effort. And that the effort was, there is only the excellence of the result to prove.

Like her husband, Nesbit not only found a distinctly new note in Housman's book, but juxtaposed his poems with those by others to point up the distinctions: only 'one or two have yielded a little to the wide and wonderful influence of Mr. Kipling, and one or two suggest Heine; a feat, this last, which no other English writer has come near to perform'. Nesbit also comments on the prominence of elemental moods within the characters in the poems. Such a gallery of characters may indeed have embodied a newness, but they might have been equally at home in early British popular ballads. A stimulus to Housman's poetic endeavours not mentioned by any of the early reviewers, though later pointed out, and not to be overlooked because of its contemporaneousness, is that of Christina Rossetti's verse.

From another commentator: 'Simplicity is the note of Mr. Housman's style – simplicity and a dignified restraint.' Interestingly, this was Grant Richards, who would bring out the 1898 edition of *A Shropshire Lad*, whence that book began to flourish. That simplicity, so intensely appealing to these commentators, was elusive, however. As Richard Le Gallienne remarked, any attempt to give an accurate sense of Housman's simplicity was as trialsome 'to convey in prose as it would be hard to convey the various charms of clear water to someone who happened never to have seen it'. He added that it was 'easy enough to note certain obvious attractions of subject matter'. Cautionary notes were sounded by a *Manchester Guardian* critic who perceived that Housman's 'verse is very artful, for all its appearance of simplicity, in the use of thesis and other subtleties', and by the *Academy* reviewer, who discerned in the poems 'a latter-day simplicity, less simple than it seems', a simplicity seldom 'combined (as it is here combined) with the self-consciousness of the modern poet, yet a simplicity without affectation'.[3]

One such obvious attraction in the simplicity embedded in *A Shropshire Lad* was local colour, as was pointed out in the first notice, a terse evaluation (by T. H. Ward) in the *London Times* for 27 March 1896.[4] The term 'local colour' has been used far more often in conjunction with American fiction during the last quarter of the nineteenth century than with British literature from the same era, but, a century later, we must not cursorily pass by its implications for the first readers of Housman's book. They would have seen local colour in *A Shropshire Lad* as a noteworthy aspect of their cultural milieu, say perhaps most readily as a team mate for Thomas Hardy's Wessex fiction. Housman, moreover, was named along with William Barnes, the Dorset poet, and T. E. Brown, who used the Isle of Man as artistic material, in creating a distinctive world within his verse.[5] Among others upheld as fine local colour writers were Eden Philpotts, H.[enry] D.[awson] Lowry and Ella D'Arcy, respectively for Dartmoor, Cornwall and the Channel Islands. Lowry and D'Arcy gained attention when his *Women's Tragedies* and her *Monochromes* appeared as titles in John Lane's notorious Keynotes Series during 1895, and both were complimented as local colourists, Lowry more so than D'Arcy, who did not restrict her settings to any one locale. Although precise critics point out that Housman was not himself a Shropshire lad, as many of his early readers supposed, he has been as emphatically associated with that part of Great Britain as Mark Twain has been with the Mississippi River – no matter that each spent most of his life in another part of his country. Not every reviewer found local colour significant in *A Shropshire Lad*. W. Robertson Nicoll, writing as 'Claudius Clear' in *The British Weekly*, 26 April 1896, states that readers must not expect to find in Housman's poems such localisms as dialect – like that in William Barnes's Dorset poems – and downplays the geographical features: 'neither is there much local colour, although here and there we come on the names of Shropshire towns and hills. The scenery of the country is not effectively rendered.'[6] From the outset, ironies were to dog interpretations of Housman's poems.

A Shropshire Lad differed from much else in its time because, unlike the poets of the urban scene, for example Dowson, Gray, Symons, Johnson, its creator turned his literary imagination chiefly to country subject matter. No London cafés, no painted women, no exotic dance themes, nor any attempts to be an 'interpreter of the ideal significance of the music halls' here! Instead we encounter ruralness that was applauded by some, for example, 'O. O.' [W. Robertson Nicoll] in the *Sketch*, who rejoiced at the 'fresh country pictures', which partake of the 'real, forcible imagination that works in folk-tales', and which come to us with 'much of the picturesque conciseness of the old ballads'. Sharply countering this praise, the American, Louise Imogen Guiney, found Housman's poems 'not merely rural, but country-bumpkinish to a degree', and too obtrusively displaying 'ugly villageous ingredients: spites, jealousies, and slit throats'. Evidently, Guiney thought that rural life should be portrayed in its bucolic aspects alone. Her critique was in the main, though, positive. Several years later, T. P. O'Connor found especially fresh and appealing in this 'memorable book' the 'echoes from country lanes [which] seem to ring out from its pages with a sincerity impossible to imitate'. O'Connor chose to illustrate his idea by quoting complete 'Oh, see how thick the goldcup flowers' and '"Is my team ploughing?"' The former he called 'a story of spring, and about it there lingers spring's own atmosphere'.[7]

British local colour did not encompass rural environs alone. The city and its impact had been gaining impetus in literature, but the 1890s witnessed a burgeoning in creative writing grounded in urban locale and concerns. We need but think of Arthur Morrison, Israel Zangwill, Hubert Crackanthorpe, Ella D'Arcy, Ella Hepworth Dixon or Netta Syrett as purveyors of fiction which featured the (usually) baneful effects of city living and employment conditions detrimental to many workers, especially those from the lower classes. In poetry, Dowson, Johnson, Binyon, Davidson, Symons, Gray and Wilde most readily come to mind for their emphases on urban materials and themes. Therefore, when in *A Shropshire Lad* the young protagonist departs the country, his experiences reflect yet another segment of life that was not foreign to the literary consciousness of the 1890s – and in the background for this book may be A. E. Housman's own course in life up to that point.

Housman's military poems serve as points of intersection for rural and urban issues. Departing Shropshire for his military service, the Lad had of necessity to engage city conditions. The soldier had long enjoyed popularity as a character in British literature; the uprisings and threats of uprisings here and there in the Empire, and the impact of the American Civil War, all contributed to maintaining his prominence. Understandably, then, Spencer Blackett, the manager at Kegan Paul, was 'particularly captivated with the military element', and wanted *A Shropshire Lad* to be reworked as 'a romance of enlistment'. Soldiers and soldiery in the book caught the eyes of readers at the start, and the military substance has long continued to be a focus in criticism. One may well wonder in this respect just what impact on Housman's creativity might have emanated from the fiction of Stephen Crane, whose work, we know, remained a steadfast favourite with the Englishman. To speculate in this matter is tempting because Crane's *The Red Badge of Courage* and *Maggie: A Child of the Streets*, to use its British title, were both much noticed during the months when *A Shropshire Lad* was in the making. Crane's writings were inevitably and inextricably connected with war and battle motifs, according to British reviewers, whose critiques of the young American author's works betrayed no mean knowledge of the literature of war otherwise, repeatedly citing his affinities with, and (often to Crane's advantage) departures from Tolstoi, who had previously seemed to be the greatest among novelists of war.

Housman's military themes elicited praise on both sides of the Atlantic, although that acclaim was directed at varied aspects of the soldier's role. As might be anticipated from a church-related newspaper, the *Guardian*, noting the sombre themes of death and endurance pervading Housman's book, complimented particularly the 'very stirring' note of endurance in some of the 'soldier poems', citing 'From Clee to heaven the beacon burns' as

illustrative. Less sympathetic, the Boston *Literary World* emphasized the decided predilections for themes of the heroes' deaths
in the military poems (singling out 'The Recruit' as 'good'), a
sentiment echoed by William Archer in *The Fortnightly Review*,
and by the anonymous reviewer, who tellingly entitled his screed
'The Funereal Muse', in *Literature*. Archer thought that the patriotic inspiration of Housman's soldiers derived from their intentness
to enhance 'the credit of Shropshire'. The critic in *Literature* added:
'[I]t is characteristic of [Housman] that he seems to value soldiering
much less for the opportunities which it offers to a young man
for serving his country than for the unique facilities which it affords
him for winning a speedy and honourable death.' *The Daily News*
concurred with Archer in noting that the soldier is never divorced
from Shropshire. *The Daily Chronicle*, by contrast, viewed the Lad's
outlooks on patriotism and war as parts of his 'wholesome sense
of life's proportions and congruities'.[8]

Another feature of the characters in *A Shropshire Lad* that places
it with much else during the 1890s is signalled by Nesbit (p. 243),
who, once again, touches on more than one of the cultural pulses
underlying the era, in comparing the fratricide who was hanged
at Shrewsbury with Cain. A composite figure, to whom were
imparted character traits from legends of Cain, Judas Iscariot and
Satan, such an outcast played important roles in the artistic milieu,
witness Aubrey Beardsley's 'A Kiss of Judas', which appeared in
the *Pall Mall Magazine* for July 1893, as an illustration for a short
story about vampirism by 'X. L.' – Julian Osgood Field. Other
notable treatments of such figures were George Moore's *Mike
Fletcher* and *Esther Waters*, Oscar Wilde's *The Picture of Dorian Gray*
and 'The Ballad of Reading Gaol', Marie Corelli's bestsellers, *The
Sorrows of Satan* and *Barabbas*, as well as in many minor productions.[9] Housman's soldiers at times thought themselves outcast,
alone, desolate, as much as they might have manifested good
nature, for example, in '"Terence, this is stupid stuff"', and thus
they join ranks with other literary characters who were more
sensationally delineated. Throughout the military poems, we
encounter two more themes that add firmness to the 1890s aura
of *A Shropshire Lad*. Housman's soldiers take their places with
the sexually liberated, and perhaps not strictly heterosexual, per-
sonages who so often peopled literary texts of the times. They
are analogous, too, to the artist figures whose early promise was
cut off by untimely deaths. Aspects of the dual 'creativity', that

is, sexual and artistic, also cannot go overlooked in reading poems like 'From Clee to heaven the beacon burns' or that perennial favourite of explicators and anthologists, '"Is my team plough-ing?"' – and others could be cited for illustrative purposes. Thus Housman's poems assuredly did fit into the 1890s, *pace* his later antipathy to the notion of their status, and in ways that many of his devotees might not immediately divine.

What some found as the 'vulgar tongue' (to use E. Nesbit's phrase) in *A Shropshire Lad* also occasioned comment pertinent to 1890s literary endeavour. Localism in language seemed to exercise reviewers in that day, and it might be another irony for association with Housman's book that Nesbit's own collection of short stories for Lane's Keynotes Series, *In Homespun* (1896), drew repeated remarks concerning its regional dialogue. Nesbit herself would therefore have had colloquial language on her mind when she addressed that in *A Shropshire Lad*, and many other books of the day also elicited special comments in regard to their colloquial language. British reviewers were unlikely to miss what seemed to them the colloquialisms or regionalisms in writings by Americans or in indigenous literary wares, as is borne out in critiques of Twain, Crane, Cable, Wilkins, Philpotts or the 'Kailyard school'.

Another aspect of *A Shropshire Lad* that engaged early critics and that has persisted is that of biographical-personal versus altogether imaginary foundations for the poems. E. Nesbit stated that, unlike so much from other contemporary poets, Housman's poems were 'not personal to himself. Though a distinct personal note is heard through all his song, that note is not of his own personality, but of another's. He is dramatic. He has conceived a character, and sees the world through the eyes of his concep-tion' (p. 242). Just how much of A. E. Housman himself informs the contents of his book we will never know with definitiveness, but many present-day Housmanians would challenge Nesbit's thinking by proposing that the poet's yearnings for his univer-sity classmate, Moses Jackson, constituted the most active inspirations underlying these poems. The first *Manchester Guard-ian* notice may unintentionally but ironically delve near the personal origin for the poems: 'There are touches of strength and manliness, but the whole is hardly masculine.' Might a passage like this characterize shy, prim A. E. Housman in contrast to the bluff, 'manly' Moses Jackson? Interestingly, Grant Richards calls *A Shropshire Lad* 'a biography in verse', which treats 'the loves and sorrows, the dramatic incidents, the daily labours of a Ludlow boy'. A concurrent attitude comes from *The Boston Evening Transcript* reviewer, who classifies Housman as a good poet because he's a 'man', illustrated by '"Is my team ploughing?"' and because he knows the 'beautiful stainless sorrows of first youth', as is evident in 'The time you won your town the race'. Of equal interest is *The Daily Chronicle* viewpoint: 'Mr. Housman is not subjective; he is dramatic. His lyrics are a revelation of personality but of a personality other than his own.'[10] For many, the non-subjective quality would have marked out these poems as something new in the 1890s, when ego all too often deliberately reared its head in the arts.

Finally, whether to read *A Shropshire Lad* as a unified long poem or as a volume of individual poems was a question in many minds. N. O. B. in *The Echo* saw no coherence in the book, although he detected signs that a unity had been envisioned if not achieved. Americans were less censorious about a unified book versus individual poems, witness William Morton Payne in *The Dial*, who found 'a collection of short poems', and the commentator in *The San Francisco Chronicle*, who referred to the 'sixty-three brief lyrical poems'. Another American, Willa Cather, when she first reviewed it in the Pittsburgh *Home Monthly* for October 1897, treated *A Shropshire Lad* as if it were a heterogeneous collection; later, however, she remarked that 'there seems to be a vague sort of plot running through them all, binding them together'. *The Nation* apprehended that the book 'gives to the American a single vivid glimpse of the average rural Englishman of the lower class [and that] it gives a continuous kinetoscopic view of the one man, the Shropshire Lad'.[11] In other words, *A Shropshire Lad* falls into line with the manifold miniaturizings of 1890s art, but in that very feature it also carries on nineteenth-century attempts to create an epic, witness *Don Juan, The Prelude, Empedocles on Etna, The Ring and the Book, Idylls of the King* and *Tristram of Lyonesse*. Housman's book brings epic scale into more compact compass, as do Meredith's *Modern Love*, D. G. Rossetti's *The House of Life* and the sonnet sequences of Christina Rossetti and W. S. Blunt. Like several of these works, too, *A Shropshire Lad* contributed to tendencies toward the collapsing or blurring of genres in its minglings of poetry with fictional methodology and dramatic techniques. Thus Housman's book looks backward and forward. His practice may be likened to that of Hardy in his Wessex fiction, to Ella D'Arcy, whose short stories offer several series possibilities, Galsworthy in the *Forsyte Saga*, Sara Orne Jewett in *The Country of the Pointed Firs*, Sherwood Anderson in *Winesburg, Ohio*, Ernest Hemingway in the Nick Adams stories and William Faulkner in the Yoknapatawpha chronicles.

To conclude one might well cite the 1898 reviewer for the *Literary World*, who expressed an enjoyment in reading Housman's book that prompted re-reading, a repetition that most other poetry of that time did not inspire. Re-reading may have been prompted by features noted above; some recapitulation may therefore be in order. The debatable 'simplicity' as a hallmark of newness in *A Shropshire Lad* may strike some as a curiously ironic feature of the book. On the one hand, that quality certainly would have gained acclamation during the 1890s, a time when the ornate phrasing, sententiousness and length of earlier British poetry were in general being eliminated from works in progress – in the face of intermittent bows toward the epic mode. From our perspective of 100 years, however, we may see the heralding of another seemingly dichotomous element in the book's undeniable 1890s configuration. What was seen as 'simplicity' in Housman's verse was coincident with 'realism' in fiction, an element for which fictionists were constantly lauded or chastised. Many other writers whose works began to appear at about the same time as Housman's were dubbed simple by some, not so simple by others. For example, H. D. Lowry, whose volume of short stories with Cornish settings and characters, *Women's Tragedies*, has been mentioned above, was applauded for the simplicity in the stories by some reviewers, whereas others found the apparent simplicity deceptive, but all the better for that very double-sidedness. Lowry's stories, like Housman's poems, were acclaimed as 'healthy studies of human nature, stories which are full of strong, deep, and simple emotions'. Like Lowry, too, like Hubert Crackanthorpe and like Thomas Hardy the poet – with whom he was teamed in the *St. James's Gazette* in late 1898 – Housman was often cited for his blendings of simplicity with pessimism, a pessimism which, in his case, was demarcated as 'no fashionable pose, but simple, strong, and sincere'. That this periodical did not think lightly of Housman's accomplishments is evident in its notice of Grant Richards's 1903 printing of *A Shropshire Lad* at one shilling a copy: 'A distinctive benefit is thus conferred upon many with more appreciation of true poetry than the wherewithal to buy books.' The convergences of tradition with newness in *A Shropshire Lad* would make it, surely, part and parcel of the 1890s, that era when experiments resulted in such yokings. We could turn again to Lowry for comparison because *Women's Tragedies* included stories of contemporary Cornish life, as well as several set in pagan days in that area, and reviewers argued the merits and demerits of each variety.[12] The penchant for the dialogue, as it might advantageously be employed in narratives of the short, hard-hitting types that were shoving aside many earlier ponderous novels, furnishes another kind of these bracketings. Housman's balladry and his concordant lyricism dovetailed neatly with these techniques; they gave the poet as singer a new artistic dimension. The dramatic texture found by several reviewers, as mentioned above, would doubtless have appealed to devotees of the renaissance in the dialogue form, just as it might now seem to us as a precursor of the dramatic as advocated by James Joyce. Housman's grotesque or sardonic humour, another feature in *A Shropshire Lad* that firmly bonds the book with the 1890s cultural milieu, also drew notice, for example in *The Daily News* and *The Echo*. The proximity of mirth to melancholy or pessimism in Housman's poems once again suggests a kinship with kindred blendings in Moore, Wilde, Beardsley, Machen (*The Three Impostors*) or Kipling. In the writings of all, and in those by many others of the era, comedy often throws tragedy into bolder relief.

To look briefly at the outreach of *A Shropshire Lad* during early years of the twentieth century is also enlightening about and affirming to Housman as an 1890s writer. For example, Douglas Goldring recounts that from his schooldays, when his Headmaster, the Rev. Arthur Clark, lent him a copy of Housman's book and related an anecdote of their days together at Oxford, Goldring took great pleasure in Housman's poetry. Subsequently, during his own years at Oxford, with companions such as Montague Summers, Goldring and his circle found in the verse of Dowson, Francis Thompson, Baudelaire, Verlaine and *A Shropshire Lad* 'our principal sources of poetic inspiration'. Goldring's first volume of verse, *A Country Boy*, was 'as the title suggests, . . . largely influenced by A. E. Housman'. Slightly later, in 1914, when he was age sixteen, Alec Waugh was introduced by his father to the poetry of 'Dowson, Housman, and Rossetti' as part of the family's customary poetry readings.[13] Many more like examples might, of course, be cited. To continue would be superfluous; A. E.

Housman was very much an '1890s writer', and that sobriquet does him no detriment.

Notes

I am deeply grateful to Roy Birch for contributing significantly to the genesis of this study, as well as to Jennie McGregor-Smith, for help far beyond the call of duty. I also thank these persons in the University of Mississippi: Ms Martha E. Swan and her Inter-Library Loan staff; John M. Meador, Jr, Dean of Libraries; John D. Cloy, Library Reference; John Pilkington, President of the Friends of the Library; and Michael R. Dingerson, Dean of the Graduate School; finally, Professor William J. Zimmer, Jr, Montgomery County Community College, for considerable assistance.

1. Several notices of the 1896, 1897 and the 1898 publications of *A Shropshire Lad* appear in *A. E. Housman: The Critical Heritage*, ed. Philip Gardner (London and New York: Routledge, 1992) pp. 58–93, though he selects few from newspapers. One should read in conjunction P. G. Naiditch's lengthy review of Gardner's book – *The Housman Society Journal* 20 (1994) 79–103. A concise overview of the first and several subsequent printings of Housman's volume may be found in '"A Shropshire Lad": A Bibliography', *The Times Literary Supplement* (30 March 1946) 156. See also Colin Dexter, *Daughters of Cain* (New York: Crown Publishers, 1994; Ballantine Books, 1996); Andrew Taylor, *An Air That Kills* (London: Hodder & Stoughton; New York: St. Martin's Press, 1994). Much earlier, E. C. Bentley included an amusing portrait of A. E. Housman in his lampoon of Dorothy Sayers's detective novel, *Gaudy Night* – 'Greedy Night: A Parody', *Ellery Queen's Mystery Magazine* 4.1 (January 1943) 27. In my Bibliography, I supplement information furnished by Gardner and Naiditch. Noteworthy, too, is that much of my thought throughout this study, though based on opinions now a hundred years old, dovetails, in matters too numerous for specific citation, with many ideas found in Keith Jebb's *A. E. Housman* (Bridgend: Seren Books, 1992) and Jeremy Bourne's *The Westerly Wanderer: A Brief Portrait of A. E. Housman* (Bromsgrove: The Housman Society, 1996).

2. Housman is likened to the earlier poets by N. O. B., 'A New Poet', *The Echo* 13 August 1896: 1 (not in Gardner). Worth comment here, to forestall needless pursuit of a chimera – a 'review' of *A Shropshire Lad* – is the fact that, although a commentator in the London *Weekly Sun*, 7 July 1896: 2, tersely outlining Housman's career, remarks that the *Sun* 'had something to say a short time ago' in regard to *A Shropshire Lad*, what we find in the 17 May issue (p. 2) is merely a reprinting of 'Far in western brookland' without comment – but with the commendation implicit toward all reprintings to be found in 'At the Sign of the Lyre' columns. A subsequent commentary,

'Poems by Two Brothers', in the literary supplement for 6 December
1896: 2, which notices *A Shropshire Lad* and Laurence's *Green Arras*,
suggests that A. E. H.'s classical background may have inspired his
'art which likes art' in his verse. I have unearthed no additional
1896 notice of *A Shropshire Lad* in *The Weekly Sun* (and there are no
missing issues at Colindale for that year). Housman's letter to Richards
is conveniently located in *The Letters of A. E. Housman*, ed. Henry
Maas (London: Rupert Hart-Davis; Cambridge, Mass.: Harvard University Press, 1971) p. 271.

3. Bland, 'A New Poet', *New Age* (16 April 1896) 37; Nesbit, 'A New
   Poet', *The National Observer* (11 July 1896) 242; Richards, 'A Shropshire Lad', *The Review of Reviews* (London) 14 (July 1896) 187; Le
   Gallienne, 'Books and Bookmen', *The Star* (London) (11 May 1896)
   1. One can only wonder what Bland would think of some recent
   critiques of 'Loveliest of trees', whence we might come away thinking how, in reality, this is one of the veriest bits of versified trash,
   in theme and technique, that has ever masqueraded as poetry. In
   this context, albeit with none of the severity that has been expressed
   in our own time, W. E. Henley, thanking Edith Nesbit for the copy
   of *A Shropshire Lad* she had given him, opined on 23 February 1899:
   'I like him well enough, here and there, to wish I'd written him.
   But I find him very monotonous. I think if I had written him I should
   have burned at least two thirds of my work, and stood to win in
   what was left. But that doesn't prevent him from being a man with
   something to say and a very distinguished way of saying it'– Doris
   Langley Moore, *E. Nesbit: A Biography*, rev. edn (Philadelphia, New
   York: Chilton Books, 1966) p. 154. See also A. R. Coulthard's 'The
   Flawed Craft of A. E. Housman', *The Victorian Newsletter* 84 (1993)
   29–31; and my rejoinder in 'The Poets of the Nineties', *Victorian
   Poetry* 23 (1995) 552–3. *The Daily Tatler* critique of 'Loveliest of trees'
   (19 November 1896: 3) anticipates Coulthard. Contrariwise, John Bell
   Henneman, in the *Sewanee Review*, noticing the 1906 American edition of *A Shropshire Lad*, singles out 'Loveliest of trees' for high
   commendation (p. 382). See, too, 'Books of the Week', *The Manchester Guardian* (4 October 1898) 9; 'Mr. A. E. Housman's Poems', *The
   Academy* (8 October 1898) 23–5 – this latter ascribed without verifi-
   cation to William Archer by Ghussan Rouse Greene, 'The Public
   Reputation of A. E. Housman's Poetry in England and America',
   dissertation, University of South Carolina, 1978: p. 156. On Christina
   Rossetti's influence see Laurence Housman, *My Brother, A. E. Housman*
   (New York: Charles Scribner's, 1937) p. 86; and Norman Page, *A. E.
   Housman: A Critical Biography* (London: Macmillan; New York:
   Schocken Books, 1983) pp. 80–1.
4. 'Books of the Week', *The London Times* (27 March 1896) 13.
5. 'Books of the Week', *The Manchester Guardian* (4 October 1898) 9.
6. Nicoll, Letter to the editor, *The British Weekly* (23 April 1896) 9. Sharper
   ironic divergences would sound decades later in the contretemps
   involving, on one side, John Carter and John Sparrow and, on the
   other, Tom Burns Haber, over implications in the texts of the poems.

7. O. O., 'The Literary Lounger', *The Sketch* (22 April 1896) 574; Guiney, 'A Shropshire Lad', *The Chap-Book* (1 February 1897) 245–6; O'Connor, 'Books and Their Writers', *T. P.'s. Weekly* (27 February 1903) 489–90. Guiney, it should be mentioned, ordered copies of *A Shropshire Lad* once she read the review in the London *Daily Chronicle*; see *Letters of Louise Imogen Guiney*, ed. Grace Guiney, 2 vols (New York and London: Harper & Bros, 1926) p. 164. Thereafter she praised Housman's poems.

8. A. E. to Laurence Housman, probably in April 1896 – Henry Maas: 36–7; Grant Richards, *Housman 1897–1936* (Oxford and New York: Oxford University Press, 1942; New York: Octagon Books, 1973) p. 337; 'A Shropshire Lad', *The Guardian* (3 June 1896) 872; 'A Shropshire Lad', *The Literary World* (Boston) (17 April 1897) 128; William Archer, 'A. E. Housman', *The Fortnightly Review* (1 August 1898) 263–8; 'The Funereal Muse', *Literature* (29 October 1898) 387–9; 'Verse', *The Daily News* (11 May 1896) 8; 'A Shropshire Poet', *The Daily Chronicle* (31 October 1896) 3.

9. See *The Letters of Aubrey Beardsley*, eds Henry Maas, J. L. Duncan and W. G. Good (Rutherford, NJ: Fairleigh Dickinson University Press, 1970) pp. 48–9; and Ewa Kuryluk, *Salome and Judas in the Cave of Sex* (Evanston, IL: Northwestern University Press, 1987) pp. 259ff.

10. *The Review of Reviews* (London) (1 August 1896) 187; rptd New York *The Review of Reviews* (14 September 1896) 371; *The Boston Evening Transcript* (14 April 1897) 10; *The Daily Chronicle* (31 October 1896) 3; 'Books of the Week', *The Manchester Guardian* (16 April 1896) 7. Companion reading that illuminates Housman's sexuality in this context appears in Ruth Robbins, '"A very curious construction": masculinity and the poetry of A. E. Housman and Oscar Wilde', *Cultural Politics at the Fin de Siècle*, eds Sally Ledger and Scott McCracken (London and New York: Cambridge University Press, 1995) pp. 137–59.

11. N. O. B., 'A New Poet: Mr. Alfred Housman's "A Shropshire Lad"', *The Echo* (13 August 1896) 1; Payne, 'Recent Poetry', *The Dial* (1 October 1897) 188–9; Cather (commenting respectively in 1897 and 1900), *The World and the Parish: Willa Cather's Articles and Reviews 1893–1902*, ed. William M. Curtin (Lincoln: University of Nebraska Press, 1970) pp. 357–8; 706–9; 'Recent British Poetry', *The Nation* (9 December 1897) 460. Gardner and Greene, mentioned above, do not give Americans just dues as regards their positive responses to *A Shropshire Lad*.

12. See reviews of *Women's Tragedies* in *The Western Daily Mercury* (4 May 1895) 3; *The Western Morning News* (10 May 1895) 7; *The Weekly Sun* (London) (23 June 1895) 2. See also 'The Literary World', *The St. James's Gazette* (31 December 1898) 4; 'Rapid Reviews', *The St. James's Gazette* (19 February 1903) 16; W. P. Ryan, *Literary London: its Lights and Comedies* [1898], rptd P. G. Naiditch, 'A Forgotten Notice of "A Shropshire Lad"', *American Notes and Queries* 21 (1982) 44; 'A Shropshire Lad', *The Speaker* (26 November 1898) 637; 'New Writers: Mr. A. E. Housman', *The Bookman* (London) (10 August 1896) 134.

13. Douglas Goldring, *Odd Man Out: The Autobiography of a 'Propaganda Novelist'* (London: Chapman & Hall, 1935) pp. 34, 55, 63; Alec Waugh, *The Early Years of Alec Waugh* (London: Cassell, 1962) p. 19.

Bibliography

Anon. 'A Shropshire Lad', *The Academy* (20 August 1898) 17–72.

Anon. 'A Shropshire Lad', *The Argonaut* (San Francisco) (15 March 1897) 9.

Anon. 'A Shropshire Lad', *The Athenaeum* (8 October 1898) 488.

Anon. 'A Shropshire Lad', *Book News* 15 (April 1897) 421.

Anon. 'A Shropshire Lad', *The Bookman* (New York) (6 July 1897) 434–5.

Anon. 'The Bookman's Table: *A Shropshire Lad*', *The Bookman* (London) (15 October 1898) 27.

Anon. 'Library and Foyer', *The Boston Evening Transcript* (14 April 1897) 10.

Anon. 'A Shropshire Lad', *The Citizen* (Philadelphia) (3 November 1897) 215–16.

Anon. 'A Shropshire Poet', *The Daily Chronicle* (31 October 1896) 3.

Anon. 'Verse', *The Daily News* (11 May 1896) 8.

Anon. 'A New Book of Verse', *The Daily Tatler* (New York) (19 November 1896) 3.

Anon. 'A Shropshire Lad', *The Guardian* (3 June 1896) 872.

Anon. 'Poetry', *The Literary World* (17 April 1897) 128.

Anon. 'A Shropshire Lad', *The Literary World* (31 October 1898) 278.

Anon. 'Books of the Week', *The Manchester Guardian* (16 April 1896) 7.

Anon. 'Books of the Week', *The Manchester Guardian* (4 October 1898) 9.

Anon. 'Recent British Poetry', *The Nation* (9 December 1897) 459–61.

Anon. 'The Literary World', *The St. James's Gazette* (31 December 1898) 4.

'Rapid Reviews', *The St. James's Gazette* (19 February 1903) 16.

Anon. 'Poems of A. E. Housman', *The San Francisco Chronicle* (14 March 1897) 4.

Anon. 'Recent Poetry and Verse: *A Shropshire Lad*', *The Speaker* (27 June 1896) 694.

Anon. 'A Shropshire Lad', *The Speaker* (26 November 1898) 637.

Anon. '"A Shropshire Lad": A Bibliography', *The Times Literary Supplement* (30 March 1946) 156.

Anon. 'Books and Their Writers', *T. P.'s. Weekly* (27 February 1903) 489–90.

Anon. 'Women's Tragedies', *The Weekly Sun* (23 June 1895) 2.

Anon. 'At the Sign of the Lyre', *The Weekly Sun* (London) (17 May 1896) 2.

Anon. 'Books and Bookmen', *The Weekly Sun* (London) (7 July 1896) 2.

Anon. 'Poems by Two Brothers', *The Weekly Sun* (London) (Literary Supplement) (6 December 1896) 2.

Anon. 'Women's Tragedies', *The Western Daily Mercury* (4 May 1895) 3.

Anon. 'Women's Tragedies', *The Western Daily News* (10 May 1895) 7.

Archer, William, 'A. E. Housman', *The Fortnightly Review* (1 August 1898) 263–8.

Beardsley, Aubrey, *The Letters of Aubrey Beardsley*, eds Henry Maas, J. L. Duncan and W. G. Good (Rutherford, NJ: Fairleigh Dickinson University Press, 1970).

Bentley, E. C., 'Greedy Night: A Parody', *Ellery Queen's Mystery Magazine* 4.1 (January 1943) 27.

Bland, Hubert, 'A Shropshire Lad', *The New Age* (16 April 1898) 37.

Bourne, Jeremy, *The Westerly Wanderer: A Brief Portrait of A. E. Housman* (Bromsgrove: The Housman Society, 1996).

Cather, Willa, *The World and the Parish: Willa Cather's Articles and Reviews 1893–1902*, ed. William M. Curtin (Lincoln: University of Nebraska Press, 1970) pp. 357–8, 706–9.

Claudius Clear (W. Robertson Nicoll), 'The Correspondence of Claudius Clear', *The British Weekly* (23 April 1896) 9.

Coulthard, A. R., 'The Flawed Craft of A. E. Housman', *The Victorian Newsletter* 84 (1993) 29–31.

Dexter, Colin, *Daughters of Cain* (New York: Crown Publishers, 1994; Ballantine Books, 1996).

Fisher, Benjamin F., 'The Poets of the Nineties', *Victorian Poetry* 33 (1995) 550–4.

Gale, Norman, 'Some Volumes of Verse: *A Shropshire Lad*', *The Academy* (11 July 1896) 30–1.

Gardner, Philip (ed.), *A. E. Housman: The Critical Heritage* (London, New York: Routledge, 1992).

Goldring, Douglas, *Odd Man Out: The Autobiography of a 'Propaganda Novelist'* (London: Chapman & Hall, 1935).

Greene, Ghussan Rouse, 'The Public Reputation of A. E. Housman's Poetry in England and America' (Dissertation, University of South Carolina, 1978).

Guiney, Louise Imogen, *Letters of Louise Imogen Guiney*, ed. Grace Guiney, 2 vols (New York and London: Harper & Bros, 1926).

——, 'A Shropshire Lad', *The Chap-Book* (1 February 1897) 245–6.

Henneman, John Bell, 'A Shropshire Lad', *The Sewanee Review* 14 (July 1906) 381–2.

Housman, A. E., *Collected Poems and Selected Prose*, ed. Christopher Ricks (London: Penguin, 1988, 1989).

——, *The Letters of A. E. Housman*, ed. Henry Maas (London: Rupert Hart-Davis; Cambridge, Mass.: Harvard University Press, 1971).

Housman, Laurence. *My Brother, A. E. Housman* (New York: Charles Scribner's Sons, 1938).

Jebb, Keith. *A. E. Housman* (Bridgend: Seren Books (Border Lines Series), 1992).

Kuryluk, Ewa, *Salome and Judas in the Cave of Sex* (Evanston, IL: Northwestern University Press, 1987).

Le Gallienne, Richard. 'Wanderings in Bookland', *The Idler* 9 (June 1896) 727.

——, 'A Shropshire Lad', *The Star* (11 May 1896) 1.

Macdonnell, Annie, 'A Shropshire Lad', *The Bookman* (London) 10 (June 1896) 83.

Moore, Doris Langley, *E. Nesbit: A Biography*, rev. edn (Philadelphia, New York: Chilton Books, 1966).

Naiditch, P. G., 'A Forgotten Notice of "A Shropshire Lad"', *American Notes and Queries* 21 (1982) 44.

Nesbit, E(dith), 'A New Poet', *The National Observer* (11 July 1896) 242–4.

N. O. B. 'A New Poet', *The Echo* (13 August 1896) 1.

O. O. (W. Robertson Nicoll), 'The Literary Lounger', *The Sketch* (22 April 1896) 574.

——, 'The Literary Lounger', *The Sketch* (9 November 1898) 108.

Page, Norman, *A. E. Housman: A Critical Biography* (London: Macmillan; New York: Schocken Books, 1983).

Payne, William Morton, 'Recent Poetry', *The Dial* (1 October 1897) 188–9.

Richards, Grant, 'A Shropshire Lad', *The Review of Reviews* (London) 1 August 1896: 187; rptd 'Notes from Our London Correspondent', *The Review of Reviews* (New York) (14 September 1896) 371.

Robbins, Ruth. '"A very curious construction": masculinity and the poetry of A. E. Housman and Oscar Wilde', *Cultural Politics at the Fin de Siècle*, eds Sally Ledger and Scott McCracken (London and New York: Cambridge University Press, 1995) pp. 137–59.

Taylor, Andrew, *An Air That Kills* (London: Hodder & Stoughton; New York: St. Martin's Press, 1994).

[Ward, T. H.]. 'Books of the Week: Short Notices', *The London Times* (27 March 1896) 13.

Waugh, Alec, *The Early Years of Alec Waugh* (London: Cassell, 1962).

3

The Land of Lost Content
Keith Jebb

Content, a thing contained; psychologically 'The totality of the constituents of a person's experience at any particular moment' (*O. E. D.*); 'The sum of qualities, notions, ideal elements given in or composing a conception; the substance or matter (of cognition, or art, etc.) as opposed to the form' (*O. E. D.*).

I am going to throw some thoughts across the space opened up by the pun *content/content*. Housman, in *A Shropshire Lad*, created not so much a myth, as a mythic space, like the wood in *A Midsummer Night's Dream* or the island in *The Tempest*. Whatever its topographical coordinates (and some of these, as I have written elsewhere, are particularly accurate[1]) the social, historical and linguistic sinews on these bones are insubstantial. It is pastoralism rather than ruralism, Philip Sidney rather than Thomas Hardy. None of this is anything but a truism of Housman studies; nor do I presume to hold a key which will unlock the lost *content*, as if there were something buried within the text which as readers we have overlooked, not dug deep enough for. If Shropshire is unreal in the poems of A. E. H. it is not, I believe, because it is serving an allegorical purpose.

We know that Housman was a homosexual. We don't know that he practised homosexuality, although we don't know for sure that he never did. And it doesn't matter. What does matter is Housman's status as a homosexual writer, a status which we may be forgiven for thinking does not exist; which may make some of us feel more comfortable with Housman, feel he is talking to us, whoever we are.

Oscar Wilde is a homosexual writer, though one may not be aware of this directly from the surfaces of his writing. Whatever he was arraigned for it was not for *writing* as a sodomite, but his works do consistently echo the social situation of the homosexual in Victorian society. In *The Importance of Being Earnest* Jack Worthing leads a double life as Ernest his supposed brother; in *The Picture of Dorian Gray* the doubling of the double life is even more intimate, Dorian Gray's double life of respectability and debauchery being facilitated by the other double of the portrait, which suffers the consequences of Dorian's moral decline. The novel in many ways mirrors Wilde's own life, occluding, of course, the issue of homosexuality, but retaining the low-life context of many of Wilde's homosexual encounters.

Wilde's writings present a number of issues of interest to us here. Firstly, there is a cloaked confessionalism about both *The Importance of Being Earnest* and *The Picture of Dorian Gray:* this confessionalism could be seen to take the form of a kind of questioning of the possibility of a homosexual lifestyle in Victorian society, or rather its impossibility. Secondly there is an interrogation of the moral codes of this society, which though it is not systematic, is far-reaching in its consequences, especially with regard to the hypocrisy inherent in the social structure which judges his protagonists for . . . hypocrisy. Thirdly there is the notion of doubling, which itself doubles as both a structural element in the writings, and the strategy of the protagonists.

How does any of this relate to Housman? On the surface, none of it does. The possibility of a homosexual lifestyle, given a disguised but real treatment in Wilde's writings, appears to be a non-issue in A. E. H.'s poetry. If we look for a similarity, however, we find a big one: guilt. The most obvious instance is *ASL* XLIV, 'Shot? so quick, so clean an ending?':

> Souls undone, undoing others, –
>   Long time since the tale began.
> You would not live to wrong your brothers:
>   Oh lad, you died as fits a man.
>
> Now to your grave shall friend and stranger
>   With ruth and some with envy come:
> Undishonoured, clear of danger,
>   Clean of guilt, pass hence and home.

That a Woolwich cadet, discovered by Housman in a newspaper article, killed himself to avoid the shame and dishonour he felt would follow the commission of homosexual acts (this is really the only scenario that fits the cadet's admissions in his suicide note), serves to express a latent guilt which shadows the rest of the poems in the volume. In this one poem it could be said that Housman 'comes out', leaving us the crucial piece of evidence by placing the newspaper cutting at the relevant page of his own copy of *A Shropshire Lad*. It is a circumstance we ignore at our peril: more than a biographical accident, it is an effective act of annotation. It is a gesture towards the lost content. But it is not a key. If it was, A. E. H. would be established as a homosexual writer in the way that Wilde is. But everything is much more shadowy. The poem celebrates the homosexual's refusal to come to full expression of himself, rather than the strategies, however compromised, by which he tries to find expression. As such, it is a kind of suicide note in itself. We must ask ourselves where the writing subject of this poem stands? If desire kills the cadet, where is the subject's desire, the desire of the speaking voice of the poem? It cannot follow the cadet 'clear of danger' passing 'hence and home'. So it is sited and cited clearly within the danger zone, what the man Alfred Edward Housman did, or didn't do, with his own desire.

It may seem strained to try to keep the difference between the subject of this poem and Housman, given the fact of the newspaper article. Perhaps that article should be seen as the thing which articulates the space between them. Because the poem – if it is about homosexuality at all (and before the emergence of the article it effectively was not) – is anti-homosexual. The cadet harbours 'The soul that should not have been born'. Nothing could contrast more with *Additional Poems* XVIII, 'Oh who is that young sinner with the handcuffs on his wrists', a poem clearly about the Wilde trials, which declares: 'they're taking him to prison for the colour of his hair.' Both poems, it should be added, were written in the same year, the Woolwich cadet killing himself a little over two months after Wilde was convicted, and probably, therefore, to some extent as a consequence of that conviction.

But a reading of *A Shropshire Lad* as a volume takes us, apparently, far away from the world of the Wilde trials. In this context, the death of the Woolwich cadet functions as yet another in a string of similar resorts to suicide or heroism, to suicide as a form of heroism and vice versa. The military theme runs throughout this, but as a poem such as 'Bredon Hill' shows, it is not necessary as a context or background to the act. Indeed, in *ASL* XLIV, the suicide is not identified as a cadet, and a link with the military could not be confidently implied without the extra-textual knowledge we have of the poem's origins. Reading these origins too glibly into the poem itself, we risk missing the fact that Housman omitted this information and that the poem's theme of honour therefore takes place in the context of a more personal morality. In fact the military theme, with one notable exception, relates to death in battle. Such a death is treated throughout the volume as a kind of expedient: if a godless world can offer no consolation, if even love is doomed to loss or betrayal, a heroic death can stand for something – although precisely what is actually less clear. In this context it becomes at least irrelevant, if not unfortunate, that the figure behind *ASL* XLIV was a military cadet. In Housman's Shropshire the only reason to be a soldier is to die for Queen and country and for one's comrades, but real soldiers in Victorian England did not always have that opportunity.

Suicide as such appears elsewhere in *A Shropshire Lad*. It is implied at the end of 'Bredon Hill' (*ASL* XXI), it is advocated in *ASL* XLV, 'If it chance your eye offend you', directly following the Woolwich cadet poem; but these are not characteristic instances. More frequently death is sought, rather than self-administered. However, the death-drive of the volume as a whole is almost inexorable, and this, combined with the moral outlook of the poems, which alternates between stoicism and a form of nihilism, has been the cause for some of the most telling and difficult-to-answer criticism of the book, and of Housman's poetry as a whole – difficult-to-answer in the sense that it can only really be disagreed with *as a criticism*, certainly not refuted or denied.

Perhaps the most celebrated of these criticisms comes from Stephen Spender:

> Housman tends to unconscious self-parody, which means he also provides other poets, and the critics, with material to ridicule him. This is partly due to the meretricious aspects of his famous pessimism; partly also to the fact that the tension of his poetry seems often to be the result of some inner contradiction, which the unsympathetic can view one-sidedly. He is classical in his feeling for the past and for form, and yet romantic in his human sympathies; austerely tight-lipped, and yet profoundly sentimental; inhibited, yet subtly and deeply self-dramatizing, and – one suspects – even self-pitying. At his best,

his poetry embodies the noble contradiction of being both cool and passionate.[2]

The contradictions that Spender identifies in Housman are interesting. What he is in fact doing is setting up a series of binary oppositions and claiming that Housman plays both sides of them, thus risking self-parody. Take classicism and romanticism, however: they are certainly different from one another, but they are basically styles or modes of art with differing historical and social origins. Romanticism could not be called a reaction and opposition to classicism. In fact the truth is the opposite. Elements of classicism reintroduced into poetry by the early Modernists (particularly by the Imagists of the 1912–15 period) were intended as an antidote to the lack of focus of much of the redundant romanticism of late nineteenth- and early twentieth-century poetry in England. In the wake of this came a tide of anti-romantic criticism, led by T. S. Eliot and I. A. Richards extolling the virtues of Elizabethan, metaphysical and neoclassical English poetry. In other words this opposition belongs to Modernism and nobody, surely (despite Eliot's praise of his lecture *The Name and Nature of Poetry*[3]), is going to call Housman a Modernist.

Take the next of these oppositions: if Spender's adjectives 'austerely' and 'profoundly' are removed, we are left with the bald statement that Housman is 'tight-lipped and sentimental', which no longer sounds so unreasonable or ridiculous, sentiment and the ability to express it being different faculties of what may be loosely called human consciousness. In the third of these oppositions, 'inhibited, yet subtly and deeply self-dramatizing', Spender seems to have got himself saying something he thinks may even be beyond Housman, so he qualifies the point with 'subtly and deeply'. But if someone's self-dramatizing is subtle and deep this suggests that it is itself inhibited, a force that wants to come to the surface but can't, a mechanism of repression, rather than a contradiction.

Indeed, Spender is actually more aware of what is going on than this list of characteristics suggests, when he ceases trying to cover the range of the Housman problem and aims straight at the heart of it: 'If one were to sum Housman up in a word, that word would be "repressed". He is the lyricist of English repression.'[4] This is a problem for Spender: the repression of a content – we are given the consequences of something without its cause. As Spender continues:

The most typical symptom of this is that his strongest, most direct statements produce in the reader's mind, the question: 'What is it all about?' Sometimes the question, less sympathetically, becomes: 'What is all the fuss about?' One certainly cannot quite believe in all these lads with hard luck stories and unhappy endings. They are neither . . . symbols for the poet, nor are they intellectual conundra.[5]

This is where Spender's interests and mine diverge. As a critical criterion, on Spender's own terms, it is effectively unanswerable. My only caution about it in this context is: what is supposed to happen when Housman's poetry embodies 'the noble contradiction of being both cool and passionate'? The complimentary affirmation questions what Spender means by repression, as it seems to describe the kind of English stiff upper lip which is itself 'English repression'. Of course it would not be difficult to produce an argument of degree to try to deal with this. But Spender has no interest in what is actually behind this repression; he asks what is this about, but he does not investigate why. He clearly sees that death in these poems is not what it appears to be, he complains that there is 'very little feeling about the dead',[6] and that Housman lacks curiosity about death as such. 'Death is simply the answer to life,'[7] which itself is characterized by loss, which death symbolizes. This sounds rather circular: if death is the answer to life, how can it also symbolize it?

In the midst of criticizing Housman for his repressions, Spender has hit upon something more crucial: the fulcrum of how this repression works, a glimpse of the operation of the lost content. What is being repressed is not simply the biographical fact of Housman's homosexuality. We know that is a repression which Housman was able on occasion to break out of, as is evident in *Additional Poems* XVIII ('Oh who is that young sinner with the handcuffs on his wrists?'), although he knew he could not publish those breaks. What is being repressed is something which is not there (his homosexuality clearly *was* there), something whose expression is made impossible from the outset, something inextricably tied in to the nature of expression itself. Death stands for this, and in a way achieves it: but we cannot expect to name it, since it has no name. In late Victorian England homosexuality had no name,[8] although the naming process was instituted by the Parliamentary Act under which Wilde was charged; but if our sexuality and the process of genderization to which that is linked is the medium through which we see and create our world, then how much more unnameable was it to be a homosexual, to be inside there: not a psychological state, but something that could only be experienced as a disjunction with the whole social and symbolic texture of the human and political world as it is lived; or in other words with the very structure and act of language itself, as it prioritizes and, of course, represses. If a language does not acknowledge your existence, how do you exist within that language?

This point demands to be placed in its historical context, in the late Victorian period during which homosexuality came to be seen less as a sexual act or proclivity, than as an identity in itself. It was the period centred, of course, on the Wilde trials.

Oscar Wilde was tried under the now-infamous 1885 Criminal Law Amendment Act, section II, known as the 'Labouchère Amendment' after its proposer Henry Labouchère. This outlawed any kind of homosexual activity, including procurement or attempted procurement. Previously homosexuality was covered by the laws against sodomy, which demanded physical proof of the act.[9] The Wilde trials were the first real test-case of the Amendment (following the botched government cover-up of the Cleveland Street 'telegraph boys' scandal of 1889–90), Wilde providing a suitably prominent scapegoat. However, both his celebrity and his own conduct at the trial, characterized by his speech to the court on 'the love that dare not speak its name', helped to turn the scapegoat into a martyr. The psychologist and pioneer researcher into sexuality, Havelock Ellis, claimed in his *Studies in the Psychology of Sex* that the trials appeared 'to have generally contributed to give definiteness and self-consciousness to the manifestations of homosexuality, and to have aroused inverts to take up a definite stand'.[10] One of these stands, founded probably in the mid-1890s, was the Order of Chaeronia, a kind of masonic organization, dedicated to the reform of sexual attitudes. It was named after the Battle of Chaeronia, at which Philip of Macedon, in defeating the Athenians, also wiped out a Theban strike force, the 'Sacred Band', who were joined together by bonds of loyalty and love. It is said that Philip, seeing the three hundred young men lying dead together, shed tears and said 'Perish any man who suspects that these men either did or suffered anything that was base.' Laurence Housman, A. E. H.'s younger brother, was a prominent member of this order, and though it is very doubtful that A. E. H. was ever involved in it, it is quite likely that he knew of its existence, and even more likely that he, the most noted English classical scholar of his day, knew of the 'Sacred Band' and what they might stand for.

The establishment of bodies like the Order of Chaeronia was a response to the need for models on which to base the new self-affirming consciousness of homosexuality. Classical Greece, with its own established homosexual mores, was both the predominant provider of these role models and the sanction for certain practices themselves, including the interest in young men and adolescent boys which characterized some aspects of Victorian homosexuality, but not, notably, the Order of Chaeronia. The idea of an army united by more than mere duty or loyalty to a cause shadows the militarism of Housman's poetry. It appears early in *A Shropshire Lad*, in 'The Recruit' (*ASL* III):

> And you will list the bugle
> That blows in lands of morn,
> And make the foes of England
> Be sorry you were born.
>
> And you till trump of doomsday
> On lands of morn may lie,
> And make the hearts of comrades
> Be heavy where you die.

It appears again in 'The New Mistress' (*ASL* XXXIV), in a rather more suggestive context, and again counterpointed with the notion of dismaying the enemy:

'I will go where I am wanted, for the sergeant does not mind;
He may be sick to see me but he treats me very kind:
He gives me beer and breakfast and a ribbon for my cap,
And I never knew a sweetheart spend her money on a chap.

'I will go where I am wanted, where there's room for one or two,
And the men are none too many for the work there is to do;
Where the standing line wears thinner and the dropping dead
lie thick;
And the enemies of England they shall see me and be sick.'

Another important poem in this respect is '1887' (*ASL* I), which has aroused a degree of controversy regarding the tone it takes towards Queen Victoria's jubilee. When Frank Harris met Housman he praised the poem for its unpatriotic attitude and was quickly rebuffed. The problem hinges on the use of 'God Save the Queen' at the conclusion of the poem, and how ironic this is seen to be:

> 'God save the Queen' we living sing,
>   From height to height 'tis heard;
> And with the rest your voices ring,
>   Lads of the Fifty-third.
>
> Oh, God will save her, fear you not:
>   Be you the men you've been,
> Get you the sons your fathers got,
>   And God will save the Queen.

Cleanth Brooks, the US critic, sides with Housman against Harris, saying that the use of the phrase in the poem 'does not necessarily involve mockery of the Queen or the young men who have helped her'.[11] But he judges that Housman went too far to say there was no irony in the poem:

The speaker clearly admires the lads of the Fifty-third but his angle of vision is different from theirs. What they accept naively and uncritically, he sees in its full complexity and ambiguity. But his attitude is not cynical and it is consonant with genuine patriotism. The irony that it contains is a mature and responsible irony whose focus is never blurred. The closing stanza, with its quiet insistence that God will save the Queen but with the conjoined insistence on the all-important proviso that they get them the sons their fathers got dramatizes the speaker's attitude to a nicety.[12]

Basically I have no argument with this interpretation. But what it misses is the close feel of commonality with the soldiers which we can find in stanzas three and four of the poem:

> Now, when the flame they watch not towers
>   About the soil they trod,
> Lads, we'll remember friends of ours
>   Who shared the work with God.

> To skies that knit their heartstrings right,
>   To fields that bred them brave,
> The saviours come not home to-night:
>   Themselves they could not save.

The sense of closeness to and affection for soldiers is docu-
mented from Housman's adolescence, in a letter to his mother
written on a visit to London when he was fifteen: 'I think of all
that I have seen, what most impressed me is – the Guards. This
may be barbarian, but it is true.'[13] Jeffrey Weeks in his book *Coming
Out: Homosexual Politics in Britain, from the Nineteenth Century to
the Present* makes the following observation:

> From the 1870s there was an attempted purge on 'school-boy
> immorality', but it was never wiped out. It might or might not
> have been the prelude to a later homosexual life-style, but it
> was acceptable within the narrow community of the school.
> The same is true of the notorious prostitution that character-
> ized the Brigade of Guards, for which there is a long history
> between the eighteenth and twentieth centuries. It could eas-
> ily be justified as 'we are only doing it for the money', and no
> identification with being homosexual was demanded, but it was
> endemic . . .[14]

Of course, how much of this was known to Housman, especially
aged fifteen, can only be guessed at. But to focus on the nexus
of events, textual events, in *A Shropshire Lad* takes us beyond
what the individual author knew into a more shadowy space in
which the poetry links social context, authorial experience (both
remembered and repressed) and what appears, on the face of it,
to be sheer coincidence. It is a matter of making connections where
they are possible, rather than trying to sift the contents of a mind
we envision behind the poems. Not that I want to ignore biographical evidence, but one cannot be limited by it. Whether he
knew it or not, the Guards were a brigade linked inexorably to
homosexuality. But in the world of the Shropshire lad, this is
beyond mention, homosexuality is outside of the language, a
hinterland of hints that may not even be intended:

> The street sounds to the soldiers' tread,
>   And out we troop to see:

A single redcoat turns his head,
   He turns and looks at me.

My man, from sky to sky's so far,
   We never crossed before;
Such leagues apart the world's ends are,
   We're like to meet no more;

What thoughts at heart have you and I
   We cannot stop to tell;
But dead or living, drunk or dry,
   Soldier, I wish you well.

(*ASL* XXII, complete poem)

Circumstantial evidence seems to link this poem to the letter written by the fifteen year-old Housman. Like *ASL* XLIV, it is one of those rare occasions when Housman's homosexuality could be said to lie directly behind the poem. On the surface, though, this moment of recognition is an acknowledgement of shared mortality, comradeship in the face of death. Nothing could be further away from the reality of the Guards' reputation for prostitution. But the real Guards belonged to a world of unspoken tolerance, the 'narrow community' to which the state could turn a blind eye. It was not the presence of homosexuality within society which was the problem, but its visibility. Wilde became too visible. The Marquess of Queensberry did not accuse him of being a sodomite but of *posing* as one. Even then, it is quite possible that the situation could have blown over if Wilde had not taken the very public action of a libel suit against the Marquess. And what *A Shropshire Lad* is about, what it ranges around, is not Housman's homosexuality, but the inexpressibility of homosexuality as such, of a homosexual community which, in its burgeoning self-awareness, was just beginning to experiment with models of possible lifestyles and interventions into the world of social and textual languages which maintain and produce these. Community is perhaps a key word. A community can build a language, or rather make effective interventions into language. An isolated figure – which accounts for both A. E. Housman and the figure of the Shropshire Lad – cannot.

Housman almost certainly subscribed to the theory that

homosexuality was an innate condition – as 'the soul that should not have been born' and 'the colour of his hair' suggest – a theory which many homosexual reformers of the late nineteenth and early twentieth centuries subscribed to in order to defend themselves against charges of criminality and depravity, on the basis that if one is born like this, how can one be to blame? You are simply a different kind of person, but one whom the mechanisms for self-expression fail to recognize, and for whom society literally has no place, no space to inhabit except its own underground, its hinterland, a border no-man's land which is always beyond the horizon. This is the lost content, but lost in a sense that it was never yet found, and so does not exist except as a potentiality, experienced in the frustration of its unfulfilment, rather than the feeling of future possibilities. It is a *terra incognita* Housman could not enter, could not even see, but could only write the frontiers of what he did not know, the buffer zones; or as if you are lost in an unfamiliar landscape, circling some place or feature you have glimpsed, but which no road or track or pass can lead you to, so that it might as well not exist. It is a situation that might just make you a pessimist.

Housman claimed his most prolific period was during 'the first five months of 1895'.[15] This of course overlaps with the period of the Wilde trials – Wilde took libel action against the Marquess of Queensberry in April; on 25 May he was convicted and sentenced to two years with hard labour. Whatever else influenced the form and content of the book – the death of Housman's father in November 1894, the state of his feelings for Moses Jackson, now married and living in India, and whatever he meant, writing to Maurice Pollet 38 years later, when he said that he composed the poems when 'the really emotional part of my life was over'[16] – so much does seem to depend upon this one crystallizing event. A glimpse that resonates in the writing on many levels: the feeling of compassion and injustice in *Additional Poems* XVIII; the sense of shame shared with the Woolwich Cadet in *ASL* XLIV; the protest at an imposed morality of *Last Poems* XII:

> The laws of God, the laws of man,
> He may keep that will and can;
> Not I: let God and man decree
> Laws for themselves and not for me . . .

These reactions are all contradictory, in ways that the so-called contradictions found by Spender in Housman's poetry are not. The outrage in *LP* XII, the sense of injustice in society's laws in *AP* XVIII, the shame in *ASL* XLIV are all entirely at odds with each other except in an alienated and confused state of crisis. Only the third of these, the shame, was ever sanctioned for publication during Housman's lifetime (although, of course, making his homosexual brother Laurence his literary executor virtually guaranteed the posthumous publication of the others). *A Shropshire Lad* is a public, and also a popular volume, it inhabits and was intended to inhabit a public space, an artistically conservative space. But this is the space which Housman also inhabited, as a scholar first, then later as a poet. And publicly Housman was extremely cautious about what lay behind his poetry:

> I have never had any such thing as a 'crisis of pessimism'. In the first place I am not a pessimist but a pejorist (as George Eliot said she was not an optimist but a meliorist); and that is owing to my observation of the world, not to personal circumstances. Secondly, I did not begin to write poetry in earnest until the really emotional part of my life was over; and my poetry, so far as I could make out, sprang chiefly from physical conditions, such as a relaxed sore throat during my prolific period, the first five months of 1885.[17]

This comes from a letter Housman wrote in 1933, in reply to questions about his life and work sent by a Frenchman, Maurice Pollet. It conforms to other public statements Housman made about his own poetry, notably in *The Name and Nature of Poetry*, Housman's Leslie Stephen Lecture of 1933:

> ... I think that the production of poetry, in its first stage, is less an active than a passive and involuntary process; and if I were obliged, not to define poetry, but to name the class of thing to which it belongs, I should call it a secretion; whether a natural secretion, like turpentine in the fir, or a morbid secretion, like the pearl in the oyster. I think that my own case, though I may not deal with the material so cleverly as the oyster does, is the latter; because I have seldom written poetry unless I was rather out of health, and the experience, though pleasurable, was generally agitating and exhausting.[18]

This may of course be true, as far as it goes – T. S. Eliot certainly thought so – but it is also a mythologizing statement, one in which the poet disclaims all conscious responsibility for his own literary productions. It forestalls awkward questions about the wider context in which they were written. It also – and we should expect this of Housman – affirms poetry as a solitary activity, a secretion, hardly a language act at all. Housman was notoriously uncomfortable in the company of other writers, and never saw himself as a figure in a writing community.

Now without trying to impose any idea of causation, this literary isolationism can be put into the frame of the alienation of the Victorian homosexual, *especially* the non-practising homosexual, and in the wider frame of the alienation from language of homosexuality as such. At every level Housman develops a strategy of not-saying, not opening himself or his situation to the process of exchange, to the economy of language as a social act. Because the currency is not there for this expression.

But to return now to the pun: con'tent / 'content. *A Shropshire Lad* is set in the scene of a pastoral idyll, or at least, so we are told:

> That is the land of lost content,
>   I see it shining plain,
> The happy highways where I went
>   And cannot come again.[19]

What figures inarticulate desire is so often the sense of having lost something, of wanting to return. The content before the rupture of adolescence is the most important scene for this nostalgia, the time before desire as such impinges. This nostalgia, of course, affects most adults at some time or another, but for the sexually isolated, inarticulate or marginalized, the pull of this pre-adolescent scene becomes stronger. I am thinking, of course, of Lewis Carroll and J. M. Barrie, two other central figures in the story of Victorian repression. What makes Housman remarkable is that Shropshire as the 'land of lost content' clearly does not work. At no point in the volume does the pastoral scene live up to the pastoral idyll, since everything is already characterized by loss. So in fact the move from Shropshire to London which takes place halfway through the volume does not effectively change anything, except that poems with the same sense of loss and disjunction as early poems now avail themselves of a feeling of nostalgia. *A Shropshire*

Lad is not – unlike (and in their very different ways) *Peter Pan* and *Alice in Wonderland* – a text about childhood: it is a text about adolescence – a common negative criticism of Housman – but even more about the consequences of adolescence, which cannot be underestimated in this context. To accuse Housman of being a poet of adolescence and therefore immature is a redundant exercise, one that even Spender, who admires Housman in many ways, falls into. But the volume is not about an individual's failure to reach maturity. It is about the way the symbolic and ideological order of a society can deny maturity to those whose desire is considered dangerous, or uncontrollable, or excessive. The repression of *A Shropshire Lad* could, in this way, be seen as a kind of mirror held up to a society in which hundreds of adolescent girls were infibulated on Harley Street because they masturbated; in which women of 'respectable' families were incarcerated in mental institutions, often for the rest of their lives, because sexual liaisons considered inappropriate for such ladies demonstrated 'feebleness of mind' (a practice which continued well into this century); and in which homosexuality was comprehensively criminalized. These are the lost contents, also. I have said that the lost content is unnameable; I have linked it to Housman's homosexuality as it cannot find open expression in *A Shropshire Lad*, but to say that it is homosexuality is, I hope I have gone some way to showing, a mistake. Because here, in this Shropshire, in this text, it cannot be expressed because it is beyond: it is a pressure impinging from without, from another society, a lived English society; and perhaps we can recognize it most clearly by its effect on the sexual mores of Housman's Shropshire, of the world of Terence Hearsay, a world where (as if in some kind of revenge, a kind of curse) *all* love is haunted by death, and is punished.

Notes

1. Keith Jebb, *A. E. Housman* (Bridgend: Seren Books, 1992) pp. 73–94.
2. Stephen Spender, *The Making of a Poem* (London: Hamish Hamilton, 1955) pp. 157–8.
3. Review in *The Criterion*, Vol. XIII, No. 50 (October, 1933) 151–4.
4. Spender, op. cit., p. 158.
5. Ibid., p. 158.

6. Ibid., p. 159.
7. Ibid.
8. This discussion relies quite heavily on the work of Jeffrey Weeks in his books *Coming Out: Homosexual Politics in Britain, from the Nineteenth Century to the Present* (London: Quartet Books, 1977), and *Sex, Politics and Society: the Regulation of Sexuality Since 1800* (London: Longman, 1981).
9. Cf. Weeks, *Coming Out*, op. cit.
10. Havelock Ellis, *Studies in the Psychology of Sex* (4 vols), vol. 2, *Sexual Inversion* (New York: Random House, 1936) p. 352; quoted in Weeks, *Sex, Politics and Society*, op. cit., p. 103.
11. Cleanth Brooks, 'Alfred Edward Housman', in *A. E. Housman: A Collection of Critical Essays*, ed. Christopher Ricks (Englewood Cliffs, NJ: Prentice Hall, 1968) p. 77.
12. Ibid., p. 78.
13. *The Letters of A. E. Housman*, ed. Henry Maas (Cambridge, Mass.: Harvard University Press, 1971) p. 6.
14. Weeks, *Coming Out*, op. cit., p. 35.
15. Letter to Maurice Pollet, 5 February 1933, printed in *Collected Poems and Selected Prose*, ed. Christopher Ricks (London: Allen Lane, The Penguin Press, 1989) pp. 468–70.
16. Ibid., p. 469.
17. Ibid.
18. Ibid., p. 370.
19. *ASL* XL.

4

Tacit Pledges
Geoffrey Hill

*It is no mere extravagance when a poet talks of a nation's soul. It is the
objective mind which is subjective and self-conscious in its citizens:
it feels and knows itself in the heart of each.*

This is perhaps the wrong kind of essay for a centennial sympo-
sium. If it honours the work of Housman – and I hope that it
does – it does so obliquely and in accordance with the terms of
my epigraph which I take, not from Housman, but from F. H.
Bradley.[1] My main concern here is with matters of style: with
particulars of syntax, rhythm and cadence, and with the problems of pitch. Considered in its negative aspect, a writer's style
is what he or she is left with after the various contingent forces
of attrition have taken their toll. Considered more positively, style
marks the success an author may have in forging a personal
utterance between the hammer of self-being and the anvil of those
impersonal forces that a given time possesses. Hammer and anvil
together distort as well as shape. None of this, I agree, bears
much resemblance to Housman's own description of making, as
given in the 1933 Leslie Stephen Lecture, *The Name and Nature of
Poetry.* It does bear some resemblance, however, to isolated
observations found variously in Housman's correspondence and
scholarly and critical writings: 'What Balfour did in his premier-
ship was to prevent Chamberlain from quite ruining the party.
Outside Parliament, Chamberlain was much the stronger of the
two';[2] 'Class is a real thing: we may wish that it were not, and
we may pretend that it is not, but I find that it is';[3] 'we . . . usually
fit our judgments not to the truth of things nor even to our own
impressions of things, true or false, but to the standard of convention';[4] 'the amount of sub-conscious dishonesty which pervades
the textual criticism of the Greek and Latin classics is little suspected

53

except by those who have had occasion to analyse it';[5] 'There is
something novel to me not only in Mr Stone's dealings with his
native tongue but in his attitude towards his customers: it opens
a vista of new relations between the producers and consumers
of commodities.'[6]

I have called these 'isolated' observations but it is I who have
isolated them, thereby doing Housman's mind and art a disservice, seeming to imply that something finally fails to cohere. In
fact his remarks on contingency and circumstance are altogether
firm and coherent although they do not exactly cohere with his
poetry. The absence of correlative which we sense in other poets
of those years is at least in part the legacy of John Stuart Mill –
the aplomb of this logician's conclusion that, whereas 'eloquence
is *heard*, poetry is *over*heard'.[7] Mill's disservice to the critical
imagination, as to the civic imagination, is in no way rectified by
his persistent harping on the therapeutic value of poetry's presentation of the emotions.[8] He marginalizes authenticity of feeling
as he pushes away the critical element of the imagination; these
qualities are given over, in Mill's commonweal, to the licensed
eccentricities that in some unspecified way check and balance
the potential tyranny of the democratic majority.[9]

One may be able to suggest the pervasiveness of the difficulty,
as well as Housman's significant but limited success in negotiat-
ing it, by a comparison with a much younger poet, Charles Sorley
(1895–1915), who admired Housman despite the 'somewhat self-
satisfied dislike of life' betrayed by *A Shropshire Lad*[10] and who
recognized as the particular strength of Hardy's *Jude the Obscure*
that 'it was [Jude's] conscientiousness that did for him'.[11] On 28
April 1915, already in the army and writing home to his mother,
Sorley took note of the public eulogies for Rupert Brooke who
had died five days previously en route to Gallipoli. 'He is far too
obsessed with his own sacrifice, regarding the going to war of
himself (and others) as a highly intense, remarkable and sacrificial
exploit, whereas it is merely the conduct demanded of him (and
others) by the turn of circumstances, where non-compliance with
this demand would have made life intolerable.'[12] Less than six
months after writing this, Sorley too was dead, killed at Loos.

When Housman declared, in his autobiographical résumé of
1933, that 'the Great War cannot have made much change in the
opinions of any man of imagination',[13] he spoke within his rights
as a man of imagination whose opinions had not changed, though

'any' is open to challenge. I see in this no grounds for radical indignation but I do claim it as admissible evidence in a debate to which I would also admit the public and private forces and restraints.

Housman's sister, Katharine E. Symons, recalled in her memorial tribute to him that he had enclosed a copy of his poem 'Illic Jacet', originally published in 1900,[14] with a letter of condolence in 1915 'when one of my sons was killed in Flanders'.[15] These nine words are set as though by a spirit level; what they both gauge and embody is a level of assent, publicly sustained and privately contained, to what Sorley called 'conduct demanded', to that which F. H. Bradley named 'the universal maintaining medium'.[16] Clement Symons was not the first member of the family to die in battle. George Herbert Housman, beloved youngest brother of Katharine and Alfred, had been killed in October 1901 while serving with the rank of sergeant in the King's Royal Rifles, a casualty of the latter stages of the Boer War.[17] Certain of Alfred's poems, in a proper sense the aftermath of that bitter loss, 'The Olive', published in 1902, 'on the conclusion of the peace' with the Boers,[18] 'Astronomy' published in 1904,[19] and – presumably – 'Farewell to a name and a number', unpublished prior to the posthumous *More Poems* of 1936,[20] have a pitch of utterance which, I would argue, sets them apart from the idealized elegiac militarisms of *A Shropshire Lad*. But it is never less than hazardous to base one's arguments on the conjectural dating of individual Housman poems.[21] Subject to that caveat, I would suggest that there is nothing in Housman that is quite comparable to the precisely held, stark and simple complexity (anger, grief, pride, love, disillusionment) in the second quatrain of 'Farewell to a name and a number'; this is the closest Housman gets to Sorley's 'it was his conscientiousness that did for him':

> So ceases and turns to the thing
> He was born to be
> A soldier cheap to the King
> And dear to me;

To say that this quatrain achieves a verbal edge unique in Housman's poetry is to contend against a range of particular felicities which have been noted many times: 'And trains all night groan on the rail', 'Where I lodge a little while', 'the lover of the grave', 'the strengthless dead', 'the coloured counties', 'the truceless armies', 'Sleepy with the flow of streams', 'The moon stands blank above', 'cloud-led shadows', 'The felon-quarried stone', 'All desired and timely things', 'The pine lets fall its cone', 'The upshot beam would fade', 'lying about the world', 'silent hills indenting / The orange band of eve', 'When the bells justle in the tower'.[22] The quality of such phrases arises from three forms of sensuous apprehension: first the capacity to present the particular in such a way that it appears to rise spontaneously from direct observation: 'And trains all night groan on the rail', 'cloud-led shadows', 'The upshot beam would fade'; secondly the ability to choose what Yeats called 'the intellectually surprising word which is also the correct word':[23] 'When the bells justle in the tower'. The two qualities are interrelated: 'The upshot beam' is at once topo-graphically accurate[24] and accurate by Yeats's criterion of the sensuous intellect. The third form of apprehension to which I referred arises from a logopoeic form of grammar and syntax – 'The lover of the grave, the lover / That hanged himself for love', 'in fields where cuckoo-flowers / Are lying about the world'. You could say that, contrasted to the finesse of these instances, there is a touch of the obvious in 'A soldier cheap to the King / And dear to me'. In order to touch the quick of the obvious in just this way, however, Housman's imagination had to retort upon deeply established characteristics of civic and spiritual patrimony, the essence and substance of Midlands Tory patriotism, such as he had acquired from his own family and its surroundings and which he never deserted: the tacit pledges made, from time to time, ceremonious and vocal, recorded as Bromsgrove's celebra-tions of Queen Victoria's Golden and Diamond Jubilees in 1887 and 1897 were recorded in the columns of *The Bromsgrove Weekly Messenger* and by such local historians as Alfred Palmer. To reduce joyous expenditure ('the town was tastefully decorated, and the display of flags and buntings was almost universal')[25] to an actual reckoning, and to bring it down to the level of such blunt speak-ing as 'cheap to the King / And dear to me' is to go against the *mores* which display their premises in 'tastefully decorated' and which find their proper eloquence in Katharine Symons's exem-plary reticence. That such bluntness was not made public until 1936 is as significant as its having been uttered in the first place. By the time the posthumous *More Poems* appeared, several more turns of circumstance had occurred, ensuring that the odd, brusque pertinence of 'cheap to the King' (Victoria having died in January 1901, nine months before Sergeant Housman fell at Brakenlaagte) is perforce returned to the marginal private domain from which it can scarcely be said to have emerged. Would one be justified in saying that, in Housman's poetry, the tacit pledges frequently become taciturn?

The term 'tacit pledges' is not mine; I take it from Henry James's novel *The Tragic Muse* (1890). It is there observed of the elderly English *haut bourgeois,* Charles Carteret, that in his presence the much younger man Nick Dormer 'found himself immersed in an atmosphere of tacit pledges which constituted the very medium of intercourse and yet made him draw his breath a little in pain when, for a moment, he measured them'.[26] So much alertness of intelligence and sensibility, so much that strikes one as somehow *distrait,* in the writing of the period, has to do with the conduct of life in such an atmosphere, such an 'intercourse', the consideration of which moves us, as it moved them, to a style in which measure can be, if only momentarily, affirmed. One way of describing Housman's particular grammar of lyric poetry would be to say that it attempts what James's syntax attempts in that sentence from *The Tragic Muse:* it seeks primarily to 'measure' and what it seeks to measure are the 'tacit pledges' and the 'pain'; and it seeks to do so with a measure of decorum. There is an additional force of irony in that the 'tacit' must further contain, for Housman as for James, the presence of that which 'dare not speak its name'[27] and the pain of accommodating the forbidden within lives which, even without that element, had given and were to continue to give emotional and moral hostages to fortune. When, soon after Wilde's release from Reading Gaol, Housman sent him a copy of *A Shropshire Lad*, that too was a tacit pledge.[28]

'Because I liked you better / Than suits a man to say' – Housman's restrained and strained characteristic as a poet is epitomized, in its negative aspect, by these 'stiff and dry' verses from *More Poems*.[29] 'We parted, stiff and dry' – the pitch of the grammar is faithful to the hurt of the occasion; the words are formal and frank, though one cannot use the latter word without recognizing the myriad social prescriptions and proscriptions, the botched diplomacies, which have, over many decades, required its special tone of euphemism. If I call *More Poems* XXXI 'frank' I mean that it says about as much as it refrains from saying and that it is so openly unrecognizant of its hostages to Freudian ribaldry.

'Freudian', possibly, one may find the reaction of the receiver
who was called in when Grant Richards, Housman's publisher,
went bankrupt. As Housman reported to his brother Laurence in
1929: 'The financial expert . . . thought that he would like to read
A Shropshire Lad. He did, or as much as he could; then, in his
own words, "I put it behind the fire. Filthiest book I ever read:
all about —".'[30] Or one may find, in this extravagant response, if
it took place as Housman describes it, a brutish but not incomprehensible denial, a disabling of the book's oblique formalities
and mannered remote intimacies. The century-long chronicle of
the varied fortunes of *A Shropshire Lad* is not without its
grotesqueries, with Laurence, A. E. Housman's younger brother
and literary executor, as guardian of the grotto. It was he who
cut as 'unprintable' the financial expert's last word and it was he
who, late in life, with characteristic prurient frankness, observed
that his brother, having invented in Terence Hearsay the 'fig-
leaf of a fictitious character', was able to 'let himself go'.[31] The
ambivalence in 'let himself go', though I doubt if Laurence
Housman considered the implications, exemplifies the difficult
relationship that can exist between a body of work, which is by
common repute instantly accessible, and the prejudicate opinions
and predilections of the reading public, a body which palpably
exists, which can be measured in gross terms of royalty returns,
which imposes, albeit passively, an undeniable power of sanction,
but which is, even so, a non-entity. The salaciously judgmental
'let himself go' – tally ho, to his true disreputable nature, to
vicarious unnatural debauch, along the fancied road to moral ruin
– dissolves into 'letting go', that other tenuous sense of self-loss, at
once dereliction and consolation, which is the benison we sparingly
receive from the most muted of Housman's valedictory cadences:

> We'll to the woods no more,
> The laurels all are cut,
> The bowers are bare of bay
> That once the Muses wore;
> The year draws in the day
> And soon will evening shut;
> The laurels all are cut,
> We'll to the woods no more.
> Oh we'll no more, no more
> To the leafy woods away,

> To the high wild woods of laurel
> And the bowers of bay no more.[32]

This lyric, the epigraph to *Last Poems* (1922), dedicates itself to letting go: letting go, by way of not going; by accepting, in the sense that metre and rhyme may imply acceptance even against the grammar of the thing, that some early promise of happiness and fulfilment has irretrievably gone. The word 'go' itself, which has its place in Housman's source, the French folk-song 'Nous n'irons plus au bois', is here tacit, eased out by the faintly archaic grammar of the first, eighth and ninth lines. Housman, moreover, lets go, or partly lets go, in the pattern of monorhyme: lines 1, 8, 9 and 12 a pattern unique in his verse. There is a full rhyme in lines 10 and 12 (*away/bay*) but it is half hidden, half heard.

The effect here is obliquely contrary to that which Housman, in *The Name and Nature of Poetry*, attributed to one of Blake's early lyrics, 'Memory, hither come' from *Poetical Sketches:* 'the stanza does but entangle the reader in a net of thoughtless delight.'[33] As is the way with contraries, each is bound to the other by implication. Blake's lyric is not thoughtless: the thoughtlessness lies in Housman's complacent description. There is 'thought' in *A Shropshire Lad* and in *Last Poems* but it is not taken through the turn of circumstances as even the most spontaneous of Blake's songs are.

And, in a sense, thoughtlessness is the desired consummation:

> When I shall lie below them,
>   A dead man out of mind.[34]
>
> For nature, heartless, witless nature,
>   Will neither care nor know
> What stranger's feet may find the meadow
>   And trespass there and go,
> Nor ask amid the dews of morning
>   If they are mine or no.[35]

This is still the poetry of amusement, according to the sense in which Addison wrote in an early *Spectator,* that he had spent an afternoon 'amusing myself with the tomb-stones and inscriptions' in Westminster Abbey;[36] and Housman's style could be found acceptable, after a brief acclimatization, by the more sceptical readers of that paper, as necessarily consequent upon the bold but tastefully sublime hypotheses of Addison's 'Ode':

> What though, in solemn silence, all
> Move round the dark terrestrial ball?
> What tho' nor real voice nor sound
> Amidst their radiant orbs be found?
> In reason's ear they all rejoice,
> And utter forth a glorious voice,
> For ever singing, as they shine,
> 'The hand that made us is divine'.[37]

It is as if Blake's genius leaps from Addison's final line to create, by law of contraries, 'The Tyger';[38] and it is equally as if the rational piety of the 'Ode' continues to run down, of its own inertia, for some considerable time, just over two hundred years, to issue in Housman's 'For nature, heartless, witless nature, / Will neither care nor know'. These words seem drawn from the tacit recesses of Addison's formal optimism, and the 'eternal shade', the 'peace and darkness', of the poem that Housman titled 'For My Funeral' (and which was sung at the collegiate service for him in 1936),[39] mitigate the cosmic witlessness only by the resigned wit, the Cyrenaic casuistry,[40] of its own final line: 'And wilt cast forth no more', 'more' rhyming with 'restore'.

For a period during the 1930s Ludwig Wittgenstein, then Fellow of Trinity College, Cambridge, was near neighbour to Housman, a resident Fellow of the same college; an anecdote recalls the occasion on which Housman refused Wittgenstein's urgent request to use his lavatory.[41] That these two men should have enjoyed such testy proximity is like a charade in which radical incompatibilities of intellect and sensibility – of intellects which nonetheless divide between them some of the most illustrious trophies of the century – are reduced to yet another clash of stereotypical minor eccentricities. In claiming here a form of parity I have in mind Housman's incontestable greatness as a classical scholar while admitting that the particular nature of his achievement and fame as a poet cannot be divorced from the body of his intellectual being or from the private and public circumstances of his life, greatly though he desired that this should be so. Housman and Wittgenstein, in common with F. H. Bradley, Bertrand Russell and T. S. Eliot, were drawn from several directions and in several ways to consider the name and nature of solipsism. It would be appropriate to say that there are as many definitions of solipsism as there are individuals who wish to waste time over a self-inflicted task. Wittgenstein sets 'Idealists, Solipsists and Realists' a-sparring 'as if they were stating facts recognized by every reasonable human being'.[42] The *O. E. D.*, 2nd edn, 1989, is succinct: 'The view or theory that self is the only object of real knowledge or the only thing really existent. Also, =EGOISM 1, and in weakened sense.' In this context Housman presents the most marked, because the most divided, example. In his capacity as a textual critic he indicted bad scholarship as a form of aggressive or torpid egoism, editorial 'self-complacency'[43] as he termed it; and he defined its moral antithesis in clear practical terms: 'to read attentively, think correctly, omit no relevant consideration, and repress self-will'.[44] Taking a phrase from Arnold, he paid his great predecessor Bentley this cogent tribute:

> *Lucida tela diei:* these are the words that come into one's mind when one has halted at some stubborn perplexity of reading or interpretation, has witnessed Scaliger and Gronouius and Huetius fumble at it one after another, and then turns to Bentley and sees Bentley strike his finger on the place and say *thou ailest here, and here.*[45]

In *A Shropshire Lad, Last Poems* and the posthumous *More Poems,* on the other hand, his poetry is imbued with solipsism and seems passively to reflect, rather than actively to reflect upon, the prevailing modes of philosophical parlance. In 1893, three years before the publication of *A Shropshire Lad,* F. H. Bradley stated, in *Appearance and Reality,* that 'it is by the same kind of argument [i.e. that I arrive at other souls by means of other bodies, and the argument starts from the ground of my own body] that we reach our own past and future. And here Solipsism, in objecting to the existence of other selves, is unawares attempting to commit suicide.'[46] In May 1895 – which marked the end of 'the most prolific period' of Housman's lyric writing, a period of five months in which he had written 'twenty-five of the poems destined for his Terence Hearsay collection'[47] – an article in the Jesuit periodical *The Month* referred to our being under spiritual penalty, 'under pain of "solipsism", of being shut up within our own subjectivity'.[48] I do not suggest that when Housman was engaged upon the 'Hearsay' poems he had necessarily heard talk of this term, made current, in 1874, by Fraser, in his *Selections from Berkeley,* or of its cognate 'solipsistic' taken up by William James;[49] I suggest merely that

one can use the word without fear of anachronism. We have
Housman's observation that, in matters of perception, 'Our bodies
are much superior to our minds.'[50] And when Sorley noted 'a
remarkable feature of [Housman's] poetry – its earthiness'[51] – I
would say that he was finding in *A Shropshire Lad* something
more akin to Bradley's 'I arrive at other souls by means of other
bodies, and the argument starts from the ground of my own body'
than to the verdict of the reader who found it the 'filthiest book'
he had ever read.

My own application of the word 'body' would relate rather
more to the body of the work than to that of the disappointed
eponymist Terence Hearsay. While keeping somewhat closer to
the Bradleian sense of 'suicide' than to that of Durkheim (1897),[52]
I would nonetheless argue that, even in the most objectively formal sense, Housman's theory of poetry, as advanced in the Leslie
Stephen Lecture of 1933, could be considered as the summation
of an attempt to commit suicide (in Bradley's sense, 'unawares').
Housman's poetic self objects to the existence of 'other selves' –
for example, to the other self of Blake. To say of Blake's work
that it 'answers to nothing real'[53] is to project upon its significant body of meaning the tyranny of one's own ethical solipsism.
I would add that, in the 26 years between the appearance of *A
Shropshire Lad* and the publication of *Last Poems,* Housman's exquis-
ite lyrical gift was balanced upon the possibility of Bradleian
dissolution; that it survived, tenuously, was due in great part to
his own form of *insouciance.* In this, as I have previously suggested,
he seems to me the disinherited heir of Mill. If Bradley is correct
in his critical description of Mill's philosophy,[54] the relation to
Housman is through 'philosophical' or 'practical' hedonism since
this clearly is the light in which Housman desires his mind to be
read.[55] For Mill 'the one unpardonable sin in a versified
composition, next to the absence of meaning, and of true meaning,
is diffuseness'[56] and, in that sense, Housman is an ideally compact
poet. Equally for Mill 'Poetry is feeling, confessing itself to itself
in moments of solitude, and embodying itself in symbols, which
are the nearest possible representations of the feeling in the exact
shape in which it exists in the poet's mind.'[57] In that sense
Housman is ideally confessional. But these qualities reduce themselves to a solipsism, an oxymoron enjoined by Mill's sentimental
rationalism. The sardonic prose of Housman's *Manilius* prefaces
is truly forensic: it is public capacity and accountability, in a sig-

nificant aspect or sector, that are on trial in these essays and Housman's eloquence is aware that it will be heard. The verse, on the other hand, is to be 'overheard' and when, finally, badgered and driven to expatiate on the nature of 'this stuff'[58] – as if it were ectoplasm or a nocturnal emission – he reacts with coy anger: 'I take no pride in it [*The Name and Nature of Poetry*]. I would rather forget it, and have my friends forget. I don't wish it to be associated with me.'[59] His instinctive judgment, at the heart of this denial, is entirely correct. The situation of the poet, as one of the licensed eccentrics exalted and belittled by the inheritors of Mill's dicta, is ultimately futile – especially when the lyric talent is itself circumscribed by those perimeters of self-knowledge and cultural judgment. In this, I would add, Housman is diametrically opposed by the poetry of Thomas Hardy, an obsessed and obsessive being who began, at the age of fifty-eight, two years after the appearance of *A Shropshire Lad,* to publish those volumes of poetry which are great lyrical dramas of sexual – particularly marital – solipsism and suicidal introversion.[60]

That quality which distinguishes Hardy's poetry from Housman's is technical rather than philosophical; or let us say that certain characteristics of 'depth' – as we might think of calling it – can be realized in terms of 'thought' only by the reach and grasp of technical perception and accomplishment. I take as my correlative an entry in Wittgenstein's *Notebooks 1914–1916*[61] which became formulation 5.64 of the *Tractatus Logico-Philosophicus* of 1922, the year in which Housman brought out *Last Poems* and Eliot published *The Waste Land:*

> Here we see that solipsism strictly carried out [*streng durchgeführt*] coincides with pure realism.
> The I in solipsism shrinks to an extensionless point and there remains the reality co-ordinated with it.[62]

The grammar of modernism in its closest matching of Wittgenstein's theory seems to me to be the semantic and syntactical catalepsis of the last poems of Paul Celan and the final plays of Beckett. But the great precursors are to be found at various points along this grammatical spectrum – Eliot, from 'The Love-Song of J. Alfred Prufrock' to, at least, 'Marina'; even the Hardy of 'Concerning Agnes'.

I could not, though I should wish, have over again,
    That old romance,
. . .
I could not. And you do not ask me why.
    Hence you infer
That what may chance to the fairest under the sky
    Has chanced to her.
Yes. She lies white, straight, features marble-keen,
Unapproachable, mute, in a nook I have never seen.[63]

My reason for claiming that even this acknowledges, by inference,
the force of Wittgenstein's perception is that the abrupt phrases
show at once the narrator's mind lapsing into solipsistic reverie
and tugging free of the lapse in the self-same grammatical place-
ment: 'I could not', 'I could not', 'Hence you infer', 'Yes'. The
coincidence is that the texture of the verse which speaks for the
'solipsism' finally remains as the reality coordinated with it. For
Hardy the proximate condition to solipsism is an ever-present
contingent circumstance, to be squinnied at, regarded askance,
ruggedly contested. In Housman's poems of subjective projection,
'Her strong enchantments failing' and 'When the eye of day is
shut',[64] the metrical-grammatical pattern is itself solipsistic, so that
the voice which sounds with allurement or menace and the voice
which defies the allurement or menace are finally indistinguishable
in the pitch and cadence of the chant. It is as if that which is
spoken in a Housman poem remains in thrall to that which is
unspoken: in this respect defiance is not the same as resistance –

        Her strong enchantments failing,
            Her towers of fear in wreck,
        Her limbecks dried of poisons
            And the knife at her neck,

        The Queen of air and darkness
            Begins to shrill and cry,
        'O young man, O my slayer,
            To-morrow you shall die.'

        O Queen of air and darkness,
            I think 'tis truth you say,
        And I shall die to-morrow;
            But you will die to-day.[65]

Housman told an enquirer that 'The queen of air and darkness comes from a line of Coventry Patmore's "the powers of darkness and the air", which in its turn is a reference to "the prince of the power of the air" in Ephesians II.2; and the meaning is Evil.'[66] It was understood by Housman's nephew Clement Symons (killed in 1915) as 'the portrayal of conflict in which cowardly fear was vanquished'.[67] If this is so, the antagonists sing an identical melody. This may eventually tell us something of significance not only with respect to Housman but also in relation to a gifted reader of Housman, Wilfred Owen (1893–1918), and his *odi et amo* struggle with the spirit of high Victorian Poetry; it may tell us something of the power of English tacit pledges; but one cannot conclude from this that Housman works at the pitch of creative understanding which we recognize in Hardy, Gurney or Rosenberg. As I have suggested, Housman's poems are full of defiance but they do not resist.

In the chapter on 'Solipsism' in *Appearance and Reality* Bradley wrote of a 'truth to which Solipsism has blindly borne witness':

> My way of contact with Reality is through a limited aperture. For I cannot get at it directly except through the felt 'this', and our immediate interchange and transfluence takes place through one small opening. Everything beyond, though not less real, is an expansion of the common essence which we feel burningly in this one focus.[68]

My suggestion would be that much minor 'lyrical' writing is minor because it is the equivalent of Bradley's 'limited aperture' and that this is particularly so with the poetry of Housman. That it is equally so of the poetry of Owen is a suggestion likely to meet much resistance, but I believe it to be the case: as much as with Housman, everything in Owen is got at through the 'felt "this"'. The 'felt "this"' must be understood as including much that James termed 'tacit pledges'; and that which is 'felt' can be interpreted in radically different ways: Owen feels things very much as Housman feels things but brings those feelings to conclusions antagonistic to Housman. Owen's 'Disabled'[69] parodies the kind of public lyrical sentiment which, among other forms of public seduction, it is implied, brought the legless and armless soldier to his plight: the poem by Housman which Owen has chiefly in mind is 'To an Athlete Dying Young':

And round that early-laurelled head
Will flock to gaze the strengthless dead,
And find unwithered on its curls
The garland briefer than a girl's.[70]

It is no mitigation, in this kind of confrontation, that the word
which gives its peculiar logopoeic strength to the quatrain is the
word 'strengthless', the word which, in the original Greek
(ἀμενηνά), in the Eleventh Book of the *Odyssey,* describes the
ghosts who flock to drink the blood of the ditch in order that
they may speak.[71] One recognizes both knowledge and judgment
in the rightness of Housman's word; to place one's words in such
a way shows distinction. Drawing upon the same episode Bradley
remarks, in one of his *Aphorisms,* that 'The shades nowhere speak
without blood, and the ghosts of Metaphysic accept no substitute. They reveal themselves only to that victim whose life they
have drained, and, to converse with shadows, he himself must
become a shade.'[72] Some sense of a metaphysical or existential
penalty being its own just price, its own tacit pledge, seems to
have been in the intellectual climate, for the German classical
scholar Ulrich von Wilamowitz-Moellendorf wrote, in 1908, in very
similar terms:

> We know that ghosts cannot speak until they have drunk blood;
> and the spirits which we evoke demand the blood of our hearts.
> We give it to them gladly; but if they then abide our question,
> something from us has entered into them; something alien, that
> must be cast out in the name of truth.[73]

The 'something alien' that Owen desired to cast out in the name
of truth was in part this metaphysical patrimony; it comprised
'many books' and much 'Poetry'.[74] To pledge the heart's blood
in any figurative sense became for him an inexpiable moral betrayal:

> Heart, you were never hot
> Nor large, nor full like hearts made great with shot;[75]

Because Owen faced the machine-guns with unflinching courage we may fancy that his opinions were carefully objective and
his aesthetics ethically superior to those of poets who, like
Tennyson and Housman, eulogized the fallen from a safe distance;

but this is not actually the case. The sensibility-in-action of 'Greater Love' is in fact no different from the sensibility-in-repose of 'To an Athlete Dying Young'. Owen wrote, in August 1917:

> I have just been reading Siegfried Sassoon, and am feeling at a very high pitch of emotion. Nothing like his trench life sketches has ever been written or ever will be written. Shakespere reads vapid after these. Not of course because Sassoon is a greater artist, but because of the subjects, I mean.[76]

This is not qualitatively different from Housman's 'I think that to transfuse emotion – not to transmit thought but to set up in the reader's sense a vibration corresponding to what was felt by the writer – is the peculiar function of poetry.'[77] It is rather that the 'turn of circumstances' has turned Owen's subjectivism to face a destructive force approaching from an entirely different direction. As I have previously suggested, if 'the peculiar function of poetry' is to be established in relation to our century it must be understood in the sense of Wittgenstein's coordinate or in the sense in which one might envisage an alternative to Bradley's 'limited aperture'.

It was Housman's ill-luck, though not a mischance peculiarly reserved to him, that, having in part succeeded in transferring a style of decorum from the magisterium of scholarship to the domain of the supposedly 'spontaneous' Romantic lyric – by way of Bridges's *Shorter Poems*[78] and the *Odes* of Horace – the very decorum should have been indicted by Owen, in the name of his 'expressionless' men,[79] as if it were no less despicable than an editorial in Horatio Bottomley's *John Bull*:[80]

> If you could hear, at every jolt, the blood
> Come gargling from the froth-corrupted lungs,
> Obscene as cancer, bitter as the cud
> Of vile, incurable sores on innocent tongues, –
> My friend, you would not tell with such high zest
> To children ardent for some desperate glory,
> The old Lie: Dulce et decorum est
> Pro patria mori.[81]

This 'famous Latin tag' (it is actually a Greek tag Latinized)[82] belongs, in its Horatian context (*Odes*, III.2), to a poem marked by 'abrupt' and unsettling changes of emphasis, which has been described as 'the most difficult, perhaps the only difficult ode, in the cycle of [Horace's] Roman Odes',[83] a poem which could be said presciently to acknowledge, both in its abruptness and 'mysterious avoidance', the force of Sorley's objections to Brooke's sonnet sequence '1914'. 'Mysterious avoidance', among other elements of making, has been part of the burden of this paper: mysterious avoidances are to be accounted correlatives of tacit pledges.

My decision to consider, under one heading, Housman in confrontation with a number of his contemporaries must itself abide the reader's question. I would hope that it is possible to show how a seemingly arbitrary collocation of authors can illuminate not only the direct and oblique features of their work but also something of the nature of tacit pledge and of the force for good or ill which this can exert, in a particular society, upon the supposedly 'individual' and 'original' voice. I would suggest that our proper desire and true aim in the critical examination of a body of work that has moved us, whether to assent or to dissent, is to satisfy ourselves, to be satisfied in our selves, that we have justly recognized the achievement of a 'particular sought pitch and accent'. In the contrary mode, when we admit that we have failed to take the 'straight measure' of the work, it is an appropriate discipline to determine, as precisely as we are able, whether the fault lies in us, in our predilections, presuppositions, prejudicate opinions, our tacit pledges, or in the fact of some '*usurping* consciousness' within the work itself, its 'displacement', for whatever rhyme or reason, from its 'indispensable centre'.

Each of these phrases – 'particular sought pitch and accent', 'straight measure', '*usurping* consciousness', 'indispensable centre', 'displacement' – I owe to the one source: the 'Preface' which Henry James wrote to *The Tragic Muse* when it was reprinted in the New York 'Definitive' Edition in 1908.[84] If I am correct in my suggestion that Housman's poetry is itself displaced from an indispensable centre, this does not in any way displace respect or deny accomplishment. Nor does it claim to have discovered an unprecedented dilemma or plight. I return for the last time upon the matter of John Stuart Mill, to the *Autobiography* and the essays on poetry where he slights poetry even as he stoops to praise its timely contribution to the recovery of his spirits;[85] and to the essay *On Liberty,* in which 'genius', which he purports to honour and which he sees, with some justice, as being perennially vulnerable to 'the general tendency of things throughout the world . . . to render mediocrity the ascendant power among mankind',[86] is nonetheless brought down to the level of his own mediocrity. Mill's conception of the context for genius diffuses into an 'atmosphere of freedom' in which alone 'Genius can . . . breathe freely'.[87]

In chapter XVI of *Essays on Truth and Reality* F. H. Bradley footnotes an allusion to Shelley's 'The Sensitive Plant', 'I do not know whether this in my case is a mark of senility, but I find myself now taking more and more as literal fact what I used in my youth to admire and love as poetry.'[88] Bradley's emphasis on 'literal fact' is hardly an improvement on Mill's 'atmosphere', although I think we are to understand the words as somehow putting Mill's kind of sensibility firmly in its place, in acknowledgment of an inescapable 'turn of circumstance'. Housman's poetry, unlike his scholarship, his textual emendations, is caught between Mill's 'atmosphere' and Bradley's 'literal fact'. What Eliot concluded, in the course of his study of Bradley, was that 'Solipsism has been one of the dramatic properties of most philosophical entertainers. Yet we cannot discard it without recognizing that it rests upon a truth.'[89] The thought here is Bradley's, from chapter XXI of *Appearance and Reality*;[90] the entertainment is Eliot's: he seems too easily pleased here by his powers of detachment though his tone does not exactly represent his conclusions on the question.[91]

James argues, in the New York 'Preface' to *The Tragic Muse*, that 'no character in a play (any play not a mere monologue) has, for the right expression of the thing, a *usurping* consciousness; the consciousness of others is exhibited exactly in the same way as that of the "hero" . . .'[92]

Transposing James's concern with drama to my own concern with poetry, I would claim that the poet in the poem is bound to take on the challenge of the 'usurping consciousness'; either he accepts it or he is the ignorant recipient of a destructive burden. There is rarely an unambiguous issue to this contest. To be wholly defeated by the challenge is to be drawn down into 'mere monologue'. Many poems move us with their knowledge of what is being exacted by such confrontation: in this sense there can be a difficult beauty of imperfection; but it is not, in such cases, a beauty of thought. It is a manifest beauty of intelligence – by which I mean, as the *Oxford English Dictionary* means, in one of its several senses of 'intelligence', 'understanding as a quality of admitting of degree'.[93] Eliot concedes that solipsism rests upon a truth; but one would add that, if solipsism is to be redeemed from mere monologue, the intelligence which is brought to bear upon it cannot be simply conceptual. What James called the 'indispensable centre' of such work must be realized within the many dimensions of language itself (though language is never, in actuality, language itself):

> A worm fed on the heart of Corinth,
> Babylon and Rome:
> Not Paris raped tall Helen,
> But this incestuous worm,
> Who lured her vivid beauty
> To his amorphous sleep.
> England! famous as Helen
> Is thy betrothal sung
> To him the shadowless,
> More amorous than Solomon.[94]

Housman's 'strengthless dead' is good; Isaac Rosenberg's 'amorphous sleep' is better. The strength of 'strengthless' momentarily holds back from the epigram 'find unwithered on its curls / The garland briefer than a girl's'; 'amorphous' is what 'vivid beauty' comes to; it is the ultimate dissolution of 'fame'; and it is the necessary condition of fame; the fame to which, in 1916, England is incestuously betrothed. 'Amorphous sleep' draws down the solipsistic beauties of English poetry into itself, the 'amorphous' transfluently becomes 'amorous'. This is not so much Blake's 'rose' that is 'sick' or his 'invisible worm / That flies in the night'[95] – though for Rosenberg that poem is evidently more than thoughtless delight – as the amorphous idea of English poetry, which 'answers to nothing real' yet is 'packed with material to set nostalgic imagination to work'.[96]

James Russell Lowell, in *Among My Books* (1870), desiderated a 'quality in man which . . . gives classic shape to our own amorphous imaginings'.[97] Housman's poems, in their several gatherings, from *A Shropshire Lad* (1896) to *Additional Poems* (1937), famously bring classic shape to amorphous imaginings. To say that they 'bring' is not to say that they 'give'. Giving, as I would understand it – particularly in the work of Housman's much younger contemporaries Gurney and Rosenberg – presupposes 'understanding as a quality of admitting of degree': the intelligence made manifest in Gurney's 'Tewkesbury' ('What is best of England, going quick from beauty, / Is manifest, the slow spirit going straight on')[98] and in every phrase of Rosenberg's brief poem, in the perceived sensual plighting of 'amorphous' / 'amorous' that is England's fatal love for herself. But intelligence, such as we find in Rosenberg, is a quality that 'England' has never been over-disposed to acknowledge, for it has never 'delighted and inspired generations of readers'.[99]

Notes

1. F. H. Bradley, *Ethical Studies* (1876), 2nd edn, (Oxford: Clarendon, 1927) p. 184.
2. *The Letters of A. E. Housman*, ed. H. Maas (Cambridge, Mass.: Harvard University Press, 1971) p. 208.
3. Ibid., p. 310.
4. A. E. Housman, *Collected Poems and Selected Prose*, ed. C. Ricks (London: Allen Lane, The Penguin Press, 1988) p. 268: 'Introductory Lecture delivered before the Faculties of Arts and Laws and of Science in University College, London, October 3, 1892.'
5. Ibid., p. 328: 'The Application of Thought to Textual Criticism', 4 August 1921.
6. Ibid., p. 421.
7. *Collected Works of John Stuart Mill* (Toronto: University of Toronto Press, 1963) vol. I, p. 348: 'Thoughts on Poetry and its Varieties', 1833.
8. Ibid., pp. 150–3: *Autobiography*, c. 1853–73.
9. John Stuart Mill, *On Liberty* (1859), ed. G. Himmelfarb (New York: Knopf, 1974; Harmondsworth: Penguin, 1985) p. 132.
10. *The Letters of Charles Sorley with a Chapter of Biography* (Cambridge: Cambridge University Press, 1919) p. 49: a paper read to the Literary Society, Marlborough College, 15 May 1913.
11. Ibid., p. 108: letter of 6 March 1914.
12. Ibid., p. 263.
13. Housman, *Letters*, ed. cit., p. 329.
14. Ricks, ed. cit. pp. 101 and 487: *Last Poems* IV.
15. *Alfred Edward Housman 26 March 1859: 30 April 1936* [Special Issue of *The Bromsgrovian*], (Bromsgrove, 1936) p. 29.
16. Bradley, *Ethical Studies*, p. 185.
17. J. Pugh, *Bromsgrove and the Housmans* (Bromsgrove: The Housman Society, 1974) lxvii–lxxiii: Appendix E, George Herbert Housman.
18. Ricks, ed. cit., pp. 223 and 499: *Additional Poems* XXIII.
19. Ibid., pp. 115 and 488: *Last Poems* XVII.

20. Ibid., 186: *More Poems* XL.
21. A. Burnett's edition of the complete poems (OUP) was published in 1997.
22. Ricks, ed. cit. p. 31: *A Shropshire Lad* IX; p. 34: *ASL* XII; p. 38: *ASL* XVI; p. 41: *ASL* XIX; p. 43: *ASL* XXI; p. 51: *ASL* XXVIII; p. 59: *ASL* XXXV; p. 60: *ASL* XXXVI; p. 76: *ASL* XLII; p. 86: *ASL* LIX; p. 122: *LP* XXIV; p. 141: *LP* XL; p. 142: *LP* XLI; p. 155: *MP* IX; p. 179: *MP* XXXIII; p. 207: *AP* IX.
23. I give this as quoted in *The Collected Poems of Sidney Keyes*, ed. M. Meyer (London: Routledge, 1945) p. 117. I once had the original reference but have long since mislaid it.
24. R. Shaw, *Housman's Places* (Bromsgrove: The Housman Society, 1995) p. 115.
25. Pugh, op. cit., p. 167.
26. Penguin Modern Classics edition (Harmondsworth, 1978) p. 199. The allusion is to *Hamlet*.
27. Lord Alfred Douglas, 'The Two Loves'.
28. R. P. Graves, *A. E. Housman: the Scholar Poet* (New York: Charles Scribner's Sons, 1980) p. 113; cf. D. Kerr, *Wilfred Owen's Voices: Language and Community* (Oxford: Clarendon, 1993) p. 182, referring to Owen's 'recent contact with the "secret men" of the embattled homosexual community in London'.
29. Ricks, ed. cit., p. 177.
30. Housman, *Letters*, ed. cit., p. 276.
31. Graves, op. cit., p. 101.
32. Ricks, ed. cit., p. 96.
33. Ibid., p. 367.
34. Ibid., p. 91: *ASL* LXIII.
35. Ibid., p. 141: *LP* XL.
36. *The Spectator*, no. 26, Friday, 30 March 1711.
37. *The Spectator*, no. 465, Saturday, 23 August 1712.
38. *Songs of Innocence and of Experience*, 1794, Plate 42.
39. Ricks, ed. cit., p. 194: *MP* XLVII; Graves, op. cit., pp. 265–6.
40. Housman, *Letters*, ed. cit., p. 329: 'I respect the Epicureans more than the Stoics, but I am myself a Cyrenaic.'
41. Graves, op. cit., p. 249.
42. *Philosophical Investigations*, trans. G. E. M. Anscombe, 3rd edn (New York: Macmillan, 1969) 122e.
43. A. E. Housman, *Selected Prose*, ed. J. Carter (Cambridge: Cambridge University Press, 1962) p. 42.
44. Ibid., p. 51.
45. Ibid., p. 27.
46. F. H. Bradley, *Appearance and Reality* (1893), second edition (1897), ninth impression (corrected) (Oxford: Clarendon, 1930) pp. 224–5.
47. Housman, *Letters*, ed. cit., p. 329; Graves, op. cit., p. 107.
48. cited *O. E. D.: Solipsism*.
49. Ibid.
50. Ricks, ed. cit., p. 432 [49: Virgil].
51. Sorley, *Letters*, ed. cit., p. 51.

52. Emile Durkheim, *Le suicide: étude du sociologie* (Paris: F. Alcan, 1897).
53. Ricks, ed. cit., p. 367.
54. *Ethical Studies,* ch. 3, 'Pleasure for Pleasure's Sake'.
55. Graves, op. cit., p. 249; Housman, *Letters,* ed. cit., p. 329. The doctrine of Aristippus of Cyrene, who established the Cyrenaic school, was that of 'practical hedonism' (*O. E. D.*).
56. *Collected Works,* I, p. 499.
57. Ibid., I, p. 348.
58. Ricks, ed. cit., p. 370.
59. P. Withers, *A Buried Life: Personal Recollections of A. E. Housman* (London: Jonathan Cape, 1940) p. 102.
60. But cf. Housman, *Letters,* ed. cit., p. 329 [February, 1933]: 'For Hardy I felt affection, and high admiration for some of his novels and a few of his poems.'
61. L. Wittgenstein, *Notebooks 1914–1916,* ed. G. H. von Wright and G. E. M. Anscombe, 2nd edn (Chicago: University of Chicago Press, 1979) 82 and 82e.
62. L. Wittgenstein, *Tractatus Logico-Philosophicus,* trans. C. K. Ogden (1922), first paperback edn (London: Routledge, 1981) pp. 152–3.
63. *The Complete Poems of Thomas Hardy,* ed. J. Gibson (London: Macmillan, 1976), p. 878; in *Winter Words* (1928).
64. Ricks, ed. cit., p. 134: *LP* XXIII.
65. Ibid., p. 100: *LP* III.
66. Ibid., pp. 486–7.
67. Ibid. The words are Katharine Symons's.
68. Bradley, op. cit., 229.
69. *The Poems of Wilfred Owen,* ed. J. Stallworthy (London: Chatto/Hogarth, 1985) pp. 152–4.
70. Ricks, ed. cit., p. 41: *ASL* XIX.
71. Homer, *The Odyssey,* trans. A. T. Murray (1919), 2 vols (London: Loeb/Heinemann 1984) I, pp. 388–9.
72. F. H. Bradley, *Aphorisms* (Oxford: Clarendon, 1930) no. 98.
73. Quoted as epigraph, H. Lloyd-Jones, *Blood for the Ghosts: Classical Influences in the Nineteenth and Twentieth Centuries* (London: Duckworth, 1982). This contains two useful essays on Housman as classical scholar. Either Wilamowitz or his translator had in mind Arnold's sonnet to Shakespeare.
74. Wilfred Owen, *Collected Letters,* eds. H. Owen and J. Bell (London: Oxford University Press, 1967) pp. 581–2. *Owen,* ed. cit., p. 122, 'Insensibility', ll. 7–8; p. 155, 'A Terre', pp. 10, 192, 'Preface'; cf. pp. 101–2, 'Apologia Pro Poemate Meo'.
75. Ibid., p. 143: 'Greater Love'.
76. *Collected Letters,* ed. cit., pp. 484–5.
77. Ricks, ed. cit., p. 352.
78. Housman, *Letters,* ed. cit., pp. 173, 294.
79. *Collected Letters,* ed. cit., p. 422. 'The men are just as Bairnsfather has them – expressionless lumps' (letter of 4 January 1917). Bruce Bairnsfather did not depict the British private soldier as 'expressionless', a fact which can be demonstrated by spending ten minutes

or so with *Fragments from France*, 1917. 'In Dixie-Land: "Well, Friday
– 'ow's Crusoe?"', to take one example, shows eight tommies, each
with a distinct, strongly realized, facial expression, each one a delineated 'character'. If there are 'expressionless' stereotypes in
Bairnsfather, they are more likely to be officers: vacant 'silly ass'
faces for subalterns, Blimpish for general staff. It is nonetheless true
that Bairnsfather has evolved an English comedy of humours as
artificial in its way as *Jorrocks's Jaunts*. Owen requires 'the men' to
be 'expressionless lumps' to establish the moral ground upon which
his war poems are based: the conviction that he alone can give a
terrible inarticulacy its voice (cf. *Collected Letters*, ed. cit., p. 521, letter
of 31 December 1917). Further discussion of this question lies outside
the scope of the present paper.

80. *Collected Letters*, ed. cit., pp. 468 n. 2, 568, 585 n. 2.
81. *Owen*, ed. cit., pp. 117–18.
82. Owen, *Collected Letters*, ed. cit., p. 500; Horace: *The Odes*, ed. K. Quinn
    (London: Macmillan Educational, 1980, corrected reprint, 1984)
    p. 245.
83. Quinn, ed. cit, p. 244.
84. H. James, *The Art of the Novel*, (New York: Charles Scribner's Sons,
    n.d.) pp. 81, 79, 90, 84, 86.
85. Mill, *Collected Works*, I, pp. 150–3, 344–5, 348–9, 403.
86. *On Liberty*, ed. cit., pp. 130–1.
87. Ibid., p. 129.
88. F. H. Bradley, *Essays on Truth and Reality* (Oxford: Clarendon, 1914)
    p. 468 n. 1.
89. T. S. Eliot, *Knowledge and Experience in the Philosophy of F. H. Bradley*
    (London: Faber, 1964) p. 141.
90. Ibid., p. 142; Bradley, op. cit., p. 229.
91. Concerning 'entertainment': when Eliot, in 'Little Gidding', predicts
    'the hedges / White again, in May, with voluptuary sweetness', how
    far is the Bradleian 'voluptuary' (cf. *Ethical Studies*, p. 270n) an implicit
    condescension to Wordsworthian 'sensations sweet' as particularized
    by the Victorian and Georgian lyric style, for instance in Housman's
    set pieces ('The hawthorn sprinkled up and down / Should charge
    the land with snow', *ASL* XXXIX, 'under blanching mays', *LP* XL)?
    For G. Grigson, *The Englishman's Flora* (London: Readers' Union/
    Phoenix, 1958) pp. 166–71, the may can be over-sweet, indeed ful-
    some: 'The stale, sweet scent from the trimethylamine the flowers
    contain, makes them suggestive of sex … Trimethylamine is an
    ingredient of the smell of putrefaction' (p.168). In Amphlett's and
    Rea's exemplary *The Botany of Worcestershire* (Birmingham: Cornish
    Bros, 1907) pp. 140–1, this is a specificity that goes unrecorded though
    they note that 'into the usages and rejoicings of the country-side
    the plant has entered largely'. Housman's art brings the hawthorn
    particularly into his necessitarian returns upon the usages and
    rejoicings of the Worcestershire ('Shropshire') countryside: 'In valleys
    green and still / Where lovers wander maying', *LP* VII; ' … the flowers/
    Stream from the hawthorn on the wind away' *LP* IX. If such verses

are a form of parody on 'usages and rejoicings', the intelligence
that dictates them is not at all remote from the decent sensibilities
of Amphlett and Rea ('Orchis... From an untranslatable word,
referring to the double tuberous root', p. 348). I am pondering here
the affinity between one style of closed meanings and another and
debating, as I have throughout the paper, the nature of the pressure which social *mores* impose upon the individual voice. These are
mutual overhearings and tacit understandings, within Mill's range
of assumptions though not with his particular emphasis. The true
genius in these restricted circumstances is Edward FitzGerald's
refusing blancmange at a wedding breakfast, 'Ugh! Congealed bride's-
maid'. Housman's table-talk can be both witty and suggestive, but
not with this kind of purchase on chance and possibility. His set
lyric melancholy ('The garland briefer than a girl's') seems at times
as vulnerable to FitzGerald's peculiar felicities of entertainment as
to Sorley's suggestion of a 'somewhat self-satisfied dislike of life'
(cf. note 10 above). But then again one might say that FitzGerald,
in the language and cadences of the *Rubaiyat*, seems at times vulnerable to the quality and scope of intelligence at work in his letters
and conversation; and that there is nothing in Sorley's verse to match
the grasp of expectation and circumstance shown in his remarks on
the occasion of Brooke's death (note 12, above). It is appropriate to
recall here Housman's own words concerning judgment, truth and
convention (note 4, above).

92. James, *Art of the Novel*, op. cit., p. 90.
93. *O. E. D.*: intelligence, sense 2.
94. *The Collected Works of Isaac Rosenberg*, ed. I. Parsons (London: Chatto & Windus, 1979) p. 105.
95. Blake, *Songs of Innocence and of Experience*, 1794, Plate 39: 'The Sick Rose'.
96. R. Shaw, *Housman's Places* (Bromsgrove: The Housman Society, 1995) back cover.
97. *O. E. D.*: *amorphous*.
98. *Collected Poems of Ivor Gurney*, ed. P. J. Kavanagh (Oxford: Oxford University Press, 1982) p. 129.
99. *Housman's Places*, op. cit., back cover.

5

'Ashes under Uricon': Historicizing A. E. Housman, Reifying T. H. Huxley, Embracing Lucretius

Kenneth Womack

In his 1911 Cambridge Inaugural Lecture, A. E. Housman alluded to the same scientific and natural laws that informed, thematically and ideologically, much of his earlier poetic *oeuvre*: 'This fright, this night of the mind, must be dispelled not by the rays of the sun, nor day's bright spears, but by the face of nature and her laws. And this is her first, from which we take our start: nothing was ever by miracle made from nothing' (26). In this remarkably Lucretian phrase, as well as in his own work as poet and classical editor, Housman reveals his great regard for Lucretius and his ancient philosophy. Housman's admiration for Lucretius has indeed been well-documented; he once praised the poet-philosopher's *De Rerum Natura* lovingly as 'a work more compact of excellence than any edition of any classic produced in England' (Graves, 1979, p. 166). Lucretius' Epicurean ontology profoundly influenced Housman's poetry, particularly in the poet's 1896 volume, *A Shropshire Lad*, while at the same time impinging upon Housman's own interest in the means of human existence and the *topos* of atomic theory – Lucretian concepts that fathered the notion of 'the stuff of life' so prevalent in Housman's poetry.[1]

A reading of Housman's work in regard to the scientific naturalism of Victorian England, particularly through the essays of Thomas Henry Huxley, reveals a post-Victorian aesthetic informed by the scientific pursuits and conclusions of another era – not only from the age of Lucretius, as previous critics have astutely noted, but from the age of Darwin as well. In this manner, then,

Victorian science informs the historical dynamic of Housman's poetics and thus merges with his latent Lucretian ideology to produce a complex historical amalgam comprising competing scientific philosophies from dramatically divergent historical moments. At the same time, such a conclusion underscores the value of Jerome J. McGann's programme for historical-literary study, originally promulgated in his 1985 volume, *The Beauty of Inflections: Literary Investigations in Historical Method and Theory*. McGann writes: 'Poems at once locate a dialectical encounter between the past and the present, and they represent, through processes of reflection, a particular instance of dialectical exchange which is taken in the present as given and through the past' (p. 5). Considering Housman's poetry as a venue for the historical interplay between ancient and Victorian scientific beliefs – particularly in regard to McGann's relevant poststructuralist concerns for matters of historicity – enables critics to revise their ideas concerning the manner in which Housman forged his aesthetic, while at the same time allowing them to unearth further the Victorian ideals embedded in Housman's remarkable verse.[2]

To understand fully Housman's appropriation of ancient philosophy in his poetics, the respective philosophies of Epicurus and Lucretius must first be elucidated. Long acknowledged by literary critics and philosophers alike as one of the greatest influences upon both the poetry of Housman and Lucretius, Epicurus, who lived between 342 and 270 BC (Copley, p. ix), employed poetry in his landmark study, *On Nature*, to advance his largely scientific arguments (Clay, pp. 56–57). In his work, Epicurus afforded particular emphasis to the notion of free will – an interest that stemmed largely from his conclusions about atoms and their tendencies to swerve of their own accord (Copley, p. xv). Epicurean philosophy *per se* functions upon three basic principles. First, Epicurus argues that all pleasure is good, while all evil is bad. The second basic tenet of Epicurean philosophy arises directly from the concepts of good and evil. Epicurus believed that death was a natural part of humanity – an experience not to be feared, but to be embraced (Rosenbaum, 1986, pp. 217–18). In *On Nature*, Epicurus argues that to the living, death remains an unknown quantity, thus producing an understandable human fear. Epicurus believed that such a fear was ludicrous because man has no basis for understanding the experience of death, only the expectation of it: 'Foolish, therefore, is the man who says that he fears death, not because it will pain when it comes, but because it pains in the prospect' (Rosenbaum, 1989, p. 82). As Epicurus argues, the fear of death is grounded merely in its expectation; without any knowledge about the experience of death, man can only wait and ponder the possibility of no longer existing.

The final principal tenet of Epicurean philosophy relates to the existence of atoms. Epicurus drew his conclusions regarding atoms from another ancient philosopher, Democritus (born 460–457 BC), who identified atoms as the basic forms of matter. Epicurus believed that atoms were both indivisible and indestructible, and thus they could not be created by man. Accordingly, Epicurus believed that the body in its living state is made up of a finite number of atoms that comprise the human soul. According to the Epicurean ontology, when the body enters a state of death, its atoms are immediately dispersed into the world, thus becoming free to form another being. In this manner, Epicurus offers an important observation about the mortality of the human soul and suggests that through death, the body and the soul enter into a permanent state of non-existence (Copley, pp. xi–xiii). Further, this observation remains one of the primary philosophical underpinnings of Housman's early poetry.

One of Epicurus' earliest disciples was the ancient poet, Lucretius, who is believed to have lived between 95 and 52 BC (Copley, p. viii). Lucretius embraced Epicureanism, especially Epicurus' three principal tenets and his forays into atomic theory (Copley, pp. xvi–xvii). Lucretius prominently features these Epicurean ideals in *De Rerum Natura*, particularly in Book Three of his long poem. In this instance, Lucretius explores the Epicurean belief that death remains an unknown experience – again, an experience not to be feared but embraced. Lucretius wrote: 'Often through fear of death men come to hate life and the sight of the sun so bitterly that in a burst of grief they kill themselves, forgetting that it was this fear that caused their cares, troubled their conscience, broke their bonds of friendship, and overturned all sense of decency' (pp. 58–9). Thus, in Lucretius' philosophical purview, the fear of death breeds a fear of living.

Lucretius also replicates Epicurus' early examinations of atomic theory. In the preface to his discussion of atoms in Book Three of *De Rerum Natura*, Lucretius defines the existence of the soul and its physical place within the body: 'First, I speak of the soul (sometimes called "mind"), in which life's thoughts and government are placed; it's no less part of a man than hand and foot and eyes are part of the total living creature' (p. 59). Atoms, in this Epicurean sense, are the virtual life-force of the living body. Like Epicurus, Lucretius also demonstrates the phenomenon of atomic dispersal when the body dies. Life, according to the Epicurean argument, creates the restraint that holds the atoms within the body. In death, however, the atoms are released to pursue their own free will. As Lucretius writes: 'Say it again: when all our fleshy husk is loosened, and the breath of life cast out, you must admit that sensate soul and mind break up; a single life links soul and body' (p. 70). In this way, then, Lucretius suggests that with the exodus of atoms, the body and the soul cease to exist. Following the philosophies of Epicurean thought, Lucretius, in addition to making observations regarding the human fear of death, alleges that immortality and afterlife are non-existent and imposs-ible entities within 'the nature of things'.

Two thousand years later, a series of essays by Thomas Henry Huxley revealed the scientist's latent Epicurean ideals in his Victorian-era criticisms of the work of British naturalist, Charles Darwin – critical studies that offer a relevant discourse on several issues of an Epicurean nature. For example, in his 1868 essay, 'On the Physical Basis of Life', Huxley considers the same ques-tions that Epicurus surely must have pondered years before:

> And now, what is the ultimate fate, and what the origin, of the matter of life? Is it, as some of the older naturalists supposed, diffused throughout the universe in molecules, which are indestructible and unchangeable in themselves; but, in endless transmigration, unite in innumerable permutations, into the diversified forms of life we know? Or, is the matter of life composed of ordinary matter, and again resolved into ordinary matter when its work is done?
>
> (p. 145)

Like Epicurus and Lucretius before him, Huxley hypothesized that atoms arise out of ordinary matter to become composite forms during life while returning to the realm of ordinary matter in death. This argument supports Epicurean notions about the cess-ation of life through death, both of the body and of the soul, and challenges the concepts of afterlife and immortality. Death, according to Huxley, is a natural state of lifelessness, as well as a process that ultimately begins with birth: 'Under whatever disguise it takes refuge, whether fungus or oak, worm or man, the living protoplasm not only ultimately dies and is resolved into its mineral and lifeless constituents, but is always dying, and strange as the paradox may sound, could not live unless it died' (p. 145).

Huxley likewise harboured substantial reservations about the concept of the human soul. In his 1874 essay, 'On the Hypothesis that Animals Are Automata, and Its History', Huxley ponders the possibility of the soul's existence:

> Either consciousness is the function of something distinct from the brain, which we call the soul, and a sensation is the mode in which this soul is affected by the motion of a part of the brain; or there is no soul, and a sensation is something generated by the mode of motion of a part of the brain. In the former case, the phenomena of the senses are purely spiritual affections; in the latter they are something manufactured by the mechanism of the body.
>
> (di Gregorio, 1984, pp. 146–7)

In addition to his theory that the soul does not exist as a separate bodily structure, Huxley concludes that the soul is simply an article of religious faith (di Gregorio, 1984, p. 146). To Huxley, a confessed agnostic, faith was a concept that operated outside of the bounds of scientific consideration (Marlow, 1958, p. 152), and his ideas about the validity of the soul, as well as his discourse on atomic matter within the body, truly demonstrate Huxley's own Epicurean-like conclusions.

In his poetry, Housman, in the tradition of Lucretius and Huxley, operated from an ontology in his work that remains strikingly Epicurean. Housman's poetry and prose contain several examples of Epicurean concepts, particularly in relation to atomic theory, mortality and the human fear of death. As his brother Laurence recalled, in religious matters Housman approved of the Church of England as an institution, yet possessed no faith in its tenets (Haber, 1967, p. 164). Critics such as Richard Perceval Graves ascribe Housman's affinity for the philosophies of Epicurus and Lucretius – and later, Huxley – to their atheism. As Graves notes, Lucretius' 'main work [*De Rerum Natura*] was a savage attack upon religious belief' (p. 203). Housman, both a contemporary of Huxley[3] and also agnostic in his beliefs, believed that the soul was as mortal as the body and had strong reservations about the notion of immortality. As Norman Marlow argues, 'One can sense in Housman, as in Huxley, Romanes, and other agnostics of the late nineteenth century, the underlying bewilderment and anguish of a soul naturally Christian, . . . yet to call Housman a Christian, as some have done, is of course nonsense' (p. 152).

Like Lucretius, Housman examined the human fear of mortality from an Epicurean stance. In his *London Introductory Lecture* (1892), for example, Housman proffered his own views about the fear of non-existence, and, in doing so, revealed the absorption of Epicurean ideals into his aesthetic:

> Existence is not in itself a good thing, that we should spend a lifetime in securing its necessaries: a life spent, however victoriously, in securing the necessaries of life is not more than an elaborate furnishing and decoration of apartments for the reception of a guest who is never to come . . . [O]ur true occupation is to manufacture from the raw material of life the fabric of happiness; and if we are ever to set about our work we must make up our minds to risk something. Absolute security for existence is unattainable, and no wise man will pursue it; for if we must go to these lengths in the attempt at self preservation we shall die before ever we have begun to live.
>
> (Marlow, 1958, p. 155)

Like Lucretius, Housman believed that the human fear of death precluded any real and productive means of existence, and an examination of his poetry reveals the manner in which he employs – again, like Lucretius – the tenets of atomic theory in an effort to demonstrate the vacuous nature of human life in the enduring face of death.

The poet also entertained similar notions regarding Epicurean atomic theory, arguments previously considered by Lucretius and Huxley. In Poem XXXI from *A Shropshire Lad*, Housman offers images of the gale of life as it blows through the fictive terrain of the poet's Shropshire, spreading the ashes and atoms of the narrator's human precursors among the shadows of his fleeting contemporary existence:

> There, like the wind through woods in riot,
>   Through him the gale of life blew high;
> The tree of man was never quiet:
>   Then 'twas the Roman, now 'tis I.
>
> The gale, it plies the saplings double,
>   It blows so hard, 'twill soon be gone:
> To-day the Roman and his trouble
>   Are ashes under Uricon.

Norman Page argues that the movements of the wind in *A Shrop-shire Lad* function as a poetic manoeuvre that enables Housman to forge a temporal link between the ancient past, a dismal present and an uncertain future: 'The wind blows not just through a human life but through history,' Page writes; 'the wind of the distant past . . . links dead Roman and Victorian Englishman' (1983, p. 195). In this way, Housman alludes – through his references to the enduring winds of ancient Uricon – to the phenomenon that Tom Burns Haber calls the 'unending cycle of atomic dissolution and recombination' prevalent throughout the poet's verse (1967, p. 164).

Housman offers similar images of the wind as a means of posthumous transport in Poem XXXII from *A Shropshire Lad*, a poem where Housman continues to posit his overarching argument regarding atomic theory. The manner in which Housman employs his Epicurean thesis across the boundaries of his various poetic entries in *A Shropshire Lad* underscores the poet's insistence upon the value of atomic theory and its ancient philosophical properties, while also affirming Page's assertion that 'almost any individual poem in *A Shropshire Lad* has a total meaning that is partly supplied by its relationship to other poems in the collection. This relationship may be thematic or it may be a matter of recurrent diction or imagery' (1983, p. 195). In the following instance from Poem XXXII, the poem's narrator again discusses the existence of atoms – the 'stuff of life' – and the way in which they combined to form his very being:

> From far, from eve and morning
>   And yon twelve-winded sky,
> The stuff of life to knit me
>   Blew hither: here am I.

In the second stanza, the narrator warns that he has not yet 'dispersed', referring to his own inevitable death and atomic dissolution, as well as to the larger, Epicurean ontological construct of atomic dispersal. Through this ancient metaphor, the narrator acknowledges the fleeting nature of his existence:

> Now – for a breath I tarry
> Nor yet disperse apart –
> Take my hand quick and tell me,
> What have you in your heart.

The images of fortuitously swerving atoms in these lines are vivid indeed, and, as Haber notes, Poem XXXII 'can be understood only in terms of Lucretius' atomistic theory' (1967, p. 162). John Bayley also argues that this instance in Poem XXXII offers additional images of 'urgency ... heightened into mysteriousness' – emotions no doubt intensified by Housman's arguments, via Lucretius, regarding the tenuous nature of human life. As Bayley concludes: 'A lifetime should be enough for any number of such exchanges, but the poem sees the whole of it as a moment' (1992, p. 34).

Yet another poem from *A Shropshire Lad*, Poem XLIII ('The Immortal Part'), echoes Lucretian and Epicurean ideals as well. In this poem, the narrator suggests that the only immortal part of the body is the bone, rather than the soul – the conclusion of the more popular religious beliefs of Housman's era. As Marlow remarks, 'Housman himself never speaks of his atheism more directly' than in 'The Immortal Part' (1958, p. 53). When the narrator refers to a voice within him, he refers not to his immortal Christian soul, but instead to his aching bones, appendages exhausted from the chores of living:

> When I meet the morning beam
> Or lay me down at night to dream,
> I hear my bones within me say,
> 'Another night, another day'.

In this instance – and within Housman's larger aesthetic – the bones trudge on, for they are the true immortal parts, and long after the narrator's life has ceased, his bones will continue to endure:

Before this fire of sense decay,
This smoke of thought blow clean away,
And leave with ancient night alone
The stedfast and enduring bone.

As Cleanth Brooks notes, 'The Immortal Part' offers a paradox because 'the immortal part of man is his skeleton – not the spirit, not the soul – but the most earthy, the most nearly mineral part of his body' (1968, p. 70). Such a conclusion is reminiscent of Huxley's own scepticism about the soul as a living feature within the human body. For this reason, Housman conspicuously avoids any explanation for the location of the soul, while instead providing his readers with the lasting image of a 'stedfast and enduring bone' – humanity's true immortal part, destined to live for centuries. As B. J. Leggett remarks, 'Here is another instance in which Housman gives us a full look at the worst, infects us with his own dark vision, yet manages to defend us against the anxiety of death and leaves us with a sense of victory' (1978, p. 149).

In this way, then, the historical and literary interplay between the poetry of Housman and Lucretius and the scientific conclusions of Huxley and Epicurus both underscore the spirit of McGann's argument regarding poetry and its propensity for creating a larger dialectic exchange. By reifying Epicurus' philosophy against the tableau of late-Victorian England and its competing philosophies of scientific naturalism, Housman, with a well-focused eye to the past, interprets and offers a critique of the scientific and ontological arguments of his historical present. In his poems about human mortality and atomic theory, Housman also reinvigorates the science and poetry of another era by reflecting his own carefully measured verse upon the ideals of Epicurus, Lucretius, and the very 'stuff of life' upon which their philosophies function. In this manner, he establishes a palpable and conscious poetic and historical interchange between his own poetry and that of his ancient precursors, while at the same time demonstrating that the creation of great poetry may be the only true avenue to immortality.

Notes

1. The author would like to thank William Baker, Roy Birch, Charmian Hearne, Terence A. Hoagwood and Alan Holden for their encouragement and advice throughout the production of this essay.
2. Notably, Housman's verse – often lauded by his critics for its simplicity of form and meaning – in fact offers little in the way of poetic resolution. As John Peale Bishop remarks: 'Despite an apparent clarity such that almost any poem seems ready to deliver its meaning at once, there is always something that is not clear, something not brought into the open, something that is left in doubt' (1940, p. 141). As this essay will demonstrate, the complexity of the philosophy endemic to Housman's opaque aesthetic finds its roots in the very confusion and doubt of which Bishop speaks, and the poet deliberately appropriates such a hazy tableau in order to posit his arguments regarding atomic theory and the fleeting nature of human life.
3. In a letter to Max Beerbohm of 16 May 1933, Housman refers in poetic jest to his Victorian contemporary. 'I also have a vision of grandpapa and great-grandpapa reading the works of Mr. Aldous Huxley, with the legend,' he writes: 'T. H. Huxley Esq., P.C. / Is this how Leonard bred his brat? / The Rev. T. Arnold, D.D. / Good Gracious! even worse than Matt' (*Letters*, 1971, p. 334).

Bibliography

Bayley, John. *Housman's Poems* (Oxford: Clarendon, 1992).

Bishop, John Peale. 'The Poetry of A. E. Housman', *Poetry*, 56 (1940), pp. 144–53.

Brooks, Cleanth. 'Alfred Edward Housman', *A. E. Housman: A Collection of Critical Essays*, ed. Christopher Ricks (Englewood Cliffs, NJ: Prentice-Hall, 1968), pp. 62–84.

Clay, Diskin. *Lucretius and Epicurus* (Ithaca, NY: Cornell University Press, 1983).

di Gregorio, Mario. A. *T. H. Huxley's Place in Natural Science* (New Haven, CT: Yale University Press, 1984).

Graves, Richard Perceval. *A. E. Housman: The Scholar Poet* (New York: Scribner's, 1979).

Haber, Tom Burns. *A. E. Housman* (New York: Twayne, 1967).

Housman, A. E. *The Collected Poems of A. E. Housman* (New York: Holt, 1965).

——. *The Confines of Criticism* (Cambridge: Cambridge University Press, 1969).

——. *The Letters of A. E. Housman*, ed. Henry Maas (Cambridge, MA: Harvard University Press, 1971).

Huxley, Thomas Henry. *Collected Essays; Volume I: Methods and Results* (Westport, CT: Greenwood, 1968).

Leggett, B. J. *The Poetic Art of A. E. Housman: Theory and Practice* (Lincoln: University of Nebraska Press, 1978).

Lucretius. *De Rerum Natura*, Introduction Frank O. Copley (New York: Norton, 1977).

McGann, Jerome J. *The Beauty of Inflections: Literary Investigations in Historical Method and Theory* (Oxford: Oxford University Press, 1985).

Marlow, Norman. *A. E. Housman: Scholar and Poet* (Minneapolis: University of Minnesota Press, 1958).

Page, Norman. *A. E. Housman: A Critical Biography* (London: Macmillan, 1983).

Rosenbaum, Stephen. 'Epicurus and Annihilation', *Philosophical Quarterly*, 39 (1989), pp. 81–90.

——. 'How to Be Dead and Not Care: A Defense of Epicurus', *American Philosophical Quarterly*, 23 (1986), pp. 217–25.

6

A. E. Housman and Thomas Hardy

Norman Page

One of the words in my title may seem to take too much for granted: Housman and Hardy is scarcely the same kind of conjunction as Beaumont and Fletcher, Wordsworth and Coleridge, Rodgers and Hammerstein or Marks and Spencer, and I shall try not to yield to that mixture of enthusiasm and desperation that often seems to activate those engaged in comparative studies. Perhaps the patron saint of such enterprises is Captain Fluellen in Shakespeare's *Henry V*, who argues for the strong resemblance between King Henry and Alexander the Great: 'There is a river in Macedon, and there is also moreover a river at Monmouth . . . and there is salmons in both.' When all is said and done, differences and uniquenesses are usually more interesting and more profound than similarities, however ingeniously teased out, and in bringing together these two writers – in inviting the reader to look here upon this picture and on this – I shall, like Hamlet, often have to dwell upon dissimilarities and disparities rather than resemblances. Lurking behind my innocent title, in fact, is a shadowy and obstinate Other: 'Housman not Hardy.' But *vive la différence*.

As poets, however, they are more than close neighbours in an index, and to put them side by side may help to provide a context in which to judge and appreciate Housman's distinctive achievement. At first glance, they certainly seem to have much in common. Though not quite of the same generation (for Hardy was eighteen when Housman was born), they emerged as published poets at about the same time, Hardy's first volume of verse, *Wessex Poems*, appearing only two years after *A Shropshire Lad*. Both had been writing poetry, almost secretly, for a long time; neither had been in a hurry to print his verses. Both favoured the short lyric and practised traditional verse-forms such as the ballad as well as making delicate metrical experiments. For both, poetry retained its primitive association with music, and both have been a plentiful source of inspiration to composers. Both created a region partly real, partly fantasized: Hardy's Wessex, like Housman's Shropshire, is a blend of topography and dream-landscape, as if a transparent imaginary map had been laid over the Ordnance Survey. More broadly, both were preoccupied with the idea of Englishness. Both were not only lovers of nature but scrupulous observers and recorders, inside and outside their poetry, of natural phenomena: in a rare moment of autobiography, Housman describes himself as 'following the progress of the seasons' on his afternoon walks around Cambridge, and notes (for instance) that the lilac is in the habit of blooming on 7 May, while Hardy too was 'a man who used to notice such things'. For both, poetry was long followed as a secondary, almost a clandestine occupation or moonlighting, and both achieved success and celebrity in other spheres, Hardy as a novelist, Housman as a classical scholar. Both had begun their working lives with a long subjection to office routine, one as an architect, the other as a Patent Office clerk. Both were unbelievers, which did not prevent either of them from having a keen and expert interest in ecclesiastical architecture, from being (as Philip Larkin puts it) 'one of the crew/ That tap and jot and know what rood-lofts were'. Though Hardy's formal education was limited, he was a natural and lifelong student who once speculated that, had things turned out differently, he might have gone to Cambridge and 'might have become a don' – might, indeed, have sat beside Housman at Trinity high table. Both were notable war poets of the non-combatant variety. Both had a keen interest in death by hanging. More generally, both wrote of love and death, were fascinated by violence, had an aching sense of the transience of beauty and human life, and were widely but inaccurately regarded as pessimists (Hardy declaring himself a meliorist and Housman insisting 'I am not a pessimist but a pejorist'). Beneath a reputation for seriousness and even glumness, both had a strong sense of humour. As letter-writers, both cultivated a formality, even a stiffness, that is occasionally shattered by startling bursts of self-disclosure. Both achieved considerable fame during their lifetimes and have retained their appeal to professional and non-professional readers alike: the late Enoch Powell remarked, rather quaintly, in the *Daily*

Telegraph that *A Shropshire Lad* still appeals to 'persons of every class', and no less can be said of Hardy, for these two proud, reserved, rather aloof men are, as writers, great democrats and levellers. The memory of both is kept green by devoted societies whose members are drawn from many different lands. Both were rather small men who dressed neatly and formally; Virginia Woolf thought Hardy looked like a retired doctor or solicitor, and Max Beerbohm said that Housman resembled an absconding cashier. Both – but this list, though not exhaustive, perhaps becomes exhausting, and the point is sufficiently clear.

Yet we must also acknowledge, inevitably, some major differences: in social origins, for instance, in sexuality, in literary productivity and ultimately in literary stature. Even so, there is enough common ground – or what is more promising, ground that seems superficially common but may on closer inspection reveal instructive differences – to justify a comparison.

Our two subjects were known to each other as men and writers, though they should probably be described as acquaintances rather than friends. They met in London in June 1899, soon after each had published his first volume of verse, and possibly at the home of Edmund Gosse, who was one of several friends they had in common. The following summer Housman was a visitor to Max Gate, Hardy's home in Dorchester. If there were other meetings during the next 13 years they are unrecorded, though when Housman in November 1912 wrote a letter of condolence to Hardy on the death of his wife Emma, he recalled meeting her 'several times' at the Gosses, and it seems likely that Hardy too had been present on some or all of these occasions. They certainly met twice in Cambridge in 1913, on 10 June, when Hardy received an honorary degree and they dined together at Jesus College, and on 15 November, when Hardy went to be installed as an Honorary Fellow of Magdalene College and (as he notes in his autobiography) Housman was present 'among others of his friends'. According to Sydney Cockerell's diary, there was a further meeting in May 1914. And in 1919, though not usually enthusiastic about producing poetry to order, Housman contributed a poem to a presentation volume organized by Siegfried Sassoon and given to Hardy on his 79th birthday. Their final meeting was of a less convivial kind, when Housman, by this time an old man himself, was one of the pall-bearers at Hardy's funeral in Westminster Abbey in 1928.

Longer and deeper than his acquaintance with the man was
Housman's familiarity with Hardy's work. Alfred Pollard, recall-
ing Housman's undergraduate days at Oxford, tells us that 'among
novelists his favourite was Thomas Hardy, and I think Hardy's
influence went far deeper than Arnold's'. This would of course
have been the earlier Hardy: *The Return of the Native*, the sixth of
Hardy's 14 published novels, appeared near the beginning of
Housman's second year at St John's College. After Hardy's death
Housman told a French enquirer, Maurice Pollet, that 'For Hardy
I felt affection, and high admiration for some of his novels and a
few of his poems' – which sounds grudging until one recalls that
'high admiration' was not something that Housman bestowed
lightly on anyone or anything. In 1922, the year of his own *Last
Poems*, he seems to have agreed to produce a selection from Hardy's
poems, and actually chose the contents, though for some reason
the project never saw the light of day. Hardy for his part is on
record as an admirer of Housman's poetry, his favourite being
'Is my team ploughing?' (Housman learned this from the second
Mrs Hardy and, passing on the information to a young admirer
towards the end of his life, he added scrupulously that 'I think
it may be the best, though it is not the most perfect'.) When
Florence Henniker gave Hardy a copy of *A Shropshire Lad* as a
Christmas present in 1902, he wrote assuring her that 'It is in
my pocket at this moment' – though this physical intimacy may
possibly tell us more about his feelings for Mrs Henniker than
about his feelings for Housman.

So much for generalities. To have a sense of the poetic identities and poetic voices of these two, we need to move closer to
the poems, and I should like to start by taking up a suggestion
already made: that Housman and Hardy are both significant war
poets. A passage in Hardy's autobiography distinguishes between
two kinds of literary response to the South African War: noting
that the war has generated 'quantities of warlike and patriotic
poetry', he adds: 'These works naturally throw into the shade
works that breathe a more quiet and philosophic spirit.' He
obviously regards his own war poems as falling into this latter
category, but we may well feel that he does not go far enough
to be fair to himself – that his meditations on war are not only
'quiet and philosophic' but critical and subversive, involving
no less than a redefinition of patriotism as well as an appalled
reaction to the horrors of modern warfare. We can also ask

whether in this matter he and Housman stand together or in different camps.

In speaking of 'warlike and patriotic poetry', Hardy no doubt had in mind the popular effusions produced by such contemporaries as Henry Newbolt, William Watson and Alfred Noyes. Newbolt, a friend of Hardy's, will serve as a representative of this kind and an illustration of what Hardy and Housman were not. (Housman, by the way, had a poor opinion of Newbolt, judging him 'too little of a poet' to be a serious contender for the Laureateship when it fell vacant in 1930.) He had become famous with a volume titled *Admirals All and Other Verses*, cannily published in the year of Victoria's Diamond Jubilee; this volume contains his best-known poem, 'Drake's Drum', committed to memory by generations of schoolboys and belted out by many a bass-baritone, and his speciality was historical set-pieces, the literary equivalent of the kind of painting that ends up on a biscuit tin or as a jigsaw puzzle. Robert Bridges, who was the friend and editor of Gerard Manley Hopkins and should have known better, declared of 'Drake's Drum' that 'It isn't given to a man to write anything better than that.'

But Newbolt, who belonged to the same generation as Housman, also responded in his own fashion to the wars of his lifetime. His fashion was to see them as further chapters in a continuing tradition of inspiring challenges to manhood and chivalry, so that, writing in 1918 ostensibly on the subject of German submarines, he was prepared to maintain that Mons and Arras are in the line of Crécy and Waterloo, the Battle of Jutland no more than a replay of Trafalgar. He seems to have had no sense of the Great War as an entirely new kind of conflict and a watershed in human history. (Curiously enough, or perhaps logically enough, he became one of the official historians of that war.) Words like honour, valour and manliness, the moral vocabulary of a late-Victorian Speech Day, fall readily from his fluent pen: the battlefield was an extension of the playing-field, and battles were won on the playing-fields not only of Eton but such minor public schools as Clifton College, which Newbolt attended and celebrated in verse. The school had a strong tradition of sending boys to the military academies, and Newbolt noted with pride that in the South African War 30 Old Cliftonians were killed in action and another 14 died of wounds or fever. His poetic response to these ghastly statistics is as follows:

> Clifton, remember these thy sons who fell
>   Fighting far over sea:
> For they in a dark hour remembered well
>   Their warfare learned of thee.

These lines appear, as it happens, in a volume Newbolt dedicated to Hardy, and one wonders what Hardy made of them.
For neither he nor Housman comes anywhere near sharing this
archaic and class-ridden sense of war as a golden opportunity to
act out the moral code instilled by one's education. Though their
attitudes are by no means identical, they share a sense of war as
tragic. Newbolt for his part might have been, and perhaps was,
shocked by the sober calculation of Housman's 'The Day of Battle'
(*A Shropshire Lad* LVI):

> 'Comrade, if to turn and fly
> Made a soldier never die,
> Fly I would, for who would not?
> 'Tis sure no pleasure to be shot.

or the bleak discovery by the dead soldiers in Hardy's 'The Souls
of the Slain' (a poem of December 1899) that what the bereaved
remember them for is not military glory but the trivial details of
their personal and domestic lives. With their unillusioned sense
of war as a trap and a con-trick, both poems, and others, might
have been written specifically as an antidote to the Newbolt ethos;
both anticipate Wilfred Owen's exposure a few years later of 'the
old Lie'.

The situation is more complex than this, however, for both Hardy
and Housman had a lifelong love-affair with what Othello calls
the 'Pride, pomp, and circumstance of glorious war', the romantic and heroic notions of battle that were never more than a
half-truth and in their lifetimes ceased to be even that. In Hardy
this was manifested in an infatuation with the Napoleonic period,
significantly located before his own birth but within the living
memory of his older contemporaries. His novel *The Trumpet-Major*,
published at the beginning of Housman's final year at Oxford,
ends somewhat in the manner of a Housman poem, with the
hero 'silenced for ever upon one of the bloody battle-fields of
Spain'. But while the South African War and the Great War did
not lead Hardy entirely to say goodbye to all that, he registers

sharply the sense of change, of modern warfare as something different in kind and difficult if not impossible to glamorize. A poem of 1915, 'Then and Now', laments the passing of a time 'When battles were fought / With a chivalrous sense of Should and Ought'. 'Chivalry', still part of Newbolt's working vocabulary, is for Hardy an item in a dead language.

Though Hardy's fullest treatment of war was historical, in his epic-drama *The Dynasts* and in *The Trumpet-Major*, his response to the wars of his own later years was unstinted. His 1901 volume *Poems of the Past and the Present* opens with 11 'War Poems', some of which again anticipate Wilfred Owen's sense of 'the pity of War'. The point of view is often that of those who are left behind, but as well as expressing war's impact on individual lives Hardy takes a long historical view, questioning the Christian civilization that has produced modern warfare:

> And what of logic or of truth appears
> In tacking 'Anno Domini' to the years?

> ('A Christmas Ghost-Story')

A generation later Hardy's bitterness has intensified: at Christmas 1924 he writes that

> After two thousand years of mass
> We've got as far as poison-gas.

> ('Christmas: 1924')

Meanwhile, he is able to envisage at the turn of the century, in the later spirit of the League of Nations, a 'patriotism' that is global and liberated from nationalistic rivalries.

Hardy also included 17 'Poems of War and Patriotism' in his 1917 volume *Moments of Vision*, and again we find him taking a historically panoramic view of the Great War, contextualizing the contemporary catastrophe with that 'hawk's vision' that Auden rightly saw as one of his leading characteristics. In a poem with the title (Owenish as well as Shakespearean) 'The Pity of It', he reminds us that the war is, among other things, linguistically and ethnographically irrational, since the Germans and the British are 'kinfolk, kintongued'. That poem was written in April 1915, the month that saw the second battle of Ypres and the first use on the Western Front of poison gas.

In comparison, Housman's poetic response to the two wars that fell between *A Shropshire Lad* and *Last Poems* seems relatively detached from the contemporary realities: Hardy would certainly not have endorsed Housman's statement, made in his old age, that 'The Great War cannot have made much change in the opinions of any man of imagination.' Like Hardy, and like many other boys who are happier reading books than playing games, Housman had always been fascinated by the life of action represented by the soldier, and one of the favourite books of his childhood was Bode's stirring *Ballads from Herodotus*. But whereas Hardy's writings on Napoleonic history had been patiently researched in the British Museum, and while, as a student of the classics, Housman would have been thoroughly familiar with Greek and Roman military history, the springs of his interest in the military life seem to lie at a deeper level, in fantasies of physical glamour, sexual power and male bonding, as well as their necessary counterparts, the loss of home, the temptation to betrayal and the likelihood of death. Certain quasi-allegorical figures – the Recruit, the Soldier-Lover, the Victor, the Vanquished, the Deserter, the Condemned – move through his poems untouched by historical change, so that the death of his youngest brother Herbert in the South African War (a closer bereavement than war ever inflicted on Hardy) makes only a limited impact on his poetic world. This fantasy-world is populated by the redcoats who became extinct during his poetic lifetime, and at times we seem to be taken back to a much earlier period: in

> Oh were he and I together
>   Locking hands and taking leave,
> Low upon the trampled heather
>   In the battle lost at eve

we are closer to Culloden than to Ladysmith, Gallipoli or the Somme.

In *A Shropshire Lad* war is not a very prominent theme, though an important exception is the very first poem in the collection, which subverts Victoria's Golden Jubilee of 1887 while appearing to celebrate it. '1887' commemorates those who had paid the price of Empire in their suffering and death. The real outrageousness of Housman's '1887', and the real audacity of its placing at the head of the collection, have not always been conceded or even recognized. For the poem takes liberties not only with the National Anthem but with the New Testament, first treating the formulaic 'God Save the Queen' as if it were actually a rational statement open to discussion, and then applying both the term 'saviour' and an allusion to the Crucifixion to a common soldier. In its finely controlled refusal to toe the patriotic line, it is a poem that bears comparison with, and is not inferior to, Kipling's great vernacular chant of protest 'The Widow at Windsor', and we surely need not take too seriously Housman's reported disclaimer: even if the informant had been a more reliable one than Frank Harris, this is surely a time for trusting the poem rather than the poet.

Elsewhere in *A Shropshire Lad* redcoats march through the streets and go off to die in distant lands, but the actuality of war is kept at a distance, and although the sense of war's pageantry is undermined by an implicit scepticism concerning the whole imperial enterprise, the romantic ideal, on the verge of brutal extinction, is still alive and kicking. At the same time, as Bernard Bergonzi has shown in his *Heroes' Twilight*, the doomed young soldier is a sufficiently prominent motif to have made Housman a significant influence on Great War poets such as Wilfred Owen and Charles Sorley. To quote a single stanza:

> You smug-faced crowds with kindling eye
> Who cheer when soldier lads march by,
> Sneak home and pray you'll never know
> The hell where youth and laughter go.

Housman could not quite have written those lines, but they sound in more than one respect like a rewriting of his own verses; they are in fact by Siegfried Sassoon.

Last Poems, as we might expect, registers the warlike and tragic history of the past generation but does so less pervasively than we might expect. In 'Soldier from the wars returning' the dead man seems to belong simultaneously to two military epochs, the archaic world of cavalry and the newly invented conditions of trench warfare ('Filth in trench from fall to spring'), while the phrase 'Kings and kesars' must refer specifically to George V and Kaiser Wilhelm as well as generally to those great ones who send young men to their death. 'The Deserter', one of those dialogue poems of which both Housman and Hardy were fond, takes up the theme of 'The Day of Battle' in the earlier volume without suggesting that public history has moved on dramatically since 1896.

The lapidary 'Epitaph on an Army of Mercenaries' is probably Housman's best known war poem, and in its controlled irony, its near blasphemy and its passionate sympathy with the unsung heroes of the ranks it looks back to '1887'. More elusive, and more readily misunderstood, is 'Lancer' (*Last Poems* VI). Vivian Pinto deals severely with this in his book *Crisis in English Poetry*, which opens with a somewhat lopsided chapter on Hardy and Housman. According to Pinto, 'Housman's treatment of the subject of war can be contrasted with Hardy's. Hardy's poem "Drummer Hodge" is a profound comment on the meaning of modern warfare. Housman's poems on soldiers like "Lancer" recall the sentimental oleographs which adorned the walls of Victorian kitchens and nurseries.'

Pinto has surely got it entirely wrong so far as Housman is concerned, for 'Lancer' is anti-sentimental, ironic, subtle, allusive and faintly improper – quite unsuitable, in fact, for the Victorian nursery. It calls into service Housman's favourite device of repetition in order to invite us to inspect, ponder and question a familiar expression or sentimental cliché, which certainly does not escape unscathed: just as '1887' had subjected 'God Save the Queen' to cross-examination and left it somewhat battered by the process, 'Lancer' introduces the euphemistic phrase 'sleep with the brave' seven times into this short poem, with a significant shift of meaning. At the outset the innocence of the original meaning is unviolated; but 'share a grave with' is only one of the meanings of 'sleep with', and quite soon another meaning is invoked. Departing troops were traditionally seen off to the strains of 'The Girl I Left Behind Me', but here the girl who's waiting for me is a reminder of what the untimely dead have sacrificed in exchange for posthumous honour and glory. Behind these anti-sentimental lines, moreover, is a genuinely sentimental and once very popular poem by William Collins, the ode lamenting those killed in the Battle of Falkirk in 1746 that begins 'How sleep the brave . . .!' Housman's rewriting of this anthology-piece reminds us that he was a brilliant parodist. One is tempted to say that 'Lancer' is not a poem that Hardy could have written, that the profound scepticism and disillusion beneath the mask of demotic gaiety are Housman's own, until one remembers 'The Ruined

Maid', a poem that has the same central ambiguity, the same subverting of a sentimental cliché, the same whiff of the infectious if slightly vulgar comic song.

That impression of gaiety is of course partly created by the use of song and ballad forms and the jaunty, foot-tapping rhythms: like Kipling, Housman served an important part of his poetic apprenticeship in the London music-halls, and we can almost imagine an exuberant audience roaring back the chorus, *'Oh who would not sleep with the brave?'* Housman was always willing to accommodate some of his deepest feelings in an atmosphere of greasepaint and gaslighting, as we find in his poem about the Oscar Wilde trials, which performs the remarkable feat of being at the same time joky and outraged: 'Oh they're taking him to prison for the colour of his hair.' Hardy shares his willingness to restore to poetry its primitive kinship with song and dance, though with Hardy the models are likely to be the hymn and the folksong rather than the literary ballad or the music-hall ditty.

In both poets this can sometimes lead to a disconcerting but strangely effective mismatch between medium and message. Take, for example, the posthumously published *More Poems* VI:

> I to my perils
>   Of cheat and charmer
>   Came clad in armour
>   By stars benign.
> Hope lies to mortals
>   And most believe her,
>   But man's deceiver
>   Was never mine.
>
> The thoughts of others
>   Were light and fleeting,
>   Of lovers' meeting
>   Or luck or fame.
> Mine were of trouble,
>   And mine were steady,
>   So I was ready
>   When trouble came.

It's characteristic of Housman to make his profound pessimism a matter for pride and even boasting, but what I want to draw attention to is the way in which the grim message – expect the worst, then you won't be disappointed, for it will certainly happen – is embodied in a dance-rhythm. What's involved is a kind of dancing on the grave, or a wilful singing of the words to the wrong tune, recalling the tone-deaf man who couldn't tell the difference between 'God Save the Weasel' and 'Pop goes the Queen'. For who, apprised of the idea the poem expresses, would have anticipated that light, energetic, skipping dactylic and trochaic verse-form?

Most other poets – Matthew Arnold and Philip Larkin, for example – convey their gloom with less apparent insouciance, but Hardy's practice is strikingly close to Housman's. The poem about his 86th birthday, 'He Never Expected Much', moves forward with an unoctogenarian nimbleness:

> 'Well, World, you have kept faith with me,
>   'Kept faith with me;
> 'Upon the whole you have proved to be
>   'Much as you said you were.
> Since as a child I used to lie
> Upon the leaze and watch the sky,
> Never, I own, expected I
>   That life would all be fair. . . .

Hardy's views on the subject are less severely uncompromising than Housman's, but an entry in his diary dated New Year's Day 1902 suggests that the two of them are not very far apart: 'Pessimism . . . is, in brief, playing the sure game. You cannot lose at it; you may gain. It is the only view of life in which you can never be disappointed . . .' The wise man, he adds, reckons what to do 'in the worst possible circumstances', and this note, unpublished until 1930, is surely not far from being a prose paraphrase of Housman's poem.

Pinto's reference to Hardy's poem about the South African War, 'Drummer Hodge', is worth returning to, especially since its sources and analogues have been recently debated by Hardy scholars. This is one of the two or three finest of all Hardy's war poems, or anti-war poems, and characteristically idiosyncratic, almost perverse, in its emphasis on the physicality of burial in an alien land:

> Yet portion of that unknown plain
>   Will Hodge for ever be;
> His homely Northern breast and brain
>   Grow to some Southern tree,
> And strange-eyed constellations reign
>   His stars eternally.

How terrible, we say, that this young Dorset labourer should have been shipped off and slaughtered in the defence of Empire. Well, not quite, says Hardy, for the really awful thing is that his decomposing body should contribute to the chemical cycle of vegetation that he wouldn't have been able to name, and that the unfamiliar stars of another hemisphere should look down on his crude grave. The poem has been compared to Rupert Brooke's 'The Soldier' and found superior in political correctness (to say nothing of poetic merit), for whereas Brooke's young man plants a flag in some corner of a foreign field, Hardy's is a reluctant emigrant suffering permanent exile in an incorrigibly alien land. An influence on Hardy has been detected in Wordsworth's 'A slumber did my spirit seal', where the girl who has lived quietly in a remote rural spot becomes in death part of the revolving globe. Much nearer in time, though, is *Last Poems* XX ('The night is freezing fast'), where another dead young man is physically absorbed by the landscape and the turning earth:

> Fall, winter fall; for he,
>   Prompt hand and headpiece clever,
>   Has woven a winter robe,
> And made of earth and sea
>   His overcoat for ever,
>   And wears the turning globe.

There is more than a touch here of Hardyan idiosyncrasy, almost freakishness, in the notion of the rustic handyman setting to and making a rough coat out of the earth itself – with, of course, underlying the outrageous fancy, the bleak awareness that no overcoat, however thick, can offer protection against the coldness of death. In *The Name and Nature of Poetry* Housman dismisses much of the poetry of the seventeenth century as 'intellectually frivolous', but he seems here, as Hardy sometimes does in his prose as well as his verse, to owe something to, or at least to have some kinship with, the Metaphysicals.

Another Housman poem, not published until 1922, makes a very similar point to Hardy's. In 'Astronomy' the editor of Manilius brings his professional sense of the stars in their courses to bear on a personal loss, the death of his brother Herbert, killed in action in 1901. Like Drummer Hodge, Sergeant Housman was buried on the battlefield in the southern hemisphere, and the poem draws attention to the strangeness of his fate, as one who 'hove the Cross to heaven, and sank / The pole-star underground'. Again, there is more than a touch of Metaphysical grotesquerie in this image of the dead soldier personally rearranging the night sky.

It is difficult to speak of either of our two poets without frequently referring to death and the dead, and this brings to mind a poignant little poem by Wendy Cope:

> I think I am in love with A. E. Housman,
> Which puts me in a worse than usual fix.
> No woman ever stood a chance with Housman,
> And he's been dead since 1936.

As far as the second of these problems is concerned, both Housman and Hardy would have wondered what Ms Cope was making a fuss about. For them, to be in love with the dead presented no problems and indeed offered many advantages: the dead are in no position to complain about our attentions or our neglect, do not change, cannot be fickle or unfaithful, and are unable to reject our love. It's not surprising that Hardy's favourite among the *Shropshire Lad* poems should have been a dialogue between the living and the dead, since this was exactly the kind of poem that he himself liked writing and wrote more than once. Hardy's world, like the world of his poems and stories, was populated by the dead as well as the living: he was a great visitor of graveyards, longed to see a ghost, and was intensely aware of the daily presence of the dead, whether through some piece of furniture that was a family heirloom or through the Roman remains that, to his great satisfaction and pride, lay beneath the foundations of his home.

As might be expected of one who devoted his working life to the study of dead languages and the ancient world, Housman shares this sense of modern life being lived in the presence of the past – a sense creative rather than antiquarian, appreciative rather than morbid. 'On Wenlock Edge' links contemporary experience with that of a Roman settler in the same spot in a very Hardyan manner:

> There, like the wind through woods in riot,
>   Through him the gale of life blew high;
> The tree of man was never quiet:
>   Then 'twas the Roman, now 'tis I.

In *Jude the Obscure* a lonely child inhabits a landscape in which 'Every inch of ground had been the site, first or last, of energy, gaiety, horse-play, bickerings, weariness'; in modern Casterbridge evidences of Roman occupation are everywhere to be found, and Susan Henchard lies in death beside her Roman fellow-townsfolk.

Many of Housman's poems, like many of Hardy's, have a kind of transparency, an artful artlessness, but 'On Wenlock Edge' is subtler in its argument as well as more intense, at moments almost Yeatsian, in its rhetoric. Today's wind blowing through today's wood becomes within a few lines first a Roman wind in a Roman wood, then 'the gale of life' blowing through 'The tree of man', and the argument of the poem is an uncompleted syllogism whose completion is too sadly obvious to need stating: the Romans who once lived here are dead; we relive their experiences on the same spot; no prizes for guessing what awaits us too.

Hardy similarly ranges from the directness of anthology-pieces like 'Weathers' and 'Afterwards' to the complexity, even the wilful obscurity, of a poem like 'During Wind and Rain' or 'Wessex Heights'. Both of these read like coded autobiography, a quality shared by some of Housman's most powerful pieces. What are we to make, for instance, of this posthumously published quatrain?

> He, standing hushed, a pace or two apart,
>   Among the bluebells of the listless plain,
> Thinks, and remembers how he cleansed his heart
>   And washed his hands in innocence in vain.

Such lines have the quality of dreams, making tolerable sense within their own self-created world but being utterly baffling in relation to a larger reality. Who is the unidentified 'He', whom or what is he 'apart' from, where on earth can one see a plain filled with bluebells: the circumstantial details are as mysterious as the emotional experiences referred to. Yet the poem, like certain dreams, has a disturbing power.

The group of 23 'Additional Poems' published by Laurence Housman after his brother's death contains a number of other quatrains that may be roughly described as verse-epigrams. Here is one that might have been the result of a collaboration between John Keats and Emily Dickinson, yet is wholly Housman's in its sense of missed opportunities and of self-reproach without self-pity:

> When the bells justle in the tower
>   The hollow night amid,
> Then on my tongue the taste is sour
>   Of all I ever did.

In using that startling verb in the first line, was Housman recalling and adapting the words of another great epigrammatist, William Blake, who wrote that

> Great things are done when men and mountains meet;
> This is not done by jostling in the street.

Hardy too practised the verse-epigram but in his hands it is likely to turn into a squib rather than a riddle, as in his adaptation of a Greek epigram:

> I'm Smith of Stoke, aged sixty-odd,
>   I've lived without a dame
> From youth-time on; and would to God
>   My dad had done the same.

Or consider the following lines, also first published in Housman's posthumous *More Poems:*

> Crossing alone the nighted ferry
>   With the one coin for fee,
> Whom, on the wharf of Lethe waiting,
>   Count you to find? Not me.

> The brisk fond lackey to fetch and carry,
>   The true, sick-hearted slave,
> Expect him not in the just city
>   And free land of the grave.

Superficially, the message is a commonplace of love poetry – a declaration of independence after the enslavement of passion. But the treatment of the traditional theme is Housman's own: for him, the life-sentence as lover carries no remission and freedom can come only in the grave. While seeming, therefore, to say 'I'm off now', the poem is really saying 'I'm yours for life': beneath its lapidary or marmoreal surface, it enacts a Laocoon-like struggle with the inevitable. This struggle is mimed in the syntax: the convoluted, rather pedantic sentence that occupies almost the whole of the first stanza poses a question that is answered in just two syllables unremarkable in themselves but in this context richly defiant and contemptuous: 'Not me' – or, as we might put it in our own time, 'Forget it' or 'Get lost'. The second stanza also leads up to a negative ('Expect him not . . .'), but the effect of these negatives is to confess or concede their opposites: while telling us that he will no longer be 'The brisk fond lackey to fetch and carry' (and the extra, unstressed syllable makes the line as brisk and busy as any fetcher and carrier), he admits that the position is not one from which he can resign. Housman uses that word 'resign' in another fine poem, 'Tell me not here, it needs not saying': there the love of nature is also seen as a kind of erotic enslavement, and Housman's use of 'possess' has a similar ambiguity to that found in Shakespeare's sonnets, but there too it seems to be death that terminates the contract.

The eight short lines of 'Crossing alone the nighted ferry', then, contain passion and torment within their tightly-controlled, epigrammatic form, and this combination of intense and sometimes complex feelings with formal severity is very characteristic of Housman. It is a note, or voice, rather different from what we encounter in the poems of Hardy: if Housman's lines seem to be uttered by a man who speaks distinctly, even boldly, but keeps his strong emotions under control by attending to the shape and form of his utterance, Hardy's often seem to be the tentative words, uncertain of which direction to take, of a man thinking or remembering aloud, though only just audibly. If Hardy's are half-way towards creating their own musical settings, Housman's demand to be inscribed on stone – for preference, a tombstone.

Both, however, can achieve some of their finest effects from the use of a single, simple but suggestive image. Hardy's 'During Wind and Rain' ends with a line that is a poem in itself, 'Down their carved names the rain-drop ploughs'. Housman too

likes to talk of graves and epitaphs, and one of the subtlest poems in *A Shropshire Lad* starts from a single churchyard image
seen in close-up:

> It nods and curtseys and recovers
>   When the wind blows above,
> The nettle on the graves of lovers
>   That hanged themselves for love.
>
> The nettle nods, the wind blows over,
>   The man, he does not move,
> The lover of the grave, the lover
>   That hanged himself for love.

Aesop's fable of the oak and the reed, which Housman must have
known since childhood, seems not far away from this poem, and
the moral is the same, though Housman substitutes for the fable's
rather bland generality a more particular and more anxious
preoccupation with love. The weak, commonplace and inferior
yield and survive, the strong are steadfast, suffer and perish: lower
forms of life have the knack of scraping through, but to have
the power of loving greatly is to risk the fate of dying for love.
In such a moral world, the possession of a fine nature is a distinct handicap; yet that handicap can also be a source of pride.
As in the opening lines of Tennyson's 'Tithonus', another deeply
personal but seemingly objectified meditation on death, the image
makes a careful distinction between vertical and horizontal states:
the nettle inclines from the upright a little, then more, but finally
regains its original state, while, wind or no wind, the man remains
immovable. So the poem, like both the nettle and the man, seems
to end up where it started – except that the plural and general-
ized 'lovers' of the first stanza becomes in the second stanza
singular and particularized. And there is surely a provocative
ambiguity in the description of 'the lover / That hanged himself
for love' as 'The lover of the grave', which can mean both the
lover *in* the grave and one who loves or desires the grave. Some
loves, the poem seems to conclude, make one wish for death
and positively embrace it as a last resort. As often with both
Housman and Hardy, death and the erotic are two sides of the
same obol. If 'love' is the most significant noun in *A Shropshire
Lad*, 'grave' is a strong runner-up, not only because death is the

inevitable end of love but because it may offer the only means of escape from its pains and sorrows.

Possibly the 'nettle' poem has an even closer kinship with Hardy, reminding the reader of the description in *Tess of the d'Urbervilles* of 'that shabby corner of God's allotment where He lets the nettles grow, and where [among others] ... suicides, and others of the conjecturally damned are laid', while Tess herself was a 'lover ... hanged ... for love'. Whether or not Housman was recalling, consciously or otherwise, the novel Hardy had published a few years before *A Shropshire Lad,* there are common areas of sensibility shared by these two writers. At the same time their poetic voices, as I have tried to suggest, are markedly different. When Philip Larkin writes that 'the unresting castles thresh / In fullgrown thickness every May', or when, in different mood, he writes 'But to sit with bricks around you / While the winds of heaven bawl ...', we have no difficulty in detecting the influence of Housman, a poet he is prepared to stretch a chronological point to represent adequately in his *Oxford Book of Twentieth Century English Verse.* Larkin was also a self-confessed admirer of Hardy, but found him less imitable, a fact that may both confirm and help to suggest the nature of the essential difference between Hardy and Housman.

7

'Flowers to Fair':
A Shropshire Lad's
Legacy of Song

Trevor Hold

I hoed and trenched and weeded
And took the flowers to fair:
I brought them home unheeded;
The hue was not the wear.

The musical settings of Housman's *A Shropshire Lad* have been discussed in print on several occasions, notably by William White,[1] A. V. Butcher[2] and Stephen Banfield,[3] while Gooch and Thatcher have listed all known settings, published and in manuscript, up to 1975.[4] In this essay, therefore, I shall be brief on *what*, and concentrate on *why*, and conclude with detailed consideration of the most important settings, particularly the songcycles of Vaughan Williams, George Butterworth and John Ireland.

No other single volume of poems published in English over the past 300 years has proved such a goldmine for songwriters as *A Shropshire Lad*. Of its 63 poems, at least 50 have been set to music. Some poems have been used time and again. There are at least 35 known settings of 'Loveliest of trees' and 'When I was one-and-twenty', 22 of 'With rue my heart is laden', 19 of 'Into my heart an air that kills' and 14 of 'Bredon Hill'. Other frequently set poems include: 'Far in a western brookland' (11), ''Tis time, I think' (10) and 'White in the moon' (10).[5] In the light of this fecundity, it is surprising that composers took so long to discover *A Shropshire Lad*. The first approach to Housman for permission to use a poem seems to have been in 1903, seven years after the poems were published, by a composer named Ettrick.[6] Nothing more is known of him, his setting or even the poem he chose. Sir Arthur Somervell's *Songcycle from 'A Shropshire Lad'*, published in 1904, can therefore claim the honour of being the first-known Housman setting. From 1904 until the outbreak of the First World War, a growing number of composers turned to the Lad for inspiration, including Balfour Gardiner ('The Recruit', 1906), Ivor Gurney ('On your midnight pallet lying', 1907), Graham Peel ('In summertime on Bredon', 1911) and most notably Ralph Vaughan Williams (*On Wenlock Edge*, 1909) and George Butterworth (*Six Songs from 'A Shropshire Lad'* and *Bredon Hill and Other Songs*, 1909–11). John Ireland's first Housman setting, 'The Heart's Desire', appeared in 1917 followed by 'Hawthorn Time' (''Tis time, I think, by Wenlock town') in 1919 and his songcycle, *The Land of Lost Content*, in 1921. By this time the trickle had turned into a flood, and the next ten years saw a spate of publications: songcycles by Gurney and E. J. Moeran and single songs by Arnold Bax, Arthur Bliss, Benjamin Burrows (13 Housman settings in 1927 alone!) as well as minor, now-forgotten songwriters such as D. M. Stewart and Christabel Marillier. From 1922 composers had *Last Poems* as well as *A Shropshire Lad* to quarry and Housman was probably the most 'set' of all contemporary English poets. By 1934, Constant Lambert was wryly observing:

> Since the Shropshire Lad himself published his last poems some ten years ago, it may without impertinence be suggested that it is high time his musical followers published their last songs.[7]

Composers seem to have heeded Lambert's advice, for by the outbreak of the Second World War the Lad's heyday was long past. From 1940 to the present day, settings of Housman have been relatively few and add little to the catalogue. Vaughan Williams' *Along the Field*, though published in 1954, was mostly written in 1927, and half the texts are taken from *Last Poems*. Two unexpected shield-bearers were Humphrey Searle and Lennox Berkeley: Searle with *Two Songs* (1948), 'March Past' ('On the idle hill of summer') and 'The Stinging-Nettle' ('With seeds the sowers scatter'); Berkeley with *Five Housman Songs* (published in 1983 but written in 1940), two from *A Shropshire Lad* (XXII and XV), one each from *Last Poems* (XXVI), *More Poems* (XXXI) and *Additional Poems* (VII).

It is instructive to note the major songwriters of the period who did *not* set Housman. These include Peter Warlock,[8] Herbert

Howells,[9] Roger Quilter and Benjamin Britten. Of all Housman-
setters the most prolific was C. W. Orr (1893–1976) and many
critics – among them Eric Sams and Christopher Palmer – claim
that no songwriter has served Housman better than Charles Orr.
In fact Orr's slender reputation as a composer stands or falls by
his Housman songs, for he wrote relatively little else. (His Housman
settings, written over a period of thirty years (1921–52), make up
24 of his total output of 35 songs.) For Orr, 'Housman was more
than an influence, he was an obsession.'[10] But, as we've seen, it
was an obsession shared, in part at least, by dozens of other songwriters.

*   *   *

So up and down I sow them
For lads like me to find,
When I shall lie below them,
A dead man out of mind.

The question inevitably asks itself: Why? Why have so many composers been drawn to the Lad's troubles and tribulations? The
answer, I suggest, is twofold: the appeal of the poems' sentiments,
and the aptness of the poems for musical treatment. F. L. Lucas,
looking back at his undergraduate days at Cambridge before the
First World War, remembers that

> One of the greatest excitements was the newcomer's discov-
> ery, everywhere in its little red binding, of The Shropshire Lad
> – the expression, so long inarticulately wanted, here found at
> last, of the resentment, the defiance, the luxuriant sadness (sen-
> timent, some will call it) of youth.[11]

Nostalgia and fatalism, a preoccupation with the transience of
beauty and the inevitability of death, embedded in English pastoral
imagery, imbued with the spirit of Rural England and set in a
clearly defined English landscape: these qualities and attributes
which define Housman's collection of poems struck a resonant
chord with the generation brought up in the shadow of the First
World War, even though the soldiers in *A Shropshire Lad* (in red
coats, not khaki) were marching to or from earlier wars in 'Asia . . .
And the Nile'. Indeed several of the composers who set Housman
were actively involved in the 1914–18 war: E. J. Moeran, Arthur

Bliss and Ivor Gurney were wounded; George Butterworth was killed. To say that it struck a chord with a generation is not quite true: in actual fact it was with only half that generation. One thing obvious to any reader is that the Lad's is a male-dominated world. As George Orwell observed:

> The women's point of view is not considered, she is merely the nymph, the siren, the treacherous half-human creature who leads you a little distance and then gives you the slip.[12]

Women, when they make an appearance, are – *pace* Rose Harland – shadowy 'shes', not identified with names like the Lad's male friends, Terence, Dick, Ned and Fred. Housman is often deliberately ambiguous about who the loved one is – could be male, could be female. Songwriters admitted access to the poems were inevitably entering an exclusive Male Country Club with male concerns and frequently male-dominated sentiments. What this means as far as the songs are concerned is that the majority were written for, and have to be sung by, male singers. There are a few 'unisex' songs, performable by either female or male singer – 'Loveliest of trees' is an obvious example.[13] But can you imagine a soprano singing 'Is my team ploughing'?

> Yes, lad, I lie easy,
>   I lie as lads would choose;
> I cheer a dead man's sweetheart,
>   Never ask me whose.

Not unexpectedly, few female composers have set the poems.

The aptness of the words for music is extraordinary for several reasons, not least on account of Housman's own knowledge of and attitude to music. Though his sister remembers that A. E. H. took some interest in music as a boy,[14] by the time he was a man he had lost that interest and showed an almost total lack of understanding of it. His friend, Percy Withers, once played him Gervase Elwes' historic recording of Vaughan Williams' *On Wenlock Edge*:

> My wife, who sat near him, was momentarily expecting him to spring from his chair and rush headlong out of the room; and the torment was still on his suffused and angry visage

when the records were finished, and I first realised the havoc
my mistaken choice had caused. I thought to soothe him by
playing some record of his own choosing. He looked rather
lost when I asked him to name one, but presently suggested
the fifth symphony [Beethoven's], for the curious reason that
he remembered to have heard it well spoken of . . .[15]

Housman was a person for whom poetry, instead of being a com-
plement *to,* was a substitute *for* music. His views in *The Name
and Nature of Poetry* (1933) bear this out. For him, poetry was
'not the thing said but a way of saying it . . . Poetry indeed seems
to me more physical than intellectual.' He could be defining Music
rather than Poetry. When, therefore, composers began to write
to him for permission to use his poems, he was put into a pre-
dicament. He could have refused permission or, like Yeats, have
appointed a 'musically-minded' censor to vet applicants. Instead,
unexpectedly, he took a much more sympathetic stance. He gave
permission to composers to set his words, but refused to accept
a fee, at the same time forbidding them to print the text of his
poems in concert programmes.[16] The reason? – he felt that words
sung were no longer poetry and should not be considered as
such.[17] Considering his total lack of appreciation of music, this
was a generous gesture.

With such an unpropitious musical background, it is amazing
that Housman managed to produce poems which are such technically fine words for music. Nearly all the great lyric writers,
from Shakespeare, Ben Jonson, Burns, Goethe, Heine through to
Cole Porter and Ira Gershwin, were *musically aware* if not *musical*. A. E. H., as we have seen, was neither. The 'musicality' of *A
Shropshire Lad* was quite fortuitous. There must have been a starting-
point though. According to Percy Withers, 'Such direct influences
as he was conscious of were . . . the old ballads, Shakespeare's
songs and Heine, and these he studied intensively before a line
of "A Shropshire Lad" was written.'[18] He could not have chosen
better models. His poetry has that crucial quality found in all
good words for music: a simple, well-defined mood painted in
primary colours. Ernest Newman summed up the matter admirably:

Never before had an English poet produced so many poems
that had all the qualities requisite to poetry that is to be set to
music – concision and intensity in tone, the utmost simplicity

of language, freedom both from involution of structure and from simile, and a general build that was virtually that of musical form.[19]

Though a classical scholar by profession, Housman deliberately avoided classically derived words. In fact he went out of his way to use short, Anglo-Saxon words wherever possible, with the result sometimes of quaintness and archaism. Words of one and two syllables predominate and, as Newman observed, there is a total freedom from involuted sentence structure and from that bane of the song lyric, the simile. Linked to this is a folk-like simplicity of language and metre. His stanzas reflect the rhythms and metres of the folk ballad:

> The lads in their hundreds to Ludlow come in for
> the fair,
> There's men from the barn and the forge and
> the mill and the fold,
> The lads for the girls and the lads for the liquor
> are there,
> And there with the rest are the lads that
> will never be old.

Occasionally this deliberate simplicity becomes too low-key and conversational for music, as in the two stanzas which Vaughan Williams omitted from his setting of 'Is my team ploughing'. Another musically attractive feature in Housman is his use of symmetrical devices such as refraining lines, repetition of phrase and sentence structures, and stanzas that reflect and balance each other. Take, for example, 'Is my team ploughing' with its symmetrical stanza-balance of question and answer, and the use of refraining lines in 'When I was one-and-twenty'.

Contrary to the usual assumption among poets, songwriters do *not* like poems written in short stanzas: they much prefer longer, more complex structures. (You have only to look at the great song lyrics from Shakespeare to McCartney to realize this.) Short stanzas, of two, three or four lines, can cause a composer difficulty particularly when the length of line is short. They do not allow him to get into his stride or gain momentum. Purcell set the four short quatrains of Dryden's 'Fairest isle' as two strophes of music, while Peter Warlock reassembled the six tiny stanzas of Bruce Blunt's 'The Fox' into three irregular strophes.[20]

Housman favours the quatrain above all, but he is capable of employing a variety of stanza shapes, though they are by no means as diverse or inventive as Thomas Hardy's:

'Bredon Hill'/'The Lent lily'	5-line stanzas	ABCBB
'Think no more, lad'	6-line stanzas	ABCCAB
'Look not in my eyes'	8-line stanzas	ABABCDCD

As with Hardy, this variety of stanza shape will always prove attractive to a composer, luring him like nectar to a bee.

Taking these technical requirements into account, it is clear that not all the poems in *A Shropshire Lad* are appropriate for musical setting, and Ernest Newman's suggestion, apropos Vaughan Williams' *On Wenlock Edge,* that a songwriter worth his salt 'would have set virtually the whole of the sixty-three poems, doing for Mr Housman what Wolf did for Mörike, for Goethe, for Eichendorff, and others'[21] is clearly cloud-cuckoo – a typical instance of Newman crying wolf. No discerning songwriter would choose to set '1887': though it *looks* like a lyric, the language is too cramped and terse, the sentiment too rhetorical.[22] Perhaps a hymn tune could be made of it, but not a song. The proof of the pudding is in the eating, and the best proof of inaptness of words for music is to list the poems that have never (as far as we know) been set and ask why not – 'To an Athlete Dying Young' (XIX); 'The Welsh Marches' (XXVIII); 'As through the wild green hills of Wyre' (XXXVII); 'In my own shire, if I was sad' (XLI); 'The Immortal Part' (XLIII); 'Loitering with a vacant eye' (LI); and 'Terence, this is stupid stuff' (LXII). XIX is too prosaic: music could hardly effect an entry, and if it could, would add nothing to it; XXVIII, like '1887', is too rhetorical for a song lyric; XLIII is a long philosophical monologue – again, hardly conducive to musical setting; while the remaining four are all in rhyming couplets which, like blank verse, is usually the medium for argumentative, conversational or philosophical poetry – all of which are, by definition, anti-lyrical. As Cecil Day-Lewis has said, 'The business of the lyric is to make words sing and dance, not to make them argue, moralise or speechify.'[23] But perhaps the most problematic element in Housman for the songwriter is his use of irony. His tongue is often in his cheek: he says one thing but means another. Music, though capable of dealing with complexities of form and language,

is in this respect an innocent. It will sing *like* the birds, but cannot
think and talk *about* them. Similarly the poetic device of irony is
beyond its comprehension. Has any composer managed to capture the correct tone of voice required for the final stanza of 'Is
my team ploughing'? Is it elegiac (as Butterworth would have us
suppose) or hysterical (as Vaughan Williams maintains)? Neither:
surely it is tongue-in-cheek, relying for its irony on the fact that
it comes unexpectedly at the end of an elegiac poem? But how
can music, which needs time to establish a mood, deal with such
an abrupt and subtle mood change without sounding melodramatic? The composer who comes nearest to solving this particular
problem is C.W. Orr in his fine 1925 setting.[24] But will any composer really be able to inflect those final lines in a way that a
good reader could do?

Linked to this is another aesthetic problem, though one more
easily capable of musical solution: the conflict between inner
turbulence and outer equanimity, the 'fine contrast of this "icily
regular" beauty with the boiling, battling thoughts below it'.[25]
Some composers swing to one extreme or the other. At their worst,
Somervell and Peel capture the classical poise but miss the inner
turbulence. Vaughan Williams on the other hand becomes almost
hysterical in his endeavour to find 'the worm within the rose'
and destroys the poise of Housman's verse. The finest interpreters,
such as John Ireland, Charles Orr and George Butterworth, have
managed to find a balanced musical solution.

*   *   *

> Some seed the birds devour,
> And some the season mars,
> But here and there will flower
> The solitary stars

Though it was not his intention, Housman produced, in *A Shropshire Lad*, one of the finest musical librettos in the English language.
In such chance circumstances it cannot be expected that every
poem will be suitable for musical treatment and the songwriter
who would plan to set all 63 poems would be foolish indeed.
What composers have done is to set individual poems or to group
several poems together into a sequence as a song cycle. Among
the 'single' songs there are many outstanding examples: Graham
Peel's 'In summertime on Bredon' ('Bredon Hill', XXI), published

in 1911, which Alec Robertson has described as 'the best – because
the simplest – of all the settings';[26] John Ireland's 'The Heart's
Desire' (1917), a setting of the last three stanzas of 'March' (XXXIX),
highly praised by both Newman[27] and Banfield;[28] E. J. Moeran's
'O fair enough are sky and plain' (XX), written in 1931 but not
published until after the composer's death – a neglected but
undoubted masterpiece, far more effective than his earlier settings
in *Ludlow Town* (1920); and Benjamin Burrows' 'Bredon Hill' (1927),
which compares well with the better-known settings of Vaughan
Williams, Butterworth and Peel. Of the Housman songs by Charles
Orr, two are particularly fine. 'The Carpenter's Son' (XLVII) (1922)
seems to be the only setting of this powerful poem. Banfield
describes it as 'melodramatic but genuinely forceful'[29] and
Christopher Palmer as 'a *via dolorosa* of mounting cynicism and
aggressive despair'.[30] And of all the versions of 'Is my team ploughing' (XXVII) (1925), Orr's reaches the heart of Housman's intentions
best of all. He treats the poem with an almost casual innocence,
though with disturbing undertones, and finds a convincing solution
to the problem of the final verse. But not surprisingly the finest
settings come in the songcycles, of which the major ones are Arthur
Somervell's *Songcycle from 'A Shropshire Lad'*, Vaughan Williams'
On Wenlock Edge, George Butterworth's *Six Songs from 'A Shropshire
Lad'* and *Bredon Hill and Other Songs*, John Ireland's *The Land of
Lost Content*, and Ivor Gurney's *Ludlow and Teme* and *The Western
Playland.*[31]

Arthur Somervell (1863–1937) had established his reputation as
a songwriter with the publication in 1898 of his songcycle to poems
from Tennyson's *Maud*. His *Songcycle from 'A Shropshire Lad'* (1904)
set a standard, indeed model, for later works. Like *Maud*, it is a
true songcycle with a carefully constructed 'libretto' which draws
the strands of the narrative possibilities of Housman's sequence
gently together. Somervell chose ten poems: II, XIII, XIV, XXI,
XXII, XXXV, XXXVI, XLIX, XL and XXIII. It is significant that,
except for the last two songs, he keeps to Housman's original
order. He also follows a hallowed tradition of the German *Liederkreis*
by subtle use of thematic cross-reference. For example, the music
of the first song, 'The Cherry Tree' (= 'Loveliest of trees') is quoted
note-for-note in the penultimate song, 'Into my heart an air that
kills', transposed down a semitone and at a slower tempo. It begins
in the piano part, with the voice intoning one note, as though
drained of feeling. Only in the second stanza does the singer

recapture the melody – coming, as it were, out of its numbed daze. Followed as it is by the valedictory poem, 'The lads in their hundreds', the effect is poignant.

Several critics have spoken highly of Somervell's songcycle. Banfield observes that Housman's poetry 'released Somervell's remarkable gift for flowing and effortless melody ... It encouraged Somervell's melodic warmth to glow as nowhere else.'[32] Arthur Jacobs thinks that Housman's verse 'has perhaps never been set better. The restraint of Somervell suits the poet much better than does Vaughan Williams' "over-emotional" treatment in *On Wenlock Edge'*.[33] The 'penillion' technique used in 'The street sounds to the soldiers' tread', with the piano providing the march of the soldiers, is a stroke of genius; his repeat of the final phrase, 'I wish you well', is for once forgiveable, because poetically appropriate. But I cannot help feeling that the settings are *too* restrained: simple-minded rather than simple, not so much flowing and effortless as bland. Though his vocal lines capture the outward mood of the poems, they do not – as in Butterworth's even simpler settings – always express the 'contour' of the poet's thought. One has only to compare Somervell's setting of 'The lads in their hundreds' with Butterworth's to appreciate this. Both adopt irregular metres (Somervell a consistent $\frac{15}{8}$, Butterworth a mixture of $\frac{6}{8}$ and $\frac{9}{8}$) and folk-like melodies. But whereas Butterworth reaches the heart of the matter, Somervell lilts along the surface. Somervell's language and style – heavily indebted as it is to his mentors, Parry and Stanford – is firmly rooted in the nineteenth century in a way that Housman's verse never is. Even so, this – the first major setting of *A Shropshire Lad* – is a considerable achievement.

The two Housman cycles of Ivor Gurney (1890–1937), *Ludlow and Teme* and *The Western Playland*, were published in 1923 and 1926 respectively. Like Vaughan Williams' *On Wenlock Edge*, a work on which they are obviously modelled, both call for an accompaniment of string quartet and piano. As well as familiar poems already set by Somervell, Vaughan Williams and Butterworth (e.g. XIII and XXVII) Gurney chooses two poems which songwriters have usually ignored, 'Reveille' (IV) and 'Twice a week the winter thorough' (XVII). Despite its late publication date, *The Western Playland* contains two songs, 'Loveliest of trees' and 'Is my team ploughing', which he had originally composed in 1908. The rest date from 1919–20, Gurney's most productive songwriting years. *Ludlow and Teme* consists of seven settings for tenor voice: VII,

LII, XXXIX, XXIII ('Ludlow Fair'), XXXV, XIII and XXIX; *The Western Playland* of eight settings for baritone: IV, II, LIV ('Golden Friends'), XVII, XXVI ('The Aspens'), XXVII, XL ('The Far Country') and X. Sydney Northcote[34] and Marion Scott[35] consider these to be Gurney's finest work, but others are less enthusiastic. Banfield thinks that *The Western Playland* borders in many places on 'structural and textual incoherence, possibly through damaging revision during the composer's asylum years'.[36] Michael Hurd, while describing *Ludlow and Teme* as an extremely effective cycle, finds *The Western Playland* less so: 'The textures are far too busy and self-defeating, and the cycle is finished off, disastrously, by a singularly vague instrumental coda.'[37] Gurney of course was himself a poet of stature and not surprisingly had a poet's awareness of the words he was setting. In his best songs his music underlines each nuance, yet remains flowing and coherent, and he achieves what many less sensitive songwriters fail to do: he allows the poems to *breathe*. He does not rush his word-setting: his songs are spacious and airy. This is particularly noticeable in 'The Lent Lily' (*Ludlow and Teme*) and 'Is my team ploughing' (*The Western Playland*).

Though the Housman settings of Somervell and Gurney possess great qualities – the Somervell for its structural planning and large-scale conception, the Gurney cycles for their lyrical intensity and sensitivity of word-setting – I think that most would agree that the most effective songcycles quarried from *A Shrop-*

shire Lad are those by Ralph Vaughan Williams (1872–1958), John Ireland (1879–1962) and George Butterworth (1885–1916). Vaughan Williams wrote *On Wenlock Edge* during 1908–9,[38] immediately after his return from Paris where he had been studying with Ravel. This, however, is hardly more than an interesting historical fact as far as the songcycle is concerned. You certainly would not think that he had been, in his own words, 'having tea with Debussy',[39] unless you count such obvious things as the use of whole-tone scales and the impressionistic bell-sounds in 'Bredon Hill' which may have been suggested by Ravel's *La Vallée des Cloches.*[40] What *is* strange is Vaughan Williams' choice of Housman in the first place. One would not think that the poet's irony and cynicism would have appealed to this normally serene, optimistic composer. This was a period when Vaughan Williams was making an intense study of English folksong and, as might be expected, there is a strong folk influence in the work, in the contours of melodic lines (for example the 'ghost's' phrases in 'Is my team ploughing', 'Oh, when I was in love with you' and the final verse of 'Clun') and the modal harmonies which imbue much of the piece. But elsewhere the feeling is highly romantic, earthy and spiritual by turns. This is emphasized by the accompaniment for string quartet and piano which is used vividly to portray pictorial and dramatic elements, at times almost overwhelming the role of the singer. Indeed the work is highly theatrical in places, a series of operatic scenes rather than a song cycle.

The composer has set six poems – XXXI, XXXII, XXVII, XVIII, XXI and L – 'two reflections on life, three on different phases of love, and one on death'.[41] One unusual feature is the relative size of the six settings. Three substantial songs – 'On Wenlock Edge', 'Is my team ploughing' and 'Bredon Hill' – sandwich two very short ones – 'From far, from eve and morning' and 'Oh, when I was in love with you' – with 'Clun' acting as a postlude. 'On Wenlock Edge' begins with a graphic portrayal of the windswept trees in Housman's first stanza, and this turbulence, like 'the gale of life', continues in the background for the rest of the song. At times the composer almost breaks the back of his fivesome accompaniment: one feels that he would have liked a full orchestra to do his word-painting justice. 'From far, from eve and morning' is one of his finest achievements. After the elaborate accompaniment of the opening song, he turns to utmost simplicity: wide-spreading piano chords underpin a vocal line

that never strays far from its home note (B natural). In 'Is my
team ploughing', Vaughan Williams, more than any other composer, marks the difference between the two poetic voices. There
is no question of the poem being an interior conversation between
self and conscience: for the composer these are two distinct people.
Over a remote, timeless chord of D minor, the ghost sings a gentle,
folk-like melody, mainly stepwise in movement, Dorian in mode.
The living friend answers in a tortured wail, a vocal line full of
tritonal and chromatic intervals (see Ex. 1).

Vaughan Williams deliberately omitted stanzas 3 and 4.
Housman, who had not been notified of this, was naturally
annoyed by what he saw as this 'mutilation' and asked, 'I wonder
how he would like me to cut two bars out of his music?'[42] Vaughan
Williams' typically robust reply was:

> The composer has a perfect right artistically to set any portion of
> a poem he chooses provided he does not actually alter the sense

adding cheekily:

> I feel that a poet should be grateful to anyone who fails to
> perpetuate such lines as:
>
> > The goal stands up, the keeper
> > Stands up to keep the goal.[43]

Ernest Newman supported Housman, observing that the omission destroyed the poet's effect of 'a gradual, almost casual,
transition from the ghost's questions about the common things
of life to the questions about his sweetheart'.[44] But Vaughan
Williams was right to jib. These stanzas are an example of Housman
at his most prosaic and low-key. They are fine when read off the
page with a slightly ironic tone of voice, but to *sing* . . .? (Even
Butterworth's masterly treatment of these stanzas is slightly
uncomfortable.) 'Oh, when I was in love with you' takes up the
same key (D minor). Lightweight in tone, epigrammatic in its
brevity, with a melody that could be an authentic folksong, it
acts as a much-needed respite between the intense emotions of
songs 3 and 5. 'Bredon Hill' is the most substantial, pictorial and
ambitious song in the cycle. In the accompaniment the composer
uses a compendium of bell possibilities, from the hazy bells of a
summer morning: alternating, unrelated 7th chords played *pian-*

issimo between strings and piano (verses 1 and 2); more animated bell sounds for piano alone (verses 3 and 4); bleak 'winter bells' (verse 5); a reiterated pedal G for 'the one bell only' (verse 6); to the frenetic, almost deafening bell-rings of the final verse. 'Clun' – which is a setting of the poem, 'In valleys of springs of rivers' – acts as a quiet, consoling epilogue to the cycle, a mood of peace and serenity which Vaughan Williams was to recapture in many later works such as the Tallis Fantasia and the 5th Symphony.

Since it was first performed, *On Wenlock Edge* has provoked extremes of praise and censure, most notably in the famous verbal duel between Edwin Evans (pro) and Ernest Newman (anti) in the columns of *The Musical Times* in June and September 1918. In a particularly vituperative essay, Newman criticizes the music on several counts: that it does not 'mate happily with the prosody of the poems',[45] comparing Vaughan Williams' setting unfavourably with Butterworth's; that the composer lacks a fine ear for the niceties of English poetic rhythm; that he is too inclined to turn lyricism into melodrama or pictorialism; and that he generally fastens upon the obvious externals of a poem at the expense of the heart of its meaning. He is particularly critical of the three 'big' settings. 'On Wenlock Edge' 'loses its purely lyrical quality and becomes a mere piece of declamation to accompany a piece of descriptive instrumental writing.'[46] In 'Bredon Hill', 'he gets the balance of his picture wrong, turning what should be background into foreground, and vice-versa ... The frame is bigger than the picture ... There is no suggestion anywhere of the illimitable, unappeasable grief of the Lad.'[47] In 'Is my team ploughing', as well as deploring the omission of stanzas 3 and 4, Newman says that 'he falsifies the very essence of the poem by exaggerating the contrast between the dead man and the living. He turns the poem into a sort of long-distance telephone conversation.'[48] Another 'falsity' is that he makes the living man melodramatically agitated, particularly in that final 'difficult' line:

What is the use of the friend saying 'Never ask me whose' in a *pianissimo* when he has just howled the 'I choose a dead man's sweetheart' at the ghost's head with a noise and an agitation that would let the most stupid ghost that ever returned to earth into the secret?[49]

It would seem from Newman's tirade that there is very little going for Vaughan Williams' songcycle and little to salvage. On the contrary, whatever the critics have said, *On Wenlock Edge* remains, with Butterworth's, the most popular of all the major Housman settings. It is a true songcycle – to take any song out of its context only diminishes it – and in its spacious, almost symphonic, matching of texts and themes it is in all senses a major work. Whatever reservations one may have about the overdramatic treatment of Housman's verses in the first, third and fifth songs, by the time the hushed tread of root position chords homes onto A major in the final song, we realize that we have experienced something quite magical.

George Butterworth's two Housman songcycles – *Six Songs from 'A Shropshire Lad'* and *Bredon Hill and Other Songs,* both for baritone and piano – have provoked similar extreme reactions. Some consider that Butterworth, particularly in his first cycle, comes nearer to the heart of Housman than any other composer. Peter Pirie thinks 'Butterworth's are closest to the simplicity and directness of the verse, and bring out most strikingly the folk-element therein'[50] and Gerald Finzi has said that Butterworth's settings are 'reminiscent of English water colour... economical in an entirely new way, and saying far more in its few strokes than any words could do'.[51] C. W. Orr, on the other hand, disliked 'all those folksy settings... Some of his so-called simplicity I am blasphemous enough to describe as infantilism. (Particularly that

Ex. 2

atrociously feeble folk tune that he has used for 'When I was one-and-twenty').'[52] Eric Sams agrees with Orr:

> Housman's heart (on his sleeve, at least) belongs to Butterworth. Nothing is said about the brain, though; and it is surely the whetstone of intelligence that gives Housman's verse . . . its steely glitter and slicing edge. This goes like a knife through Butterworth, whose bland absorption often misses the point.[53]

I'm not so sure that Butterworth is such a butter-pat as Sams would have us believe. There is in his settings a balance between passion and poise, between artlessness and artifice, and the simple folk-like language of the old folk ballads, which Housman admitted were his models, are reflected in Butterworth's songs, with their folk-like, modally inflected vocal lines and their simple piano accompaniment, particularly in the first cycle. What critics often fail to realize is that a successful song is not just a matter of poet and composer, but of poet, composer and performer. Butterworth allows his performers space to give a deep, penetrating interpretation, something that Gerald Moore has pointed out[54] and which even Eric Sams admits.[55]

The background to the composition of the two cycles was complex, as Stephen Banfield's documentation shows.[56] The music was written between 1909 and 1911 and Butterworth clearly gave much thought and planning to its composition. In his own copy of *A Shropshire Lad* he listed numerous possible choices of poem, in the end selecting 14 which he placed in an order that suggests he was thinking (like Somervell) in terms of one large-scale songcycle with a narrative outline. By the time he had made his first MS copy (early 1911) he had cut out four poems, but was still intent on a single cycle, beginning with 'O fair to see' and ending with 'Bredon Hill'. In the end he divided the songs into two groups, adding a setting of a poem not on the original list, 'On the idle hill of summer'.

In *Six Songs from 'A Shropshire Lad'* Butterworth sets II, XIII, XV, XLIX, XXIII and XXVII from Housman's sequence. Though it was never called a songcycle by Butterworth himself and lacks the narrative shape of Somervell's work, it is a songcycle to all intents and purposes in that each song leads naturally on to the next through a careful juxtaposition of poem and tonality. Individual songs can stand independently, but they make a stronger

impact when heard in the sequence that Butterworth devised.
Songs about the fleetingness of life (1 and 5), the folly of falling
in love (2 and 3), the folly of being earnest (4) lead to a final
dialogue between the Lad and his dead friend. This sequence is
reinforced by a subtle arrangement of tonalities: E major – E minor
(Dorian) – F major – G sharp minor – F sharp major – C minor
(Dorian).[57] The opening song, 'Loveliest of trees', is the key to
the sequence and the key to all Butterworth's Housman settings
in that it forms the basis of his orchestral rhapsody, *A Shropshire
Lad* (1912). Motifs from this song reappear in later songs – indeed
the opening vocal lines of the first four songs bear a remarkable
similarity (see Ex. 2).

Though the song gives the impression of improvisation, its structure is highly organized and subtle. The three stanzas are set as
a bow-shaped ternary form, in which the final verse mirrors the
first. This mirroring also takes place within the verse itself. The
opening phrase – 'a pictorial image of a blossom already falling
from the cherry tree'[58] – is immediately mirrored by inversion in
the third line of the poem:

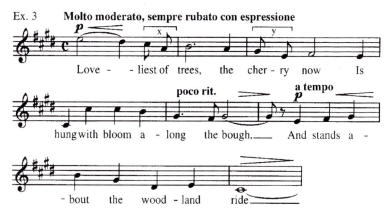

Ex. 3   **Molto moderato, sempre rubato con espressione**

In the third verse these two phrases change places: the second
heard first ('And since to look at things in bloom'), the opening
phrase last. The reason is plain: Housman has framed his poem
with references to the cherry tree; Butterworth has simply (i.e.
artfully) followed Housman. In the second verse Butterworth picks
up the 'cuckoo' motif x̄ for both vocal line and the very sparse
piano accompaniment. All is low-key – a sensible solution to a
tricky stanza, where the Lad's emotions are at a standstill while

he does some finger-counting. (It is as though the cuckoo is calling unheard while the Lad is caught up in his mathematical reverie.) Yet, despite the careful control of its structure, the final effect is not one of intellectual cleverness but of an almost trance-like extemporization. What is more, it is the *singer* who bears the weight of musical responsibility, and in doing so makes us concentrate on Housman's words. 'When I was one-and-twenty' finds Butterworth at his most simple and folk-like. Under the title of the song he has written 'Tune Traditional' – Orr's 'atrociously feeble folk tune' – but does not identify it. Nor has anyone else been able to do so.[59] It is in the Dorian mode and has the ABBA shape typical of so many English folksongs (for instance, 'The Lincolnshire Poacher'). This is perfect for Housman's poem, which follows the same pattern. The modal tune, however, is harmonized tonally, predominantly with first inversion chords and with implied 'modulations'. Butterworth takes the hint from Housman's repetition of the poem's final phrase, ' 'tis true, 'tis true', to extend the music by a further repetition, intoned *pianissimo* over a bald plagal cadence. In 'Look not in my eyes', he chooses, not the expected duple (or triple) metre, but an irregular $\frac{5}{4}$ time signature, which he shifts flexibly between 2 + 3 and 3 + 2. This gives him an 'extra note' to play with, which he uses to give two-note melismas to crucial words. During the song, these two-notes-a-syllable appear at almost every point in the bar. So instead of a metric straitjacket we have a flexible, flowing line. The vocal line is again modal (here Mixolydian) and, as with the second song, the accompaniment sometimes agrees with it and sometimes not. Butterworth again uses *tonal* devices – for example the 'modulation' to the dominant at the end of the first verse and the song's unexpected final cadence onto F-major, when the ear has been expecting B flat major. Butterworth treats the cynical verses of 'Think no more, lad' in appropriate throwaway, mock-jolly style, but rather naughtily makes a ternary pie out of Housman's two stanzas by repeating verse 1, with slight variations, at the end.[60] There is, for the usually reticent Butterworth, some explicit word-painting at the end of the first verse, where the phrase 'falling sky' drops downwards like a rocket.

Of the many fine settings of 'The lads in their hundreds', Butterworth's is undoubtedly the best. Housman's poem, with its dactylic, folk-like metre and monosyllabic language, is perfectly matched by Butterworth's music. The four stanzas are set strophically but with subtle variations for stanzas 2 and 3. There is no introduction: the voice leads the way from the outset and the accompaniment is kept to a minimum to allow the vocal line to speak for itself. The piano's predominantly high tessitura – until the final cadence, the lowest note is G sharp below middle C – imbues the setting with a dream-like aura. The song ends with a poignant piano epilogue in which the ritornello, which has linked the verses, strives for and eventually reaches its climax-note (f" sharp) before making a gentle cadence – a mixture of plagal and perfect – onto the home chord.

In 'Is my team ploughing', Butterworth characterizes the question-and-answer dialogue between the dead youth and his living friend in both vocal line and piano accompaniment:

Q: High tessitura of vocal line; *molto moderato, senza rigore: pianissimo;* the piano a legato chain of 7th chords drifting downwards over a span of an octave, concluding unresolved but pointing towards B flat major.

A: Lower-pitched vocal line: *poco piu mosso; forte;* the accompaniment consisting of block triads with a moving bass, ending conclusively on a plagal cadence in C minor.

These musical cadences effectively mirror the question and answer of the poem by the most simple means. Butterworth adds his own interpretation by the finality of the even-numbered verses: as though the living man were loath to say anything more, but eager to conclude the conversation as soon as possible. This is reinforced by the subtle way in which the composer suggests growing hesitation between the pairs of strophes by gradually lengthening the pauses: first (end of verse 2) by a simple comma break ('), then (end of verses 4 and 6) by a bar's rest for the voice.[61] How does Butterworth deal with the problem of the poem's ending? Initially by making a break between the last two lines, slowing the tempo (*Lento*) and reducing the friend's dynamics to *piano;* next by cadencing the voice onto the final of the mode (C) instead of G as previously; and finally by gently slipping from the stark triads of the friend's accompaniment into the chain of chromatic chords associated with the dead man (see Ex. 4).

The magical effect of this passage is difficult to define. It is as if the ghost and the living man, the Lad and his *doppelgänger,* are fused into one spirit. The chromatic chords, instead of drop-

ping down the octave as before, slow down to a halt half way down the scale, suspended as it were in air. A 'cadence' is effected by the deep anchoring note of the piano's lowest C, forming an added 6th chord which is only resolved when the upper notes are removed, leaving the low C 'vibrating in the memory'. But is this the resolution which Housman would have wished? As so often, Butterworth leaves the interpretation to the singer. That final phrase can be (and has been) sung in a variety of ways: with a smile on the lips, or with guilty sadness. Whatever the view, Butterworth has found a satisfying answer to a difficult problem. Of the other composers who have set this poem, only Charles Orr, to my mind, finds such a satisfactory solution.

The *Six Songs from 'A Shropshire Lad'* has homogeneity and unity: directness of expression, folk-like simplicity of vocal line and a piano accompaniment pared down to the bone. It was something new at the time and highly welcome in English music after the overwrought complexities of much late romantic music, and was due in no small part to Butterworth's study of English folk music. But no one should misinterpret this simplicity: it is art concealing art. Butterworth's second songcycle, *Bredon Hill and Other Songs* (published 1912) – settings of XXI, XX, VI, XXXV and LIV – lacks this homogeneity. Of the five songs, numbers 2, 3 and 5 share the folk-like character of the first cycle. Indeed, 'With rue my heart is laden', which he was later to quote at the end of his *Shropshire Lad* rhapsody, is one of the most hauntingly beautiful of all his songs. The remaining two songs, however, are quite different. 'Bredon Hill' is one of the weakest. It lacks the intensity of Vaughan Williams' setting, and the continuous shifts of key-centre break down the poem's unity. 'On the idle hill of summer', on the other hand, is one of Butterworth's most profound songs, anecdotally assured – the summer haze, the drums, the bugles and the fife are brilliantly evoked and integrated – and harmonically one of his most advanced conceptions.[62] In this it looks forward to the Rhapsody but, by the same token, away from the style of the other songs.

John Ireland's *The Land of Lost Content,* for tenor and piano, was composed during 1920 and 1921 and is generally considered to be the composer's finest vocal work. It is a true tenor cycle, with a predominantly high tessitura – unlike so many English 'tenor' songs, which are really for high baritone – and this feature flavours the entire work. Ireland has taken his title from a poem which he does not set[63] and uses his own titles for all songs except the first.[64] The six songs which form the cycle – XXIX, XV, XVII, XXXIII, XXII and LVII – are subtly integrated, notably by the recurrent cadential figure of a falling fifth, which haunts the whole work (see Ex. 7). The cycle begins in a 'celebration of transience' with 'The Lent Lily', but in the subsequent songs it becomes clear that 'happiness is in the past'.[65] Many would agree with Sydney Northcote that 'The Lent Lily' is one of Ireland's finest songs. Above a piano accompaniment of flowing and eddying 3rds within a metre oscillating between $\frac{3}{4}$ and $\frac{2}{4}$, the singer sings a gentle, Dorian-inflected vocal line. The first three verses are set strophically and, following Housman's unusual enjambement between stanzas 3 and 4, the composer runs the last two verses together, the eddying 3rds reaching a richly dissonant climax at the words 'spring's array' (see Ex. 5).

A criticism – and it is a valid one – is that the composer interprets Housman's unusually joyful words in too melancholy a manner. He had done the same thing ten years earlier in his famous setting of Masefield's 'Sea Fever', which has very little fever about it. ('Sea Melancholy' would be a more appropriate title.) It is as though he is forcing onto this song the fatalistic mood of the later songs. Singers will always have a problem giving

Ex. 5

sal - ly Up - on the spring's ar - ray,

the opening phrase, ''Tis Spring: come out to ramble', any vernal conviction. 'Ladslove' (= 'Look not in my eyes') had already been memorably set by Butterworth, but Ireland emphasizes the frustrated, homoerotic undertones of the poem better than anyone. This is a sensuous, passionate song whose vocal line is always straining upwards. This is noticeable from the very opening line and even at the cadences – something unusual in English song, where cadences tend to fall, but entirely effective in this context:

Ex. 6

And love it and be lost____ like me.

'Goal and Wicket' (= 'Twice a week, the winter thorough') shares the footballing imagery of 'Is my team ploughing', linked in this case with cricket to form a winter/summer contrast. Ireland sets the poem strophically, with complex harmonies over an energetic, striding bass, and underlines the poem's ironic unease with a disturbing pattern of tonalities. It is impossible to predict where the pianist's opening ritornello is going to halt: it starts with a D minor^7 chord, and then goes through B flat minor^7, A major and F minor^7 before reaching a chord of F sharp minor^7. E minor – the home key according to the key signature – is not properly reached until the verse's cadence. The song ends with a tonal version of the striding bass line which rumbles on to the final, surprisingly defiant cadence: a pre-echo of the *basso ostinato* of the fifth song. 'The Vain Desire' (= 'If truth in hearts that perish') is a poem that has had little attraction for composers – Gooch and Thatcher mention only Ireland's setting. He sets the four short stanzas as two musical strophes (1/2; 3/4). The tonality veers constantly between E flat major and A minor – i.e. tonalities a tritone apart – with the 'motto' motif of a falling 5th prominent both in the vocal line (bars 4, 8, etc.) and the piano bass (bars 2–3, 20, etc.). The piano ritornello which appears between the strophes and as a postlude (bars 18–20/36–8) is the emotional heart of the entire cycle, reflecting not only the tritonal relationship of the basic tonalities (E flat major/A minor) but also incorporating the falling fifth motto $\overline{x}$:

The singer's cadential phrase should be noted, as Ireland brings

it back at the end of the cycle. 'The Vain Desire' is one of the bleakest songs in the repertoire, the more so since it is so subdued in tone. In 'The Encounter' (= 'The street sounds to the soldiers' tread') Ireland, following Somervell's example, uses 'penillion' technique, giving the piano self-contained material – a robust, insistent march-like idea – above which the singer declaims an equally robust line, sometimes doubling, sometimes in descant with the pianist's right hand. Ireland makes effective use of bitonality throughout. The singer has a modal G major/D minor, with no accidentals and no F; the pianist a very chromatic (almost Hindemithian) tune over a striding four-note ostinato, F – G – A – B, with ambiguous tonality, outlining as it does the tritone. Somehow the composer manages to guide the song into C major for the final cadence. This song is one of Ireland's most original inventions. The 'Epilogue' (= 'You smile upon your friend today': another seldom-set lyric) acts as a short, quiet coda to the cycle, all passion spent. The two stanzas are set as a binary unit (verse 1: D flat major – B flat major; verse 2: back to D flat major) which has the effect of one long, through-composed strophe. Between stanzas, after the words 'happy is the lover', a musical phrase blossoms out which must have had a special meaning for the composer, for he had already used it in two earlier songs, 'My true love hath my heart' and 'The Trellis', where it symbolizes 'reflections of past happiness':

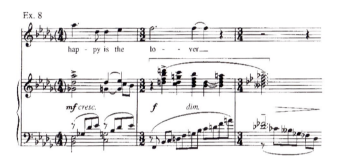

In keeping with its epilogal function, the song echoes ideas from earlier songs: the flowing thirds of 'The Lent Lily' (bars 2 and 3, etc.), the ubiquitous falling fifth (bar 10), and the singer concludes with exactly the same cadence as in 'The Vain Desire'.

The Land of Lost Content is not for the faint-hearted: its bleak fatalism is not likely to attract a large popular audience. Yet, as many critics have pointed out, it captures the mood of Housman's poetry perhaps better than any other work. Peter Pears has said that Ireland's 'edgy pessimistic nature matched the poet's perfectly',[66] while Alec Robertson has written that 'Ireland more than any other of the composers, catches the lonely, frustrated, and often bitter mood of the poems.'[67] Certainly no songs have captured the homoerotic undertones of Housman's verse more effectively.

* * *

The Housman cycles of Vaughan Williams, Butterworth and Ireland are all of a high musical quality: entirely characteristic of their composers, yet faithful to Housman's texts and illuminating them. There is no point in choosing which is 'best' or putting them into pecking order: art is not a competitive game. Each has its own unique qualities and will attract according to one's mood or to the stance one prefers to take to Housman. *On Wenlock Edge* is operatic in quality, full of drama and word-painting. Butterworth's *Six Songs* are, as Finzi aptly described them, 'water colours', folk-like and gently poetic. Ireland's vision in *The Land of Lost Content* is of sexual frustration and dark-hued pessimism. The three stand as pinnacles in twentieth-century English song and musical monuments to *A Shropshire Lad.* For, as I've suggested, the Golden Age of Housman settings has been and gone. *A Shropshire Lad,* first published in 1896, with its imagery of red-coated soldiers of pre-Boer War days, was prophetic of what was to happen twenty years later and had an immediate urgency for the generation brought up in the shadow of the First World War. For a time, the poet and his Shropshire double were the darling of English songwriters. A generation of Georgian composers found its poetic voice in the poignant, heartfelt lyrics of this reclusive Cambridge Professor of Latin. But, as is the nature of such spates of interest, it quickly subsided and I have a feeling that the lyrics will never appeal to large numbers of composers in the future.[68] They are very much of their particular age, their viewpoint limited. They do not have the emotional range and universality of feeling of (say) Shakespeare's song lyrics which can, and need to be, reinterpreted by each new generation of songwriters. The bulk of Housman, I would suggest, has now been set, the Shropshire Lad's legacy of song complete. In a lecture given in 1955, Gerald Finzi, discussing the future of Housman settings, said, 'He would be a bold man who would set Housman, or, much more likely, he would have no impulse to do so,' reminding us at the same time that 'those poems remain the same and we must recognise that it is we, not they, who have changed'.[69]

What is that musical legacy? It is not the quantity, though there is plenty of it, but the quality which is important and, as I have endeavoured to show, this is extremely high. Housman's lyrics attracted nearly every major songwriter in an age which we now see as a Golden Age of English song. I could name four superb settings of 'Bredon Hill', while the settings of 'Is my team ploughing' by Butterworth and Orr are masterpieces by any standard. And the major Housman-inspired works, the songcycles of Somervell, Vaughan Williams, Butterworth and Ireland, rank not only high in their composers' achievements but among the glories of twentieth-century English song. Take Housman away, and English music would be infinitely, inconceivably the poorer.

> And fields will yearly bear them
>   As light-leaved spring comes on,
> And luckless lads will wear them
>   When I am dead and gone.

Notes

1. 'A. E. Housman and Music', *Music and Letters,* 24 (1943) 208–19.
2. 'A. E. Housman and the English Composer', *Music and Letters,* 29 (1948) 329–39.
3. *Sensibility and English Song* (Cambridge: CUP, 1985) ch. 9 and Appendices II and III.
4. *Musical Settings of Late Victorian and Modern British Literature: A Catalogue* (New York and London: Garland, 1976) pp. 365–97.
5. Gooch and Thatcher, op. cit. Gooch and Thatcher were relying in their catalogue on *published* songs and information from composers on their unpublished (i.e. MS) settings. There must be many more settings of Housman that went unreported.
6. Grant Richards, *Housman, 1897–1936* (OUP London: Humphrey Milford, 1941) p. 54.
7. *Music Ho!* (London: Faber & Faber, 1934) p. 284.
8. Two early settings from 1913 are lost.
9. Again some Housman set but destroyed: see Banfield, *op. cit.,* p. 239.
10. Banfield, op. cit., p. 302.
11. 'Few, but roses', in *Authors dead and living* (London, Chatto & Windus, 1926) p. 172.
12. 'Inside the Whale', in *Collected Essays, Journalism and Letters of George Orwell,* I (London: Secker & Warburg, 1968) p. 553.
13. 'The Lent Lily' and ''Tis Time, I think' would work too; even, at a pinch, 'When the lad for longing sighs'.
14. K. E. Symons, *Correspondence* 'A. E. Housman and Music', *Music and Letters,* 25 (1944) 60–1.
15. Percy Withers, *A Buried Life: Personal Recollections of A. E. Housman* (London: Jonathan Cape, 1940) pp. 82–3.
16. Grant Richards, op. cit., pp. 54, 81, etc.
17. Percy Withers, op. cit., p. 69.
18. Percy Withers, 'A. E. Housman: Personal Recollections', *The New Statesman and Nation,* n.s. 9 (9 May 1936) 700–1.
19. 'Mr Housman and the Composers', *The Sunday Times* (29 October 1922) 7.
20. See my article, '"Words for Music": an old problem revisited', *Music*

Review, 47 (November 1986/7) 283–93, for a discussion of these matters.

21. 'Concerning *A Shropshire Lad* and Other Matters', *Musical Times*, 59 (1918) 393.
22. See Banfield, op. cit., pp. 239–40.
23. Cecil Day-Lewis, 'Introduction', *A Book of English Lyrics* (London: Chatto & Windus, 1961) p. 11.
24. No. 4 of *Five Songs from 'A Shropshire Lad'*.
25. A. H. Fox Strangways, 'Ralph Vaughan Williams', in *Cobbett's Cyclopedic Survey of Chamber Music*, II (Oxford: OUP, 1929) pp. 584–6.
26. Sleeve-notes, 'Butterworth: Settings of Poems from A. E. Housman's *A Shropshire Lad'*, DLP 1117, 1956.
27. (1918), op. cit., p. 398.
28. (1985), op. cit., p. 237.
29. (1985), op. cit., p. 304.
30. 'C. W. Orr: an 80th Birthday Tribute', *Musical Times*, 114 (1973) 692.
31. I exclude Graham Peel's *Songs of a Shropshire Lad* (1911), E. J. Moeran's *Ludlow Town* (1920) and C. W. Orr's various published collections as these are song*books* rather than song*cycles*.
32. (1985), op. cit., pp. 52–3.
33. 'The British Isles', in *A History of Song*, ed. Denis Stevens (London: Hutchinson, 1960) p. 158.
34. *Byrd to Britten: a Survey of English Song* (London: John Baker, 1966) p. 105.
35. 'Ivor Gurney' in *Grove 5*, ed. Eric Blom (London: Macmillan, 1954) 3, p. 195.
36. (1985), op. cit., p. 405.
37. *The Ordeal of Ivor Gurney* (Oxford: OUP, 1978) p. 209.
38. Michael Kennedy suggests that some songs had been started as early as 1906: see *The Works of Ralph Vaughan Williams*, 1964/2 (London: OUP, 1964, 2nd edn, 1980) p. 116.
39. See Vaughan Williams' 'A Musical Autobiography', in *National Music and Other Essays* (London: OUP, 1963) p. 191.
40. Edwin Evans, 'English Song and *On Wenlock Edge'*, *Musical Times*, 59 (1918) 249.
41. A. H. Fox Strangways, op. cit., pp. 584–6.
42. Grant Richards, op. cit., p. 181.
43. Grant Richards, op. cit., p. 221.
44. 'Concerning "A Shropshire Lad" and other Matters, *Musical Times*, 59 (1918) 397.
45. Op. cit., p. 394.
46. Op. cit., p. 395.
47. Op. cit., pp. 396–7.
48. Op. cit., p. 397.
49. Op. cit., p. 397.
50. Peter Pirie, 'Introduction', *Eleven Songs from 'A Shropshire Lad'* (London: Stainer & Bell, 1974).
51. Unpublished *Crees Lectures*, given at the Royal College of Music, May 1955: typescript, p. 7.
52. Banfield (1985), op. cit., p. 399.

53. Record review, *Musical Times*, (117), 1976, 659.
54. *Singer and Accompanist* (London: Methuen, 1953) p. 33.
55. Eric Sams, op. cit., 659.
56. '"A Shropshire Lad" in the making: a note on the composition of George Butterworth's songs', *Music Review*, 42 (1981) 261–7.
57. Banfield (1985), op. cit., says that the fourth song is in D sharp minor and the sixth B flat major. I think that he has confused key signatures with tonalities. Many of Butterworth's key signatures are modal, e.g. the second song, which has two sharps, is definitely a *Dorian* E minor, not B minor. Butterworth himself is not consistent in this matter. Why does not the third song have two flats in the signature? The vocal line is *Mixolydian* F throughout.
58. Banfield (1985), op. cit., p. 401.
59. Michael Dawney, who has written about Butterworth's folksong collecting, has been unable to identify the tune, nor has the great folksong authority, Maud Karpeles, with whom he discussed the matter. (Conversation with the author, 3/4/95.)
60. In his original MS version, Butterworth treats the two verses strophically: see Banfield (1981), op. cit., p. 267.
61. Any performers worth their musicianship will ensure that the pause between verses 6 and 7 is longer than between 4 and 5.
62. It was almost certainly the last Housman setting he composed.
63. First line, second stanza of XL. He had intended to print the entire poem as an epigraph to the cycle, but Housman had refused permission (Richards, op. cit., p. 185).
64. Again a practice which Housman had tried to forbid, but without success: see Butcher, op. cit., pp. 336–7.
65. Banfield (1985), op. cit., pp. 172–3.
66. Sleeve-note 'Twentieth Century English Songs', ZRG 5418, 1964.
67. Sleeve-note, 'Butterworth: Settings of Poems from A. E. Housman's *A Shropshire Lad*', DLP 1117, 1956.
68. To mark the centenary of the publication of *A Shropshire Lad*, The Housman Society commissioned new settings of Housman's poems from five contemporary British composers: Simon Bainbridge (''Tis time, I think, by Wenlock Town'); Michael Berkeley ('Grenadier'); Robin Holloway ('Song of Defiance' – 'Stand back, you men and horses', a MS poem completed by Robert Conquest); David Matthews ('Loveliest of trees'); and Howard Skempton ('Into my heart an air that kills').
69. The *Crees Lectures*, op. cit., typescript, p. 7.

8

Housman's Manilius

G. P. Goold

'LET us now praise famous men!' cries the author of *Ecclesiasticus*, and a commendation of this practice, *Clarorum virorum facta moresque posteris tradere*, constitutes the exordium of Tacitus's *Agricola*: it is a good thing that the deeds and ways of famous men should not be extinguished with their mortal lives but be recorded, so that they may continue to inspire those born after them.

Naturally, among scholars, particularly among classical scholars, whose unspectacular lives are more apt to be devoted to commemorating others than to performing themselves deeds meriting acclaim, it will not often be the case that a figure emerges to capture lasting attention with his personality. Usually it is the scholar's lot to be commemorated by his books: Lewis and Short have secured immortality through their dictionary, as Cruden through his concordance; but no one has ever been moved to write biographies of them so as to protect their personalities from the encroachment of oblivion.

But, remarkably, beyond any classical scholar of this century – even taking into account the advent of the *Festschrift* and the increased ease and attractiveness of self-biography – Alfred Edward Housman, who died in 1936 and is generally recognized as the foremost Latinist of this century, still excites an enormous amount of interest. I say 'remarkably' because he shunned the public gaze, rejected friendly approaches by strangers and expressly forbade in his will the publication of his collected papers: did everything he could, in fact, to discourage posthumous commemoration. Yet he nursed within him a strong desire to shine, as he confesses in a marginal note 'This is me' written against the following passage of T. E. Lawrence's *Seven Pillars of Wisdom:* 'There was a craving to be famous; and a horror of being known to like being known. Contempt for my passion for distinction made me refuse every offered honour.'[1]

Of course the general public knows of Housman more as a poet than as a scholar: certainly it is interest in his poetry rather than his scholarship that accounts for his appeal to biographers. Still it has to be emphasized that he ranks significantly higher in the hierarchy of scholars than of poets. Not that Housman's is to be thought of as a Jekyll-and-Hyde personality; his was an exceptionally solid and integrated one: the characteristics of his scholarship are reflected in his poetry and vice versa.

Shortly after his death in 1936 there appeared A. S. F. Gow's *A. E. Housman: A Sketch*, essentially an appreciation, by a scholar in the first rank, of one rather greater; in 1937 the recollections of his brother Laurence quoted above, himself not undistinguished in the field of literature; in 1940 the memoir of Percy Withers, significantly entitled *A Buried Life*; and the following year, the most engaging and enjoyable of all the books about him, *Housman 1897–1936*, a rambling and anecdotal account by his roguish publisher, Grant Richards. These books, and scores of contemporary articles recalling Housman, have one undisputed advantage over later biographical accounts, however superior these may be in factual accuracy or critical acumen: their writers actually knew Housman, and in every case, if perhaps they reveal a different profile to us, the actuality of their experience shines through.

The 1950s brought into the open some frank discussion about Housman and homosexuality, first and best in George Watson's *A Divided Life* (1957). In the year 1979 appeared what was intended to be the definitive life, certainly one which deployed far more data than anything earlier, *A. E. Housman, The Scholar-Poet*, by Richard Perceval Graves. His book is an invaluable contribution, but the most arresting item he has to offer is the theory on page 155, which even before the end of the sentence he transmutes into fact, that on one visit to Paris Housman engaged in a number of encounters with male prostitutes. The exact details I do not claim to know; but I think it can be shown that Graves's theory is improbable to the last degree.

This is the story. After his death part of Housman's library was sold at Blackwell's bookshop in Oxford; in one of the books was found a small card on which is written, undeniably in Housman's handwriting, a list of 15 days given as Monday, Tuesday, Wednesday, and so on, finishing with Monday, beside each of which (except for five days marked with a zero) is given a number and a description. So, for example, we have Tuesday 9

Boxeur; Thursday 3 Marin 1; Friday 9 Danseur; and, the week
after, Tuesday 9 Marin 2; Thursday 3 nègre; Friday 10 Danseur.
All told there are ten items, and at the side written vertically the
note '10 in 15 days'.

Graves interprets this (associating it with a remark in a letter
of Housman's dated 1909, when he was 50) as

> references to a number of male prostitutes, including sailors
> and ballet-dancers, together with a note of the price paid on
> various occasions for their services, and a marginal note in which
> Alfred refers with some satisfaction to the large number of these
> homosexual encounters which he had enjoyed in the space of
> a little over a fortnight.

This is a mischievous and irresponsible charge, and it is false.

The document may be dated with exactitude. A letter of
Housman's written on 18 May 1932 to Grant Richards[2] states: 'I
shall be in Paris at The Continental from May 29 to June 14.'
Assuming that Housman included at each end his date of arrival
and departure that would mean that his full days at the hotel
numbered 15, 30 May to 13 June. In 1932 30 May fell on a Monday. When Grant Richards further informs us that this 1932 visit
of Housman's to Paris was for him unusually long, I think we
can be absolutely certain that the actual days specified in the
document belonged to 1932, when Housman was in his 74th year.

We can discover more. In his letter of 18 May to Grant Richards
Housman also said: 'I cannot offer you anything of an invitation, for I shall have a friend with me who would not mix with
you nor you with him.' We learn from Graves, corroborated by
postcards from Housman to Richards:[3] 'with this unidentified
companion, he motored around Paris, travelling usually 150 kilo-
metres a day, visiting Chartres, Neuilly, Vincennes, Fontainebleau
and other places, and sampling the wines of new restaurants';
and from a letter of 15 June to his sister Katharine: 'In this last
fortnight I did not spend any night outside Paris.'

Besides a strenuous daily schedule of gastronomic field-trips,
clearly his main purpose, he was accompanied by the companion
he was reluctant for Grant Richards to meet. It is a reasonable
surmise that this was the same person that accompanied Housman
on a similar tour of Anjou and Touraine in the following year,
when he wrote to Katharine: ' . . . I shall have with me a French

companion, a nice young man, not much educated, who regards me as a benefactor' (obviously the companion was a previous acquaintance) (18 August); ' . . . I have been wretchedly ill . . . My companion has been as kind and helpful as can possibly be imagined' (24 August); 'I am weak and low, but my companion takes all trouble on his shoulders, and really does not seem to be bored' (31 August).

This makes it fairly plain that Housman's companion of June 1932 was someone like his Venetian gondolier Andrea, probably a young Parisian whom he had got to know as a chauffeur and had taken a liking to. That his liking went beyond pleasurable friendship seems excluded by the manner in which Housman describes him to his sister and to Withers.[4] But the young man may have been a homosexual and amused Housman with details of incidents (real or exaggerated), and he as a *jeu d'esprit* noted them down, the figures representing locations (for example night-clubs): zeros were added on days devoid of activity, enabling Housman to tot up the reckoning at the side. The use of English elsewhere in the document suggests that the French words came from his companion's lips, especially as Housman seems to have had some trouble in writing *Nicois* (if that is what it is).

In fine the document affords absolutely no evidence for questionable behaviour on Housman's part, and his conduct in Paris must be reckoned entirely blameless, unless the indulgence of a connoisseur's taste for good food and drink be deemed sinful.

Let us at this point review some landmarks of Housman's career. In 1879, twenty years old, he took a first in Honour Moderations at Oxford. Two years later he failed his final examination in Greats. He subsequently entered the Patent Office and until his appointment to the Chair of Latin at University College London in 1892 prosecuted his classical studies in what was virtually an academic exile. For the next five years he poured forth a profusion of articles on Latin and Greek authors which comprise volume I of his Classical Papers.[5] We can follow in detail the studies occupying Housman at this time and even surmise from the low output of 1895 and 1896 that some factor of circumstance had adversely affected his classical productivity. These were the months of gestation of *A Shropshire Lad*.

Now throughout the 400-odd pages of his classical *oeuvre* up to 1897, wherein he is, apropos of this textual point or that, surveying and appealing to the usage of the Latin poets, he sooner or later necessarily refers to all the classical authors, not only the one with whom he is dealing, but all those having some bearing, however remote, on the text he is endeavouring to settle. For example, in his most brilliant paper 'Emendationes Propertianae' (published in 1888) he is at one point discoursing on the operations of magic and music in connection with rivers: within the space of a single page he refers to Virgil, Tibullus, Ovid, Petronius, Seneca, Lucan, Calpurnius, Silius Italicus, Valerius Flaccus and Claudian. Glancing over the four pages of his article 'Adversaria Orthographica' we may extend this list to include Plautus, Cicero, Lucretius, Catullus, Horace, Propertius, Persius, Quintilian, Martial, Juvenal and Priscian. One casually turns the pages of *CP* I and here and there lights on yet a fresh name (I restrict myself to Latin writers): (p. 47) Pliny the Elder, Servius, Velius Longus, Donatus, Charisius; (p. 152, expressly quoted from the lexicons) Terence, Ausonius, Acron, Celsus, Livy; (p. 155, taken from Nettleship) Jerome; and presently the Elder Seneca, Apuleius, Tertullian, Aulus Gellius, Statius, Livius Andronicus, Vegetius, Lucilius, Nonius and – but let me no longer delay my point. It is this. In all Housman's published work there is not a single reference to Manilius until the year 1896–7 when, almost at the end of his dazzling set of articles on Ovid's *Heroides* (p. 409), he brings in, rather unnecessarily, Manilius 1.795 and proposes, to solve a metrical corruption in that line, two solutions, neither of which in the event found a place in his edition.

It follows that Housman had no firsthand knowledge of Manilius until this date. True, he must have known the existence of Manilius's poem; he had included an encomium of Bentley in his London *Inaugural Lecture* (1892) and must have read Monk's *Life of Bentley* and Jebb's monograph (1882), wherein Bentley's Manilius receives handsome attention. Nevertheless, there is no evidence to show that Housman had conceived a special interest in the astrological poet before close to the end of the century: there are two references to Manilius in 'Lucretiana' published in 1897 (*CP* II, pp. 431 and 439), but the former certainly and the latter possibly had come to Housman's notice out of context.

Marcus Manilius is the author of the earliest astrological treatise extant, *Astronomica*, a Latin hexameter poem in five books, composed in the second decade of our era probably in Rome. A mediocre poet, he is an outstanding poetaster, memorable for witty rhetoric and 'that eminent aptitude for doing sums in verse which is the brightest facet of his genius'.[6] Antiquity records neither work nor author. The earliest manuscripts, of the eleventh century, are so corrupt as to be barely intelligible; not surprisingly the poem received little attention. But the implicit challenge to make sense of it provoked first Scaliger and then Bentley, the greatest of classical scholars, to put forth their utmost powers in editions which in the event showed them capable of performing miracles of elucidation. Notwithstanding these achievements Housman was later to match their feats.

We must be careful to disavow the assumption that Housman, interested in astronomy from childhood, was specially drawn to the astrological poet Manilius, for he believed in astrology even less than he believed in God. He relates himself[7] that interest in astronomy awoke in him as a child, and his brother Laurence tells[8] us of a game he once arranged on the garden lawn: 'I was the sun, my brother Basil the earth, Alfred was the moon. My part in the game was to stay where I was and rotate on my own axis; Basil's was to go round me in a wide circle rotating as he went; Alfred, performing the movements of the moon skipped round him without rotation.' But Housman (perhaps about ten years old at the time) did not continue and deepen his astronomical interest, which never, to the end of his life, rose above an elementary level or was pursued farther than sufficed to elucidate references to celestial phenomena in ancient literature. Laurence goes on to say: 'In the later years of our youth it was Robert, not Alfred, who gave most time to a study of the heavens, and devised for his own use a large telescope ingeniously made out of cameralenses.'

How Housman's interest, and indeed his life's consuming passion, were engaged in Manilius will be revealed clearly enough if we consider the state of Manilian studies in the Victorian period. The standard text was that of Friedrich Jacob (Berlin, 1846), a useful if unlovely book, but marred by much error and a highly obscurantist text, which made Manilius appear a most forbidding author.

In 1891 Robinson Ellis, a Fellow of Trinity College, Oxford, brought out his *Noctes Manilianae*, textual notes written in limpid Latin on several hundred passages in the *Astronomica*. He was a very strange man. One contemporary[9] wrote that, as remarkable for the size of his boots, whose toes turned up in a peculiar way, as for his ill-fitting coats, he appeared to live in a world of his own, from which he would suddenly emerge with devastating observations, as for example a remark he addressed to a colleague just married to an attractive bride: 'I wonder how long it will take you to get as tired of your wife as I am of my sisters.' My favourite Ellis story concerns a journey he made to Paris to collate manuscripts in the Bibliothèque Nationale: he was so anxious not to waste a moment that he took a taxi from the Gare du Nord to his hotel, dropped his bags there and proceeded by the same taxi to the library. There he spent several happy hours until closing time, when, firmly ushered to the exit, he there realized that he had not the faintest recollection of the name or location of his hotel, and he remained in something of a trance on the front steps until he was arrested by the police for loitering. The resources of the Parisian gendarmerie proved equal to the occasion: when the professor's story eventually came out, it was realized that the cab driver who had transported him could hardly forget so singular a creature: the cabbie and through him Ellis's hotel were located within the hour. I have thought this preamble justified, for in the realm of Latin textual criticism also Ellis cut a bizarre figure, and Housman did not exaggerate when, looking back on the *Noctes Manilianae* many years later, he remarked: 'The corrections of Ellis were rather more numerous, and one or two of them were very pretty, but his readers were in perpetual contact with the intellect of an idiot child.'[10]

Ellis's dealings with Manilius were not finished when in 1893 he lighted on a fifteenth-century manuscript of the poet in Madrid (M), which he saw to be full of new and interesting readings; and in several fascicles of the *Classical Review* for that year he published a collation of its text. In 1897, the year in which, as we have seen, Housman first refers to Manilius, the prominent Cambridge Latinist J. P. Postgate brought out – this too in Latin – his *Silua Maniliana*, a tract of some 70 pages, to which we should add a continuation of eight pages, *Siluae Manilianae Appendix*, which he published in the *Journal of Philology* for the following year.

Ellis seems not to have apprehended that in M he had found the most valuable of the extant MSS of Manilius. Nor was this any more apparent to Postgate, though Part 3 of his treatise was devoted to an appraisal of the manuscript's worth. Housman, however, realized it at once and proceeded to take advantage of his deeper perception. In 1895 he had conducted with Postgate an acrimonious debate over the MSS of Propertius.[11] His address as a controversialist enabled him to leave the field with dignity, and scholars unfamiliar with this complicated and even today not wholly settled problem might fancy that Postgate got the worse of it. But if we consider impartially the propositions at issue and forget the personalities, we shall be forced to conclude that Housman's cause was dealt a lethal blow: his genealogy of the Propertian MSS, which had to date constituted his most ambitious thesis, was after his encounter with Postgate left in ruins. Henceforth his interest in Propertius declined precipitously: the wonderful edition of this poet for which he had prepared the world and for which many continued to entertain hopes was in fact abandoned.

Some of Housman's admirers imply that he was preternaturally gifted with the desire for truth. At the risk of splitting hairs I venture to disagree, and suggest that what they really have in mind is an insistence on accuracy and a hatred of inaccuracy. 'Accuracy is a duty and not a virtue,' he famously declared:[12] but this is arrant casuistry; one might as well declare that virtues themselves are duties and thus do not merit praise, that only blame can be earned, when duty has been neglected. Indeed, he seems to say as much in his review of volume 3 of Postgate's *Corpus*: 'I have spent most of my time in finding faults . . . because finding faults is the most useful sort of criticism.'[13] Strange that in 95 years no one has objected that the positive aim of finding merits may be an equally useful and in certain respects a more important province of criticism. Housman's strength was intellectual not moral. I do not of course mean to question his essential integrity and nobility of soul, but many others possess these qualities. When he castigates lesser scholars with a spiteful scourge, we should not exculpate his infliction of pain by irrelevantly endowing him with the purest reverence for truth: this does not dwell in a soul habituated to fierce passion and intemperate invective.

There is nothing like a jaundiced view of a rival for giving a spur to one's desire to shine and for galvanizing one's determination to slaughter the opposition. Foiled in his ambition to build on Propertius a reputation as a scholar of the highest rank, Housman seems about 1897 to have conceived that Manilius offered the ideal means of realizing his dearest ambition. Here was an author who, even after Scaliger and Bentley had exerted their full powers to elucidate his text, still remained so perplexing as to be beyond the generality of classicists. Moreover, a precious new manuscript had just been discovered with none likely to anticipate him in mining the gold it contained.

This account of the process by which about 1897 Housman single-mindedly decided on his life-work in scholarship is corroborated by his own statements and action.

> When I first sat down to read Manilius through, I provided myself with the Delphin edition, Thomas's collation of G, and Ellis's so-called collation of M; and thus equipped I found out for myself more than half of those emendations of Scaliger which Fayus did not record, about one-third of Bentley's, and almost all of Breiter's and Ellis's and their fellows.[14]

Boastful, but there is no reason to doubt his word. In the *Journal of Philology* for 1899 appeared a short article placing on record and without argument Housman's conjectures (some 50 in number) for Manilius, Book 1. This first book may be described as a Latin counterpart of Aratus, and being nothing if not thorough, Housman published in *Classical Review* of 1900 such a comprehensive article on the text of Germanicus's *Aratea* that it is virtually an edition on its own. A similar paper concerning the *Aratea* of Cicero and Avienus occupied six pages of *CR* in 1902. In *JP* for 1901 appeared his conjectures on Manilius, Book 5, again without argument, these numbering just under 40. By this method of publication Housman was able to establish his claim to priority for these emendations. On a point of separate interest we note that he passed from Book 1 (which, as I said, is like Aratus's *Sphaera* and deals with a description of the heavens, that is elementary astronomy) to Book 5, which, in sharp contrast to the technical astrological nature of Books 2, 3 and 4, may be regarded as a collection of character sketches typifying the kinds of men born under the influences of various constellations.

In 1903 appeared the first instalment of Housman's Manilius, a full-scale edition of Book 1 with commentary, together with an appendix consisting of his emendations of Books 2, 3 and 4 given, as with the emendations of Books 1 and 5 published in *JP*, without argument: these amounted to over 150. In the actual text of Book 1 many conjectures previously published by himself were abandoned, but continued endeavour to restore the text led to his claiming some 46 conjectural readings.

Irrespective of the truth of all these conjectures (and obviously it is not possible to invoke some infallible touchstone to serve as an objective means of measurement), the quality of Housman's work soared high above anything in contemporary scholarship: in England one had to go back to Bentley to find a parallel to the astonishingly original detection and solution of problems; in Europe one could cite Lachmann's Lucretius as the most epoch-making edition of the nineteenth century (though this had done more for Latin philology than for Lucretian studies). Housman's Manilius was a work which silenced criticism. Nevertheless, its nonpareil scholarship was not the feature which riveted the attention of the academic world. The edition was prefaced by a dedication poem of 28 lines in Propertian elegiacs of such polished artistry and emotional power that Gilbert Murray declared it was the only modern Latin verse he had ever read that might have come from the lips of a classical poet, and then – here was the bombshell – the introduction proper, 75 pages of sustained and all but actionable abuse of the editors of Manilius, the editors of other Latin authors, Latin scholars as a whole, mankind in general and indeed even God.

The peerless elegance and wit of Housman's style and the knockout punches he landed made it impossible to brush aside this sort of criticism as one might a discontent's hot abuse. Consider this treatment of one of Germany's foremost Latinists. The manuscripts of Manilius offer at 5.609 the form *renauit*: attempting to justify the initial long syllable Friedrich Vollmer suggested that it was to be interpreted as *re-enauit*, 'swam forth again'. Says Housman: 'A very pretty verb, formed, I presume on the analogy of reeo, reintegro, reoleo, reundo, and rearguo.' (Sarcasm, as the verbs are in fact *redeo, redintegro, redoleo, redundo* and *redarguo*.) Now comes the sledge-hammer: 'Mr Vollmer has been appointed editor in chief of the Thesaurus Linguae Latinae.' Occasionally the sledge-hammer was discarded in favour of the pillory:

Its original leaders [he is talking of the fashion for conservatism], as usually happens to those who instruct mankind in easy and agreeable vices, are far outdone by their disciples ... The apprentices proceed to exegetical achievements of which their masters are incapable, and which perhaps inspire those masters less with envy than with fright: indeed I imagine that Mr Buecheler, when he first perused Mr Sudhaus' edition of the Aetna, must have felt something like Sin when she gave birth to Death.

The morose and resentful attitude to life which one frequently comes across in Housman's poetry is no less common in his Manilius:

> Chance and the common course of nature will not bring it to pass that the readings of a MS are right wherever they are possible and impossible wherever they are wrong: that needs divine intervention; and when one considers the history of man and the spectacle of the universe I hope one may say without impiety that divine intervention might have been better employed elsewhere. How the world is managed, and why it was created, I cannot tell; but it is no feather-bed for the repose of sluggards.

What must have staggered the classical world was the whole-sale onslaught on editors of Latin texts: hardly any Latinist of note escaped unscathed – one such was Postgate whose special form of insult was that his *Silua Maniliana* was listed by title without comment – but the rest (and omitting Manilian scholars), Ehwald, Hosius, Klotz, Vahlen, Birt, Leo all came under the lash; Mayor, whom he was to succeed in the Cambridge chair, can hardly have felt flattered to read 'To Mr Mayor's edition [of Juvenal] one resorts for other things, but not for help in difficulties.' And a particularly cruel attack is made on S. G. Owen.

Savageness of criticism was not a new phenomenon in the academic world, but it had never been exercised in quite this unprovoked fashion. One has to remember many factors to arrive at a reasonable explanation of this violent outburst. Housman knew well enough that he had performed dazzling feats and in an ideal world would have received the instant accolade of universal recognition; but he also knew that among his contemporaries his genius might pass unnoticed or, if noticed, unacknowledged: many would permanently judge him by his failure in Greats. Beside himself with chagrin at this prospect he decided to assert his own rank in the hierarchy of scholarship by speaking out rather than condoning the ignorance of others by keeping silent.

On page 19 of *A. E. Housman, A Sketch*, A. S. F. Gow asserts that Housman had not at the time of publication of Book 1 (that is 1903) decided to embark on an edition of the whole poem. This is demonstrably incorrect, as I pointed out in an early article,[15] drawing from Gow an angry letter saying that Housman had told him so and 'that settles the matter'. The matter is worth settling because H. W. Garrod, thinking, like Gow, that Housman had finished with Manilius, embarked in 1907 upon an ambitious edition of Book 2, which appeared in 1911: he was intensely mortified when in the next year came Housman's very much superior one.

The facts are these. In a number of places in his Book 1 Housman announces that he is proposing to continue his edition: p. lxxiii: 'The sacred name of Posidonius, if I remember right, is not once mentioned in my notes; and when I come to II 96 I shall not pretend that Manilius, or Catullus either, imbibed from the manuals of that Rhodian sage the daring theory that the moon's light is borrowed'; bottom of the same page: 'I will here transcribe my note on IV 451' (and transcribes the Latin note of nearly 50 lines which in 1920 appeared in his Book 4). Immediately at the end of Book 1 he pre-publishes his note on 2.3. In the body of the Latin commentary he occasionally looks ahead to future annotations (implying that these were already composed): for example, at 1.76 in his note on *orbes* glossed as *terras* he quotes 4.677 and says *ubi plura dicam* ('where I shall say more'); likewise at the end of a very long note on 1.245 he emphasizes that he has omitted discussion of cases like 2.541, *ad quem uersum plura apponam* ('where I shall give more examples'). Moreover, on 10 September 1903 he wrote to Grant Richards, who had just offered Housman an annotated copy of Manilius from his father's library:

> If I can find sufficient industry, I hope to go on with the Manilius; but not immediately, because at this moment I am rather sick of writing and want to read; moreover Book 2 is the most serious job of the whole lot. I am sure your father's annotations would be valuable.

A man of Housman's reserve would not wish to disclose to a gossip like Grant Richards that he had resolved to make an edition of Manilius his life's work. No doubt what he said to Gow (whom I do not disbelieve) similarly closed the door on further discussion.

The interval which elapsed between Book 1 and Book 2 is

sufficiently explained in the letter to Richards; the background reading necessary for editing Book 2, the chief astrological part of Manilius's poem, occupied Housman for several years; some indication may be gleaned from Housman's paper in *CQ* 1908 on Dorotheus of Sidon; and since the material on which this paper is based is Kroll's edition of the *Catalogus Codicum Astrologorum Graecorum*, volume 6, 1903, it is likely that throughout this period he was laying the foundations of his unrivalled knowledge of Greek astrology. Another paper 'Astrology in Dracontius' (*CQ* 1910) points in the same direction.

At all events, when in 1912 Manilius 2 appeared, Housman's mastery of the field was evident. This time the prefatory material in English was devoid of general polemic and consisted of an astrological introduction of 31 pages not merely expounding Manilius 2 but collecting parallels from the Greek astrological writers of antiquity. No reader, from page 1 onwards, was left in any doubt about Housman's easy familiarity with what in 1912 was a library of very rare Greek books: Paulus Alexandrinus (ed. 1586); Ptolemy's *Tetrabiblos* (ed. 1535); Porphyry's commentary on Ptolemy (ed. 1559). To these add Firmicus Maternus, Vettius Valens, Maximus, the scholia on Germanicus, Sextus Empiricus, Hephaestion of Thebes, Geminus, the ancient commentaries on Aratus, Manetho, and all the volumes so far published of *CCAG*; and not only the primary but the secondary sources, Bouché-Leclercq's *L'Astrologie Grecque* and, much more impressive, Salmasius's *De annis climactericis.* All this erudition is very lightly carried.

In Book 3, published in 1916, a 28-page English preface continued this stupendous display of learning in Housman's beautiful and witty prose. A few extracts suffice to show its readability:

p. vi   Liars need not have long memories if they address themselves to fools, who have short ones; and an astrological poet writing his third book may safely forget his second, because an astrological reader will never remember it. But the impious and attentive sceptic will not fail to remark that some of the goods now packed in these compartments have already been stowed elsewhere.

p. ix   Pingré's attempt to wrest the words out of their sense is repeated by Breiter, who assists our calculations by figuring a nocturnal geniture, tafel II 4, in which the sun is high overhead and the hour is about ten o'clock

in the morning: the 12 athla, in not unnatural conster-
nation, have hereupon abandoned the order which
Manilius in verse 168 declares to be immutable, and
are chasing each other round the circle hind-before. No
stranger night-scene was ever witnessed by Walrus or
by Carpenter.

p. xxi (on finding the horoscope: an apostrophe to the poet)
Alas, alas! This alternative method of yours, my poor
Marcus, is none other than the vulgar method which
in 218–24 you said you knew, and which in 225–46 you
exposed as false. The wolf, to whom in his proper shape
you denied admittance, has come back disguised as your
mother the goose, and her gosling has opened the door
to him.

Book 4 duly came out in 1920 and the last book in 1930.

I have so far not much referred to the Latin commentary. I
have to admit that when in Housman's centenary year I referred
to his Latin style[16] I contrasted it unfavourably with Scaliger's
and Bentley's and even with Robinson Ellis's, judging their Latin
to be more spontaneous. But I was unfair to Housman: his Latin
is invariably idiomatic and elegant. It may be said that intoler-
ance of his predecessors' shortcomings often strikes a discordant
note as we proceed through the work. After having definitively
explained a matter, he will add, for example, *dico propter Fayum*
('This note is prompted by Fayus's error'), and often garnish his
comment with opprobrious remarks. Thus at 4.653 in rejecting a
conjecture of Bentley's he says that even though they knew it
came from him, Jacob, Bechert, Breiter and van Wageningen were
able to accept it *propterea quia inutile esset ac falsum* ('only because
it was futile and wrong'). I have noted about a hundred gratui-
tous insults of this kind. Sometimes there is a feeble attempt at
humour, e.g. 5.552 *qui ridere uolet, legat Fayum eiusue uerba mutuatum
Wageningenum* ('If you want a laugh, just read Fayus's note, which
van Wageningen took over verbatim'). Housman's contempt for
lesser scholars induces him to ridicule where he might have
applauded: at 1.895 the new-found M had facilitated the correction of a difficulty in the text which Housman had missed but
van Wageningen had spotted; this is acknowledged in the words
Wageningeno semel accidit ut probabilem coniecturam faceret ('Once
and once only did van Wageningen make a probable conjecture');

and the same ungenerous spirit obtrudes again at 5.463, where a neat but unobvious conjecture of Ellis's elicits the following shameful compliment: *hic enim Ellisium largius solito ineptiarum copia exuberantem miseratus deus semel ei emendationem subiecit quam a sagaci critico inuentam credideris* ('Here with Ellis wallowing in an excess of stupid ideas God for once felt pity for him and slipped him the emendation of a discerning critic'). Housman's mordant wit had plenty of scope: at 4.422 Manilius says *cadit post paulum gratia ponti*, 'the grace of the seashore soon comes to an end'. Now the scribe of GL, his mind on church liturgy, miscopied this as *cadit post paulum gratia Christi*, whereupon Housman says *gratiam Christi post Paulum cecidisse tam uerum quam generi humano luctuosum est*, 'that the grace of Christ came to an end after St Paul is as true as it was disastrous for mankind'. We meet the same alertness at 5.168 *pilarum* 'of balls': here one manuscript has the variant *pilatum*. Housman tersely observes *Pontii procuratoris Iudaeae cognomen*, reminding us of the mental associations of medieval scribes and suggesting the reason for the miscopying.

Just as Housman, on the eve of releasing Manilius 1 and conscious that his abilities and achievement far outshone those of any rival, and conscious also that the academic world as a whole showed inadequate awareness of the fact, had abandoned all restraint and unleashed unprecedented personal attacks on those rivals, forcing the world to take notice of him, so in 1930, preparing to let go the final volume of his work, containing, besides text and commentary to Manilius's fifth book and two appendices about the manuscripts, detailed addenda and corrigenda to the previous four books, he was overwhelmed by a similar frenzy of emotion. His first paragraph discloses that all these volumes were produced at his own expense and offered to the public at much less than cost price and that, in spite of this and a small run (only 400 copies being printed of each), the first alone had been exhausted. In a retrospective survey he gives vent to his feelings as he had done in Manilius 1.

By this time Latinists had got to know and fear the edge to his tongue, but few of these can have been quite prepared for the crushing indictment systematically piled up over decades. The severity of the criticisms of the three scholars who had edited Manilius since 1903 has few parallels in the history of learning. Garrod, whose performance was distinctly meritorious, came off less bloodied than the rest. But that his treatment of Garrod was merciless may be demonstrated without quotation by the fact that the publisher of the volume was so alarmed that he wrote to Housman, saying that he thought some statements might be actionable and requesting him to take another look at what he had written. I have seen the letter but do not know what action Housman took in reply. A few samples will serve to give his opinion of Breiter's edition:

> ... his use and choice of emendation was haphazard, and his own new conjectures, extorted by the task of editing, were without exception worthless ... His eyesight was evidently feeble, and did not serve him well in collating MSS or correcting proofs; but that is not enough to account for the bucketfuls of falsehood which he discharged on an ignorant and confiding public ... Breiter's chief purpose [in his commentary, vol. 2] was to explain for novices the astrology of the poem, but his knowledge of the subject was neither original nor adequate ... Falsehoods, blunders of every sort and size, self-contradictions, misinterpretations, miscalculations, misquotations, and misprints leave few pages undisfigured.

'It is comprehensible' he continues, 'that Breiter and Mr Garrod should aspire to edit Manilius or a book of Manilius, and should attempt the enterprise; but why Jakob van Wageningen took it into his head that the world would be better for an edition from him, and fetched his paste and scissors to this particular spot, I cannot imagine.' His indictment of van Wageningen's Manilius, though it extends over several pages of small print, is not as long as Cicero's Second Philippic, but it is just as devastating, because the charges, against his intelligence and his moral character, are unanswerable. Unlike Pliny the Elder, who believed that every book contained something of value, Housman had become, where his own scholarly reputation even remotely came into question, pathologically hostile to colleagues; he approached every book of theirs not as a grateful recipient of their contributions, but as a criminal prosecutor out for the death penalty.

However, my concern is not to judge the vituperation in Housman's Manilius[17] but to try to explain its psychological causes. What gave most offence to Hugh Stewart, Professor of Latin at Nottingham, who reviewed Manilius 5 in *CR* 1931, was not so much the ferocity of his attacks as the self-praise Housman permitted himself in laying down the qualifications for being a textual critic and then giving himself full marks for possessing them. Let one example suffice of his excessive confidence in his own powers. On p. xxxiv of Manilius 5 we read: 'If I had to name three of my own conjectures which I judge to be quite certain, I should be inclined to choose I 423 *eguit Ioue* for *esurcione*, IV 800 *ubi ab his ope sumpta* for *ubi pisces uruptor*, and V 461 *uix una trium* for *atri luxum.'* The first, let us concede, is quite certain; but the second is doubtful, and, as for the third, well, let us see. Here the poet is classifying Aquarius babies born when Cepheus is rising; among them will be tragedians: † *atri luxum* † *memorare sepulchri* (0^2: −*a* O) . . . *iuuabit* 'they will love to tell . . . a grave'. The context makes clear that Manilius is alluding to the awful banquet of Thyestes, to whom his brother Atreus served up the cooked bodies of his sons. From his very début as a scholar Housman was much intrigued by the way individual letters of words showed a propensity to become transposed: Manilius 1, pp. liv–lix are filled with examples, and he was quite justified in putting forward emendations which presuppose this kind of corruption (at 5.689 *sed nota* is felicitously emended to *detonsa*). Here his anagrammatic skill leads him to conjure out of the transmitted text *uix una trium memorare sepulchra* (which might lead to *liixun atri um* and then *atri luxum*): noting the antithesis of *una* and *trium* and remembering that Thyestes had three sons he concluded that his emendation was quite certain: 'They will love to tell of scarcely a single grave for three.' But this is not merely a cryptic allusion to the Thyestean dinner, it is a clumsy and inadequate one, unworthy of Manilius's rhetorical dexterity. Housman explains 'scarcely' by the fact that the sons were not wholly eaten (as grotesque as pedantic a modification). Then the plural *una sepulchra*, though it can be paralleled, is awkward in antithesis with *trium*. Even so Housman intimidated me (and doubtless others) into accepting his solution, and it was left to W. S. Watt (one of the foremost of living Latinists) to point out (in *CQ* 1995) that the most appropriate rhetoric would have been for Manilius to say 'they will love to tell of burial in a living grave', which is what Bentley conjectured nearly 300 years ago: *uiui bustum memorare sepulchri*. Here palaeography is an unsafe guide, for *atri* is less likely a corruption of the irrelevant (un)*a* tri(um) than a gloss *Atr(e)i*, the villain of the piece (*atri* otherwise would be an astounding coincidence). Of the variants *sepulchri* is that given by the corrector of the archetype, *sepulchra* by the archetype itself: the former was rejected by Housman on the grounds that it was interpolated under the influence of *atri*, but *sepulchra* was just as likely interpolated by someone wanting to supply an object for the verb. Bentley aptly quotes Lucretius 5.993 *uiua uidens uiuo sepeliri uiscera busto*.

Ironically, Housman, who too confidently claimed his conjecture as certain and placed it in the text, was also capable of excluding from the text much more cogent emendations of his own. In 1932 Housman produced (with the Cambridge University Press) a plain text of Manilius with a brief apparatus criticus. The work is chiefly noteworthy for the beauty of its typographical presentation (which from Housman's letters we are able to confirm was his main aim). That old age accentuates tendencies towards conservatism I should not aver as a general truth, but this edition marks a regression so far as his textual acumen is concerned. Let me give two examples. At 5.663 the poet is talking about fishermen: they catch tunny, according to the archetype, *macularum nomine*: in his large edition Housman had explained that, if sound, this means 'by that which we term meshes', 'by so-called meshes', and had illustrated this particular Latin usage. However, in Caroline minuscule *o* and *e* are confused on every page, and after we have got deep into Housman's note we are electrified to be informed that he nurses a suspicion that what the poet wrote was *macularum nemine*, *nemine* from the rare word *nemen*, 'by a network of meshes'. Of course! This is clearly what Manilius wrote, nor was a more certain conjecture ever made. But for all that, the emendation (one of Housman's best) is, so far from being placed in the text, not even mentioned in the apparatus.

Similarly at 3.228: the signs of the zodiac rise in an upright or slanting posture in proportion as a sign is close or distant from us: *ut propius nobis aliquod uel longius astrum est*. This, however, is factually quite false, and in 1903 Housman had transposed the line in an attempt to reconcile it with truth. In his *editio maior* (1916) he inclines to attribute the error to the poet, citing some similar loose thinking from Geminus. However – and again the attentive reader is thrilled at the brilliant and totally satisfying nature of the emendation – Housman observes that what Manilius should have said was that the perpendicular or oblique stance of the zodiacal sign varies in proportion with its proximity to the equinoctial points or nodes. That is, Manilius should have said *ut propius nodis aliquod* and so on. Lucretius uses the word in this sense and it occurs in Manilius's vocabulary: it seems decidedly more probable that the poet wrote *nodis* than *nobis* and on that basis I have placed the word in the text: but in Housman's *editio minor* the emendation is not even mentioned in the apparatus.

To conclude: Housman's Manilius is not the flawless work of scholarship that one might gather from the laudations it has received. Housman hardly embarked upon it in an entirely disinterested spirit: he aspired to build himself a monument, and in the process of this achievement – fearing it might not be justly appreciated – he certainly did not spare his fellow-toilers in the field, emphasizing their shortcomings and their inferiority to himself. Throughout his attacks upon inaccuracy and incompetence, as throughout his poetry, we frequently hear the Leitmotif of the unjust universe, which it is difficult not to ascribe in some measure to awareness of his homosexuality: some see even in his failure in Greats the emotional upset caused by this realization. It is not improbable that his criticism was honed to a sharp edge by his condition, just as his poetry may have been to some extent precipitated by the same source. I repudiate the charge that he was a practising homosexual, for everything goes to show that he fought valiantly and successfully to transmute his tendencies into energy fuelling his consummate scholarship and his matchless poetry. His edition of Manilius, like all his classical work, even the flawed disquisition on the manuscripts of Propertius, will for the aspiring student never become antiquated. In studying Housman, even when we disapprove of his tone or sense that he is in error, we are constantly made to recognize that we are in the company of a brave and commanding presence; and if this is Housman's immortality and, for those of us who share his interests, the joys of paradise, as near as we can approach them, let us not disdain to dwell in this heaven or think it less real than the hereafter of men's prayers.

Notes

1. Laurence Housman, *A. E. H.* (London: Jonathan Cape, 1937) p. 99.
2. Relevant information bearing on the whole matter is provided by Grant Richards, *Housman 1897–1936* (London 1941) pp. 260–3.

3. Richard Perceval Graves, *A. E. Housman The Scholar-Poet* (London: Routledge & Kegan Paul, 1979) p. 250.

4. Housman's correspondence is quoted from *The letters of A. E. Housman*, ed. Henry Maas (London: Rupert Hart-Davis, 1971): to Katharine Symons, see pp. 339, end para. 1; 340, end para. 1; and 341, para. 2; and to Percy Withers, see p. 346, end para. 3.

5. *The Classical Papers of A. E. Housman/collected and edited by J. Diggle and F. R. D. Goodyear* (3 vols continuously paged, CUP 1972), hereafter referred to as *CP*.

6. *Manilius* 2, xiii.

7. *The Letters of A. E. Housman*, edited by Henry Maas (1971) p. 328.

8. Op. cit. (n.2), p. 22.

9. Sir Charles Oman, *Memories of Victorian Oxford* (London: Methuen, 1941) p. 203 ('But his eccentricity was more than external: he was one of the oddest psychological problems that I ever met').

10. *Manilius* 5, xxiii.

11. Postgate in *Transactions of the Cambridge Philological Society* IV, 1 (82 pages), Housman in *CR* 9 (1895) 19–29 (*CP* I 351–68).

12. *Manilius* 5, p. 105 (= *Manilius* 1^2, 87).

13. *CR* 14 (1900) 469 (= *CP* II 531).

14. *Manilius* 5, xviii, footnote †.

15. 'Adversaria Maniliana,' *Phoenix* 13 (1959) 94. I later discovered that my correction of Gow had been anticipated by P. Hedley in the *TLS*, 30 January 1937, 76 and that Gow (ibid., 6 February 1937) had answered him as he answered me.

16. Op. cit. (n.15), p. 95.

17. The vituperation in the Juvenal (1905, 1931^2) and Lucan (1926) prefaces is to be similarly explained.

9

Lewis Carroll in Shropshire

John Bayley

What sort of a man would write to a colleague, not a close friend but someone he did not know very well: 'I rather doubt if man has really much to gain by substituting peace for strife, as you and Jesus Christ recommend'?

Doesn't it sound as if he might be a thoroughly tiresome person, theatrical, a show-off, perhaps wearing a beard and a velvet collar, the sort of aesthete who might have frequented the Café Royal in the 1890s, sending occasional bad and daring poems to avant-garde magazines? The sort of man who would have been proud to claim acquaintance, say, with Frank Harris, the hard-drinking journalist who boasted of his sexual conquests in *My Life and Loves*?

Well, it is easy to get things wrong; and particularly easy where Alfred Edward Housman, poet and classical scholar, is concerned. I once thought, and indeed wrote, 'we always know where we are with Housman'. Now I don't feel so sure. One of the most fascinating things about that ever-fascinating man is that his personality is both extremely definite and remarkably evasive. And nowhere does he both conceal and reveal himself more effectively than in his own writings.

And yet he is so direct, so ironically absolute. Particularly at the expense of other poets, and other scholars. His shock tactics here could make him highly unpopular, but the *persona* they made feared, and frequently disliked, is the man whom Alfred Edward H. was quite prepared to put on show for the purpose. This is how he went on, in the letter to his colleague Gilbert Murray, the Oxford liberal humanist professor, and translator of the Greek classical playwrights:

> Last Easter Monday a young woman threw herself into the
> Lea because her dress looked so shabby amongst the holiday

crowd; in other times and countries women have been rav-
ished by half a dozen dragoons and taken it less to heart. It
looks to me as if the state of mankind always had been and
always would be a state of just tolerable discomfort.

'God is not mocked', he mocks the good Guardian-minded
Murray, with his humane views. If society and civilization succeed by their well-meaning efforts in improving the lot of human
beings, 'nature soon sets to work' and makes 'seven pounds as
heavy a burden to bear as fourteen pounds used to be'.

Gentle Gilbert Murray may well have been shocked by the tone
of Housman's letter; and yet it seems clear that Housman was
genuinely sorry, in his own peculiar way, for the sad if rather
silly young woman who had drowned herself on Easter Bank
Holiday. Clearly he took an interest not only in the case itself
but in the girl's reasons for doing what she did, insofar as they
could ever be known. Not exactly vanity was her undoing but a
kind of self-respect, a wish for the graces of life that others –
herself too no doubt – felt were their due in the modern world.
Her response was a timeless one, but what brought it about was
– in Housman's view at least – too high an expectation of what
life owed her.

Housman knew from his own bitter experience that life never
gave you what you most longed for, whether it was a new dress
for a holiday, or the fulfilment of mankind's deepest wish: to
love and to be loved. When an army cadet at Woolwich committed suicide, leaving for the coroner a note of remarkable dignity
and pathos, Housman wrote a poem (*A Shropshire Lad*, XLIV)
addressing the dead young man with passionate feeling and congratulation.

> Oh soon, and better so than later
>   After long disgrace and scorn,
> You shot dead the household traitor,
>   The soul that should not have been born.
>
> . . .
>
> Now to your grave shall friend and stranger
>   With ruth and some with envy come:
> Undishonoured, clear of danger,
>   Clean of guilt, pass hence and home.

The cadet had written: 'There is only one thing in the world which would make me thoroughly happy; that one thing I have no earthly hope of attaining.' That is in itself a moving statement by a man who has died for love, and Housman in particular knew very well what sort of love it was that the cadet had died for. And yet both the statement and the poem are moving documents – moving in terms of their art, which in both cases seems wholly unconscious and spontaneous, for the poem echoes wonderfully well, and perhaps quite consciously, the simple feeling in the statement. It is art in a different sense, notwithstanding, the kind of art to which, as Dr Johnson said of Gray's 'Elegy', 'every bosom returns an echo'.

In much the same way that Housman's letter to Murray, mentioning the suicide of the girl on Easter Monday, sounds as if it might have been written by quite a different sort of person, so the Shropshire Lad poem might have been written by a poet with no specific interest in why a young man had killed himself, but with a hearty interest in maintaining uprightness and moral integrity. Whatever it was the young man of the poem had done, he had felt himself to be on the verge of infamy in some form, and the poet who speaks to him does so in a tone of fervent and heartfelt congratulation. He dies as befitted a man.

But did Housman really feel death to be a proper way out in such a case? For all its air of frank and strong feeling, the poem is really very elusive, turning what had inspired it into a manly generalization. In the same way the poet Gray had turned his own personal feelings, of possibly much the same sort as Housman's, into the quiet authority and resignation of the elegiac stanzas, pursuing 'the silent tenor' of an individual doom which is also, and by extension, the general lot of man.

When Housman was Professor of Latin at London University he accepted a lunch invitation from Frank Harris and some of Harris's other journalist cronies. The lunch does not seem to have been a success. Like many others they had been impressed by the poems of *A Shropshire Lad*, whose reputation was beginning to make its way among readers and critics, and Harris in particular had been greatly taken by the opening poem, which commemorated the Golden Jubilee of Queen Victoria in 1887. Harris and his friends assumed it must be a mock celebration. What they felt they were appreciating was what they called 'the bitter sarcasm' of the poetry. Housman was not only greatly put out by this, but from the sound of it quite confounded as well, as if he had fallen into his own trap. He was furious at their attempt to flatter him by assuming he held the same views on royalty, patriotism and the British army as they did.

Harris and his pals of course turned the poet's anger to their own advantage. When he came to write his memoir, *Contemporary Portraits*, Harris professed great amusement at the indignant reply Housman had allegedly given to their complimentary bonhomie. 'I never intended to poke fun, as you call it, at patriotism, and I can find nothing in the sentiment to make mockery of: I meant it sincerely; if Englishmen breed as good men as their fathers, then God will save their Queen.' Admiring, but also mocking, laughter, no doubt, from those who heard him. Isn't the Professor too quaint?

So, on the basis of his own writings, Housman could appear quaint, or could appear almost diabolical. Both the raffish Frank Harris, and the good and hopeful Gilbert Murray, could, and did, in their different ways, get him wrong, or at least misunderstand him. Indeed it is the complex power of making itself possibly misunderstood, and in a variety of ways, which gives such remarkable flavour and personality to the poetic 'feel' of *A Shropshire Lad*. Any 'soldier poet', or poet writing admiringly about soldiers, in the nineteenth century, might have written about the 'Lads of the Fifty-Third', the Shropshire Light Infantry and their achievements in peace and war, in the same fervently admiring way that Housman seems to do, and indeed does so uncompromisingly. He loved soldiers, because for all his solitariness he was naturally patriotic, and even more importantly because soldiers represented for him a whole world of romance and love. They were quintessentially 'the lads', a word that for Housman expresses everything that love and yearning and heartbreak can mean. So the 'lads of the Fifty-Third' are a sacred talisman, inconspicuously placed by the poet at the front of his book.

But where a poet like Sir Henry Newbolt would have been rapt in simple (and self-congratulatory) enthusiasm for the 'Lads of the Fifty-Third', as he was for those exhorted to 'play up, play up, and play the game' of war, Housman introduces a much odder note into his poem, a more serious but also more sardonic one. And suddenly we see a flicker of the poet's own guarded but at moments quite confidential personality. He seems at such moments almost to be giving his reader a wink, an effect quite different

from the studiously sardonic tone for instance of the letter to
Gilbert Murray. This is all the more remarkable because it comes
at the very moment when he is celebrating 'the glorious dead',
as they are piously commemorated on so many war memorials.

> Now, when the flame they watch not towers
>   About the soil they trod,
> Lads, we'll remember friends of ours
>   Who shared the work with God.
>
> To skies that knit their heartstrings right,
>   To fields that bred them brave,
> The saviours come not home tonight:
>   Themselves they could not save.

(ASL I)

In his masterly essays on Housman, Christopher Ricks has
suggested that the poet is positively, and deliberately, blasphemous here; and all the more so because the reference to the
supreme sacrifice of Christ is so deadpan and unobtrusive. 'He
saved others; himself he cannot save'. And yet in terms of his
own poetry and personality Housman is being not so much blasphemous as quietly and even innocently sober. He is indeed dead
serious, and yet a joke lurks in this very seriousness, for the idea
of giving God a hand in this work of saving the Queen is surely
one that would have given the troops themselves a certain amount
of ribald amusement.

More important in the tone is what misled Harris and his friends.
In one sense they were right: the poem *is* irreverent – about Queen,
soldiers, the army, the Empire, life itself: none of its honours
and glories can or will be saved. The poem contains its own ir-
reverence inside the very deep and fervent reverence it feels for
the Queen and her army. Housman's own complex private and
public personalities intermingle in a manner that is both heartfelt and humorous. Christopher Ricks adds a further arresting
point, which brings Housman as classical scholar into a special
personal collusion with Housman the poet. In his introduction
to Housman's *Collected Poems and Selected Prose*, he suggests that
the poet can sometimes resemble a classical scholar, who is actually engaged on his own act of editorial imagination in the poem,

and putting an unexpected construction on the meaning of the poem while, as poet-editor, he is glossing it. He is artfully conjecturing, so to speak, his own text, making unexpectedly alive that something that generations of public men and years of public taking for granted have left poetically and linguistically for dead. The National Anthem has for years called on God to save the King or the Queen, but what does this really mean, and who in practice is doing the saving?

In an inspired metaphor the American critic Cleanth Brooks made the same sort of point in even more startling fashion. He suggested that what was normally a 'pious sentiment' and a 'patriotic cliché' was suddenly compelled, and as if to its own astonishment, to work in a normal English sentence. And this is as bizarre and even shocking, in its calm way, as if a bishop carrying his symbolic crozier had suddenly made use of it 'to lay hold on a live sheep'.

Housman's personality, in fact, is always a matter for surprise. He surprises us in many different ways, and not least by a kind of doubletake. Frank Harris, for instance, really did meet the Housman he expected to meet – the sardonic and sarcastic poet – and yet Housman happened to be not prepared to play the game according to Frank Harris principles. Intensely his own man, Housman never does, or seems to be, anything that is quite expected.

He does not even write comic verses in any vein which the genre normally produces, but makes the comic seem to depend on his own ordinariness, his very *lack* of oddity.

> Though some at my aversion smile
> I cannot love the crocodile

begins a poem which goes on to suggest that the crocodile is an admirable and public-spirited animal, because by eating unclad children by the banks of the Nile it helps to maintain the proprieties. That little fantasy, and the satire that goes with it, is conventional enough, but those two opening lines are pure Housman, gravely maintaining as they do that the poet is unique in disliking the reptile. The insinuation is that this very normal reaction is in some way ridiculous and peculiar, even though most people may be prepared to take a fairly tolerant attitude towards it. Housman is a perfectly normal person accused, and sometimes self-accused, though quite good-naturedly, of being abnormal: a comic version of the strange and haunting ambivalence in *A Shropshire Lad*. There, as the title indicates, the poet is just 'one of the lads', except that he is not; he is a character rather improbably called 'Terence', who writes verse that 'gives a chap the belly-ache.'

> Pretty friendship 'tis to rhyme
> Your friends to death before their time
> Moping melancholy mad:
> Come, pipe a tune to dance to, lad.

> (*ASL* LXII)

The poet longs passionately to be one of the lads, and yet he can't be: such is his personal make-up, which he is not going to inflict on his friends and the public except through the medium of verse.

Housman's insistence on his ordinariness, an insistence contradicted by everything in his personality and his art, none the less contrives never to become a pose. And the methods by which he escapes from the self-contended human acquiescence in being a striking or an unusual person are always in some way funny. When his publisher wrote to him in 1921, at a time when his fame and notoriety were at their height, that there were constant enquiries from admirers who longed to express their admiration face to face, Housman advised him to say that 'some men are more interesting than their books, but my book is more interesting that its man'. What stumps one about this judgement is that it is true, not just a modest disclaimer. *A Shropshire Lad* is of course more interesting than the man who wrote it, but in saying so the man who wrote it does not so much dissociate himself from the book as disappear into it, like Alice into Wonderland.

And it is a kind of wonderland, when the poet solemnly but quizzically informs us (*A Shropshire Lad* XVII) that he used to be a goalkeeper twice a week, and that 'Football then was fighting sorrow / For the young man's soul'. This element of absurdity masquerading as complete straightforwardness crops up again and again throughout Housman's writings, often accompanied by echoes from the Old Testament. The idea of 'the man of sorrows' having to choose between his dedication to grief and his prowess on the sports field ('See the son of grief at cricket / Trying to be glad') has a deadpan absurdity which ends in what seems a serious attempt to be reasonable and take a philosophical view of the matter:

> Try I will; no harm in trying:
>   Wonder 'tis how little mirth
> Keeps the bones of man from lying
>   On the bed of earth.

The tone – that of the little man of ordinary tastes and practices, faced with a situation appropriate to romantic despair – has the same comic reasonableness as the fate of the man whose aversion to crocodiles earns him nothing but tolerant amusement. Throughout all the range of his writing, Housman maintains the same deadpan use of comic incongruity, of the one who only wants to take an average man's reasonable view, and yet seems always to find himself in the position of odd man out. There are moments when one feels that Housman is most himself as the Lewis Carroll of Shropshire, a place populated by the rustic equivalent of White Knights and Red Queens.

The reasonable man who reads poetry, that usually crazy and incomprehensible stuff, is himself not seldom doomed to become the 'man of sorrows'. On the question of his poetry, Alfred Edward was as reasonable with his brother Laurence – a much more self-consciously odd and flamboyant character – as Terence, the Shropshire Lad, is reasonable with himself about seeking comfort on the cricket field. When Laurence produced a poem in which a group of fiery horses romantically, if obscurely, figure, his brother was not slow to point out the verbal difficulties, and the objections to mere good sense, in which he had landed himself. What tended to make the poem incomprehensible was that his brother did not put himself in the reader's place

and consider how, and at what stage, that man of sorrows is to find out what it is all about. You are behind the scenes and know all the data, but he only knows what you tell him. How soon do you imagine your victim will find out that you are talking about horses? Not until the thirteenth of these long lines, unless he is such a prodigy of intelligence and good will as I am.

The victim, the man of sorrows, is steadfast in his role, even when he is on the receiving end of an obscure poem and faced with the task of understanding it. Housman usually dealt with rival classical scholars, and their many learned imbecilities, in the same spirit, if a good deal less charitably. His pieces in the *Classical Review* or the *Journal of Philology* are always clear and incisive, easily understood by those who know little of the subject, and they are often very funny as well. In a good many of such cases there is the same impression that an Alice is loose at last in the wonderland of textual emendation, casting the still small glance of irreverent common sense on the mad mazes of Germanic conjecture. Nor are Germans the only target. An eccentric English scholar and Latin professor, W. J. Stone, once proposed a new method of translating classical hexameters into English. Since the genius of the English language is essentially monosyllabic, or so his opinion held, he maintained that it was both necessary and proper to do the job of naturalizing the hexameter as much as possible to fit English style and cadence, putting as many monosyllabic endings to the lines as possible. The good professor was quite prepared to admit that the results were not always satisfactory, and even confessed that they frequently sounded awkward, but he fell back on the curious argument that if we do not much care for such peculiar and discordant effects at first, 'we must get used to them'. The bee in his bonnet insisted that translation depended not on what sounded right, but what was most faithful to a fixed principle.

This gives Housman his chance. What an interesting idea it was that one could, and should, always try to get used to the difficulties and disadvantages of doing things a new way! Just because a translation, or indeed a work of art, may seem ugly and bad, that is no reason to take against it. We must just get used to the inconvenience of its being bad. Then why don't we do the same thing when it comes to building houses and living in them? Why not, for example, use gingerbread as a substitute for bricks and mortar? There might be some practical drawbacks, it is true, but when the householder fell through the floor, or when the rain came in on him, he had only to tell himself that it was necessary to get used to this novel and interesting method of construction.

There is a link between Housman's curious personality as the Lewis Carroll of Shropshire, and the distance that he always set between his professional and his poetic life. As himself a Shropshire lad in fantasy, he was fully aware of the absurdity of his position: a scholar and a man of reason who was condemned both to a hopeless and fiercely private love, and to the creation of a world of lads and chaps, soldiers and suicides, that were the visionary and public properties of that love in his poetry. And yet he strove, and always with success, for common sense and logic, honesty and reason. The unique thing about his poetry, and himself as a poet, is that he creates a completely romantic world, and yet himself inhabits it as a sceptical and even derisive spectator.

The world of romantic poetry had never produced that twist before. And yet it accounts in part for Housman's very great popularity. Philip Larkin followed him, perhaps unconsciously, and produced a comparable romantic world, and a popularity almost as great. In both cases what makes the spell – and it is a potent one – is the sensible, unillusioned intruder, who yet cannot do without the romantic world-landscape his poetry creates. The poet cannot forbear showing that he is not impressed by the things he most depends on emotionally: and yet, of course, they continue to inspire and fascinate him.

As romantic poems written from this new perspective, it is illuminating to compare *A Shropshire Lad* XXIII, 'The lads in their hundreds to Ludlow come in for the fair', with Larkin's poem 'The Whitsun Weddings'. The lads of Housman's poem are as deeply and seductively romanticized in their setting as are the just-married brides encountered by Larkin, on a slow train from Hull to King's Cross. The brides inhabit another world, and their appeal for the poet is precisely because they do inhabit it and the poet does not. Larkin's brides have all the mystery and charm of elsewhere, of the *Princesse lointaine*, that archetype of romantic longing; and this charm is ironically increased by the down-to-earth and highly unglamorous detail with which they, and their clothes, and their new husbands, are described. Larkin is bleakly though not bitterly amused by his own fascination with this unknowable life that is coming to its mysterious fulfilment somewhere else, in the peculiar and obscurely powerful metaphor which concludes the poem

> We slowed again,
> And as the tightened brakes took hold, there swelled
> A sense of falling, like an arrow-shower
> Sent out of sight, somewhere becoming rain.

The unknowable mystery in the equally commonplace background of Housman's poem is that at the fair he is full of the exciting knowledge that 'there with the rest are the lads that will never be old'.

> I wish one could know them, I wish there were
> tokens to tell
>   The fortunate fellows that now you can
>   never discern;
> And then one could talk with them friendly and
> wish them farewell
>   And watch them depart on the way that they
>   will not return.
>
> But now you may stare as you like and there's
> nothing to scan;
>   And brushing your elbow unguessed-at and
>   not to be told
> They carry back bright to the coiner the mintage of man,
>   The lads that will die in their glory and never be old.

The crowning metaphor here is equally mysterious, and in a sense equally illogical. A flight of arrows, a shower of rain, bright coins never worn with handling: the emphasis is not on what they signify, but on their potency as emblems of difference, things too separate to be known and understood. For Housman, as for Larkin, commonplace reality is itself the ultimate romance, which yet depends for its allure on its unattainability. And the power of their poems to thrill and to beguile the reader depends on the complex manner of their engagement with romance, and the highly individual personalities they display in the process. Housman as professor, Larkin as librarian, are both prosaic and often sardonic Lewis Carrolls in the wonderland of their romantic imaginations. Their meticulous and exacting temperaments are a foil to what they feel, and to the knowledge of a private impossibility which electrifies their poems.

The gulf between the land of Shropshire, where in Housman's imagination the denizens treated him as one of themselves, and the world of real chaps and lads with whom he did not mingle, is about as wide as it can be. Housman knows it; and it is this awareness, sometimes poignant, sometimes derisive, which creates his vivid variety as an individual. But in all circumstances he remains both reasonable and disenchanted, knowing his wonder-land for what it is. His own experiences there amuse him, and he creates a variety of tones in writing of them. The young man in *A Shropshire Lad* XIII, 'When I was one-and-twenty/ I heard a wise man say', is not the same young man at all as the gloomy fellow in the following poem. ('There pass the careless people/ That call their souls their own'.) He recites the platitudes told him by a wise man ('Give pearls away and rubies/ But keep your fancy free') and then caps them with his own pert comment:

> But I was one-and-twenty,
> No use to talk to me.

The sudden spurt of derision – at himself, at both young and old, at received wisdom and thoughtless folly – suggests that the world of romance and wonderland are never truer and more tyrannical than when they are there to be laughed at. So far from discred-iting them, disillusion shows their own true and terrible worth; and their power to break the heart that has seen through them:

> And I am two-and-twenty,
> And oh, 'tis true, 'tis true.

The poem began in tones of familiar and light-hearted artificial-ity – a 'pretence poem', full of the lightness of cliché ('keep your fancy free'). It is like so many that purport to give good advice, while keeping the reader diverted and amused. And so far from being transformed by a sudden contrast, that tone is maintained to the end, as it was in Housman's letter to Murray, or in the opening poem of *A Shropshire Lad*. The tone remains the same, but the import of the words suddenly changes; and the reason-able, observant, uncommitted man has a sudden tormented cry torn out of him. Both poems express what Susan Sontag has called the 'theatricalisation of experience'; but XIII is far more in keep-ing than its successor with Housman's native temperament, and with the uses his poetry makes of it. It is a perfect expression of the poet's own peculiar 'derision therapy'. The shock effect can be on a very long fuse, as it is in the opening poem of *A Shropshire Lad*, but is here on a very short one.

Housman is not usually thought of as an original or an inno-vative poet. His metres, his vocabulary and sentiments, are wholly traditional, steeped as they are in classical precedent and in the legacy of English and German poetry – Shakespeare and Blake, Burns, Heine and the ballad. But there is an important sense in which he added to this tradition not only the dimension of an unmistakably powerful and unique personality, that of a stricken lover and a professional scholar, a quietly rational humorist and 'pejorist', but a poet who added a new enclave to the traditional world of romantic longing. Like his great successor poet, Philip Larkin, he made the world he created all the more replete with an exactness of longing, a rough magic and a touching strangeness, by not seeming to take it very seriously. He is the supremely romantic poet who denies every tenet of romanticism: the rapt and yet unillusioned wanderer in his own wonderland.

10

The First Edition of
A Shropshire Lad in
Bookshop and Auction Room

P. G. Naiditch

I

Do the varying prices paid for the first edition of *A Shropshire Lad* reflect Housman's popularity at large?

Before addressing this question, it is necessary to define what is meant by the first edition and to discuss those factors, basic to the antiquarian book trade and to the auction market, which complicate the investigation of the sales of any book.

To identify the first British edition of *A Shropshire Lad* is easy. It is a work that exists in two forms. The earlier group, bound in February 1896 and numbering some 250 copies, carries what is called 'Label A'. The later group, bound around November 1896, carries what is called 'Label B'. This later group consists of about 100 ordinary copies and, with a cancel-title leaf dated New York 1897, numbers about 150 copies.[1] The first British edition therefore consists of some 350 copies. From this number a dozen had been taken by the author, another dozen sent to his friends; five were deposited with the Public Libraries; and 23 were sent for review. At length, in 1898, Laurence Housman purchased the last 'six copies of the first edition'.[2]

Investigation of the prices brought by copies of the first edition of *A Shropshire Lad* is complicated by several factors.

First, it needs to be remembered that interest in book collecting varies from place to place and time to time. Most people are uninterested in books; of the remainder, only a small portion collects rare books or first editions; and even these individuals may be unable to develop their collections according to their intentions and desires. Wars, pestilence, civil unrest, economic depression, devaluation of currencies, private misfortune, collusion, incompetence, bad weather and bad luck can affect the price a collector will pay for a book.

Secondly, fashions change. The topic that charms one generation of collectors may fail to interest another. For example, until the twentieth century, collectors had relatively little interest in rare medical writers. The result was that prices were low.[3] Conversely, in this century, interest in Christian sermons appears, among ordinary educated individuals, small in comparison with earlier days. But English literature seems, over the past hundred years, neither to have gained nor to have lost much of its standing. If the proportion of readers interested in it has declined, the actual number of readers seems to have been increased by the doubling and tripling of the population in Britain and North America respectively. Even so, inevitably, the valuation placed on different subgenres and on individual writers has fluctuated. With special reference to Housman, the movement away from lyrical verse towards free verse, at least among influential critics and practitioners of verse-craft, contributed for a time to Housman's unpopularity in certain quarters.[4]

Thirdly, it is not so much the rarity of a book as the amount of demand *vis-à-vis* the number of copies accessible that influences the price; and the amount of demand is a function of the romantic interest a book excites. There are some 48 copies of the Gutenberg Bible, but only a dozen of so of Blakeney's *A. E. H. W. W.* The last Gutenberg Bible to come to the market brought (including the 10 per cent buyer's premium) over five million dollars ($5 390 000 or about £3 147 000). The last *A. E. H. W. W.*, though nominally four times as scarce, commands not even two-hundredths of one per cent of that price.[5] The amount of interest in Housman's donation to the William Watson fund is, understandably, paltry.

Fourthly, even supposing a book is in demand, no two copies are precisely alike; and in their differences may be found elements affecting the volume's desirability. With regard to the first edition of *A Shropshire Lad,* presentation copies, copies with wrappers, unopened copies in superb condition and signed copies are, when recognized as extraordinary, likely to command higher prices than the usual first edition with label chipped and corners bumped and pages beginning to brown.[6]

Fifthly, the prices recorded in catalogues have to be used with care. A price listed in a bookseller's catalogue carries with it no guarantee that the volume found a purchaser at that price. It may not have been sold; it may have been sold for less than the listed price, or more, or made part of an exchange with another bookseller, scout, institution or private client; or it may have been lost, stolen or destroyed. With auctions, there are additional factors to take into account: reserves; skill in lotting; the auctioneer who takes bids from the 'chandelier'; rings, whether formal or informal; the status of a purchaser, for a dealer may act as an agent for a client; and, inevitably, the vagaries of fortune. With regard to the last, every bookman will have his favourite stories. The late Seymour Adelman has described his success in the Sotheby & Co. sale of 9 July 1968. He had decided not to bid, because he knew that the Lilly Library would want the same items as he and must be able to outbid him. The night before the sale, Adelman changed his mind. He rang a New York dealer who was in London for the sale, and gave him instructions to bid on a good many of the lots. In the event, the Lilly's representative was delayed by fog and only arrived as the sale was ending. 'I trust you agree with me', wrote Adelman, 'that nothing in all nature is so beautiful as fog.' Examples of books bringing more than the 'market value' likewise will be known to anyone interested in the subject. And of course one needs to be mindful, for example, of premiums, taxes and costs of packing and carriage.[7]

Sixthly, it has to be said that the record of sales is incomplete. Few copies are so described that, when they come once more onto the market, it is clear that they are to be identified with those offered before. Of some sixty copies of the first edition of *A Shropshire Lad* that have come my way, I have been unable to trace even half in the records of the marketplace. And only a handful have full and detailed histories from 1896 to the present.

II

Over the past century, first editions of *A Shropshire Lad* have been offered for sale or at auction over 220 times. This seems to be large enough a sample to allow trends in its pricing to be recognized.

During the first quarter century of its existence, *A Shropshire*

Lad was low priced. The earliest instance of a first edition changing hands occurs in 1897, while the book was still in print at half-a-crown. In that year, Housman's friend Henry Jackson, having arranged for the Trinity Book Club in Cambridge to acquire the first edition of *A Shropshire Lad* for 2s.6d., purchased it at the Club's auction for a shilling. Until the 1920s the first edition brought relatively little. Witter Bynner, likely enough before the first World War, purchased a copy for eight shillings. In 1916, Geoffrey Keynes obtained one for nine shillings.[8] Following the war, the price for the first edition began slowly to rise. In November 1919, a copy sold at auction for four pounds. In the next year, one sold for seven pounds. As late as March 1923, another was purchased at auction merely for £8.15s.[9]

It was the Quinn sale of 10 December 1923 that marked the beginning of the rise of prices for the first edition of *A Shropshire Lad.* It brought $157.50.[10] The comparative market value of *A Shropshire Lad* in this period is suggested by the prices sought for first editions of works such as Melville's *Moby Dick,* which was offered for sale at $100; Wilde's *The Picture of Dorian Gray* at $135; and Mark Twain's *Celebrated Jumping Frog of Calaveras County* at $125. A few years later, when Quaritch sought £63 for *A Shropshire Lad,* that firm asked £50 for the first edition of Jane Austen's *Mansfield Park* of 1814; £55 for the first edition of Chesterfield's *Letters* of 1774; and £60 for the Strawberry Hill edition of *Odes by Mr. Gray* of 1757.[11]

Until 1929, prices gradually rose. The increase was not constant, as additional, if occasionally battered, copies came not infrequently onto the market; but prices rarely fell below $100. From 1923 to 1929, copies changed hands at least forty times. Early in 1925, a copy brought at auction $202.50; in November of that year, a bookseller offered one for $300. In June 1926, another copy fetched £44 at auction. In February 1927, a copy brought $320; in July, Quaritch sought £54. In 1928, Drake asked $400, Quaritch, as noted, £63.[12] About this time A. Edward Newton wrote:[13]

> Of books of yesterday: de la Mare's *Songs of Childhood,* Masefield's *Salt Water Ballads,* Housman's *Shropshire Lad,* Sheila Kaye-Smith's *Tramping Methodist,* Morley's *Parnassus on Wheels,* keep on advancing in price, to the bewilderment of their authors. How long they will hold their present value, or whether they will go still higher, nobody knows; but it would seem safe to say

that an author's first book, if his subsequent work survives the critics, could be bought with impunity.

The highest price brought at auction in this period was $625 at the Jerome Kern sale in January 1929. 'The sale of Jerome Kern's library... was Kennerley's greatest auction,' noted Matthew J. Bruccoli; 'it remains the most glamorous literary sale held in America. The 1912 Hoe sale had more and better books, but the Kern sale marked the peak of bibliomaniacal fever before the Crash.'[14]

The decline in price for ordinary copies of *A Shropshire Lad* anticipated the Stock Market crash of 1929. In the United States, the decline began in the beginning of 1929, and continued unevenly to the close of the Second World War. The price then regains the lower levels of the early 1930s before falling again in 1949. Copies remain available for under $100 until at least 1961, a low point being reached in 1956 when a copy sold for $27. In 1962, there is a slight climb, which accelerates around 1973; accelerates again in 1983; and, once more, in 1987, when an American dealer sought $1500.

In Great Britain, the decline starts in 1930. Just after the Second World War, however, the price again reached £40: thereafter, though a low point is reached in 1958 with £17, the price is usually above £40 until perhaps 1963, when the price doubles. In the late 1960s the price doubles once more and, a decade later, nearly doubles yet again to £300. In 1980, a copy was offered for £500; in 1987, £600. Only two years later, in 1989, Quaritch asked $2750 for a copy.[15]

The current level of prices can be inferred from the following selection:

> $3000 (*c.* £1546–£1910): *Bromer Booksellers* cat. 63, 1990, no. 91 (very fine).
> $1500 (*c.* £773–£955): *MacManus* cat. 310, 1990, no. 205.
> £1500 (*c.* $2550): *Howes Bookshop* cat. 249, 1991, no. 484 (accompanied by first editions of *Last Poems; More Poems;* Laurence Housman's *A. E. H.;* and an autograph letter).
> $1800 (*c.* £918–£1118): *19th Century Shop* cat. 17, 1991, no. 116.
> $1500 (*c.* £757–£875): *MacManus* cat. 321, 1992, no. 441.
> £600 (*c.* $1140): *Christie's,* 24 June 1992, no. 147.
> $600 (*c.* £397): *Sotheby,* New York, 17 December 1992, no. 308.

$850 (*c.* £548–£582): *Argosy Book Store* cat. 799, 1994, no. 279.
$1500 (*c.* £968–£1027): *Ximenes* cat. 98, 1994, no. 155.
$1000 (*c.* £649): *Oinonen Book Auctions*, 23 August 1994, no. 81.
$1000: *David Mason* (Canada) cat. 69, 1994, no. 236.
$2500 (*c.* £1572): *Wm Reese Co.* cat. 141 (January 1995), no. 486 ('An unusually nice copy for this book, about fine').
£1800 (*c.* $2880): *Ulysses* cat. 41, July 1995, no. 234.
$1100 (*c.* £691): *Swann Galleries*, 14 December 1995, no. 169.
$950 (*c.* £633): *Lorson's Books and Prints,* Fullerton, California (February 1996).
$1000 (*c.* £666): *Heritage Bookshop and Bindery,* Los Angeles (February 1996): very good copy.
$3000 (*c.* £2000): *Bromer Booksellers,* Boston (February 1996): Bradley Martin copy.
$3500 (*c.* £2333): *Bromer Booksellers,* Boston (February 1996): accompanied by signed photograph of Housman.
£1500 (*c.* $2250): *Howes* cat. 269 [March] 1996, no. 1147: ASL 1896 + LP 1922 + MP 1936 + autograph letter, signed.

These are mostly ordinary copies. It is not possible to trace all or even most of them in earlier sales.

Special copies, such as presentation copies, have mostly brought higher prices. On publication, Housman was given 24 copies, of which apparently a dozen were sent out accompanied by typed slips with the compliments of the author. From his own stock, in 1896, Housman inscribed copies to Lucy Housman, his stepmother; to Elizabeth Wise, his godmother; to M. J. Jackson, his greatest friend; and to John Maycock, a close Patent Office friend. Latterly, he inscribed copies in his possession to Mrs Sherburne Prescott and A. S. F. Gow, and perhaps to Laurence Housman. Of these, that to Laurence was destroyed in part and possibly discarded. A seventh – or eighth – copy of the 12 is known to have been kept by Housman in his rooms. A copy sent to his brother Basil was not inscribed, and this suggests that Housman likewise may not have inscribed the copies given to his other brothers and sisters, with the probable exception of George Herbert Housman. Of the dozen sent out on his instructions, however, only one copy with a presentation slip seems to survive. Of course, Housman also inscribed later editions.[16]

Financial information is on public record for two of the original presentation copies. As long ago as 1936, the copy inscribed to Elizabeth Wise came onto the market, being sold by the American Art Association/Anderson Galleries. It was described as 'apparently the first presentation copy to appear at public sale in this country'. Nearly a quarter century later it reappeared at Parke-Bernet in the Charles C. Auchincloss sale. Then, another twenty-odd years later, it surfaced anew in Perry Molstad's Housman collection, when it was estimated to bring between five and seven thousand dollars. It is now in a private collection. In 1936, this copy fetched $345; in 1961, $1150; and, in 1984, $8000.[17]

In 1964, the Maycock copy was auctioned by Charles Hamilton. Hamilton had estimated it would only bring $650. Mrs Wise's name was known to Housman specialists; John Maycock's name was not. Adelman told me that, at that time, he was the only collector in America who was familiar with Housman's handwriting in the 1890s, and consequently recognized that the presentation was contemporary with the book. He obtained it for $525 plus the premium. It is now in the Adelman Collection, Bryn Mawr.[18]

The copy inscribed to Laurence was, as noted, at least partly destroyed. Laurence had asked his brother to inscribe a copy to him, and Housman did so. Possibly, Housman used one of his own copies; possibly, he inscribed one of Laurence's copies. Then, probably between 1928 and 1930, Laurence sold the book. The American bookseller C. A. Stonehill purchased the volume. It included, he noted, a superb full-page inscription to Laurence; he paid, he thought, perhaps $600 or $750; and he sold it to Mrs Sherburne Prescott. At this point, a letter from Housman arrived asking Stonehill to return the book, and additional correspondence elicited the information that he had been tricked by Laurence into inscribing it; that he had supposed it would never be sold; and that he did not wish the book to remain in existence. Stonehill discussed the matter with his client, who sent the book to Housman with her compliments. Housman destroyed the leaf with the inscription and then, not to be outdone, sent Mrs Prescott one of his own copies: 'Presented to Mrs Sherburne Prescott by A. E. Housman in gratitude for an expensive act of kindness.' It seems unlikely that the censored copy was preserved.[19]

In 1981, the Prescott copy was sold at auction in New York for $9500; in 1984, it was again auctioned, fetching, however, only $7500. But, nine years later, it appeared in a catalogue at $17 000 and then, in 1994, having been obtained in trade for works of equivalent value, in another's catalogue for $15 000. It has since been sold.[20]

With regard to ordinary copies, the pattern of rise and fall and recovery resembles that of the antiquarian book market as a whole. With the Depression, prices fell. As comparison, one might note a book similar to *A Shropshire Lad*, Wilde's *Ballad of Reading Gaol*. At auction in 1929, its ordinary first edition was bringing $220 and $300; thereafter, until about 1964, it usually fetched less than thirty dollars, not reaching or surpassing the 1929 high until the early 1980s. Even works dissimilar to *A Shropshire Lad* present a similar pattern. *Moby Dick* in its first edition rose gradually to a high point in 1929, reaching $925, then fell: in 1931, most copies brought around $450. Two years later, the price had halved and, by the Second World War, it was unusual for a copy to bring even fifty dollars. With 1946, an increase begins but it was not until the late 1960s that *Moby Dick* regularly matched the prices it brought in the early 1930s. By the mid-1980s the 1929 high was usually achieved. At present, it often brings at least $5000.[21]

III

Curiously, the rise and decline and recovery of the price of *A Shropshire Lad* has another parallel: the critical reception of the work.

Interest in the reception of A. E. Housman's verse reaches back half a century, and almost everyone who has investigated the subject has limited himself to the 'critical heritage'. This was perhaps almost inevitable. Most investigators are academics. Those who publish on Housman have been in the main professional critics and members of colleges or universities. The bibliographical aids, to which investigators naturally turn, provide citations only to publications.[22] But, as noted, Housman was a popular author, and the question consequently arises whether the evidence of the critics accurately reflects the general popularity of his verse.

The reception of Housman by the critics does not lend itself to brief summary. One can, however, remark one special change in the reception. The evidence shows that, by the early 1930s, a reaction against Housman's work had begun. What a previous generation had mostly taken for granted – that *A Shropshire Lad* evidenced courage and maturity – a new generation often could not or did not perceive. For them, the book revealed little but an adolescent's self-pity.[23] There are exceptions, of course; and it may be that, even in this period and after, those who emphasized individuality continued to think well of the book; but it took little time before this new attitude, unquestioned and unexamined, had taken hold.

At length, in 1961, John Carter's *Selected Prose* heralded a revival of admiration for Housman. The 1957 biography by George L. Watson had been hostile. In 1958, the life by Maude M. Hawkins proved sentimental, irritating and incompetent, while Norman Marlow's appreciation was too dry to attract many readers. So also Otto Skutsch's 1959 lecture and the Carter-Scott exhibition catalogue seem not to have circulated widely enough to have had much effect. But Carter's selection, published by the Cambridge University Press in both cloth and stiff paper, proved popular, a second edition being issued in 1962. And, thereafter, interest in Housman's life and works rose.

This suggests that ordinary book collectors generally allowed their taste to be governed by the critics. By this reasoning, when the critics admired Housman, collectors paid well to have him in their libraries; when the critics ceased to admire him, the willingness of buyers to obtain *A Shropshire Lad* in its first edition was reduced and prices declined. Consequently, the decision to include the work in a collection of books notable in English literature would be due less to a collector's own taste than to his adherence to that of the professional critic. That the price was obedient to the critics' praise or dispraise is, however, apparently beyond demonstration. The changes in valuation may only be coincidental with the fortunes of the market at large.

IV

The varying prices paid for the first edition of *A Shropshire Lad* do not in fact reflect Housman's *general* popularity.

Tracing the popular reception of the book is rendered the more difficult by the absence of data and by the presence of false and misleading information. Thus, statistics on sales exist but they are deceptive. In 1979, Richard Perceval Graves used a chart, preserved in the Grant Richards Papers at the Library of Congress, which seemingly records Richards' sales of *A Shropshire Lad* from mid-1905 to mid-1925. Graves notes:

Sales in 1905 only amounted to 886 copies; but in 1906 the book at last began to sell really well, and from then until 1911 the average annual sale was more than 13,500 copies, on which the 10 per cent royalty which Richards had once offered to its author would in itself have been worth at least £150 a year.[24]

The chart leads one to believe that it was in November 1905 that sales began to rise. In July, August, September and October of that year, according to the chart, monthly sales had consisted respectively of three copies, one copy, one copy and nine copies. In November they rose to 406 and, in December to 416. In 1906, the year's sales reached 10 064; in 1907, 15 395; in 1908, 18 247; in 1909, 16 359; in 1910, 9932; and, in 1911, 12 180. From July 1905 apparently to June 1925, the chart records sales of over 317 000 copies of *A Shropshire Lad.*[25] But there is strong reason to believe that the chart is an imposture, whether innocent because of incompetence or culpable because of plan cannot be stated with certainty.

The first difficulty is the implication that, each year, so many copies were necessarily produced. It is of course not impossible that they were; but anyone acquainted with the numbers of surviving copies will be uneasy. For instance, no British printings for 1909, 1910 and 1911 are known, and in consequence one wonders whether these are meant to be the remains of the 1908 printings. But why, having *ex hypothesi* sold 15 395 in 1907, would one have produced in 1908 at least 38 471 copies? It is unbelievable, the more so since sheets from the 1908 Hyde large post octavo were reissued in 1912 in tan boards.

Then, too, even when a printing or issue is known, it is difficult to explain why so few copies survive. The chart records sales of 9094 and 14 644 for 1915 and 1916 respectively; for my part, I know only five copies of the 1915, two of the 1916.[26] Of course, there probably are more; and, when a book is not a first edition, or a limited edition, or possessed of some special feature, one naturally does not expect it to survive well; but a fair number of enthusiasts have endeavoured to bring together collections of *A Shropshire Lad*; and it consequently should cause suspicion that these are scarce when the chart promises that they should be common.[27]

Finally, there are other statistics from Grant Richards' records summarized at the Lilly Library. According to these statistics, in

December 1908, editions amounting to 5000 copies were produced; in November 1912, another 5000; in December 1915, yet another 5000; in December 1918, 4540; and so forth. Thus, in this ten-year period, 19 540 copies were produced. But the chart records sales of 126 444 copies.[28]

Now, unfortunately, the first independent statistics to come to hand postdate the chart. On 18 July 1927, Housman authorized the Richards Press to print 5000 copies of the small edition of *A Shropshire Lad*. This agrees with the Lilly statistics; other letters of authorization, though they do not all precisely agree with Lilly, are at any rate far closer to the Lilly statistics than to those recorded on Charles Richards' chart.[29]

And, most obviously, despite these statistics, Housman latterly recorded: 'It is a great exaggeration to talk about a boom in connexion with the second edition [of *A Shropshire Lad*, 1898]: such boom as there was began with the war of 1914.'[30] Another method is consequently wanted.

At least in broad terms one can say something about the popularity of *A Shropshire Lad*. True, despite sixty years of bibliographical investigation, no one at present knows how many editions and reprints of *A Shropshire Lad* have appeared; none, how many copies of all these printings were issued. Of copies printed and bound, none can say how many were sold. The problem may be illustrated by a text frequently found on the shelves of bookshops. Elinore Blaisdell's illustrated edition of *A Shropshire Lad* was copyrighted in 1932 by Illustrated Editions in New York. The Illustrated Editions version alone presents various title pages and formats.[31] And William White has quietly warned that 'these sheets were reissued by Grosset & Dunlap, Three Sirens Press, Concord Books, Hartsdale House, Halcyon House, Arden Book Company, Deluxe Editions, and other imprints with various bindings'.[32] He thus rightly implies that they were not all issued in 1932. But White himself seems to have made no sufficient effort to assign these versions to their proper years, and his listing does not in fact reflect the correct ordering of their appearance. Here it will suffice to remark that those issues with alternative title pages belong to different times: for example, the Arden Book Company issue does not seem to predate 1936 and probably belongs to *c.* 1944; the Hartsdale House issue, 1946; and the issue of Halcyon House in Garden City, 1947, perhaps belonging to *c.* 1951.[33] But the Blaisdell illustrated editions have this advantage, that mechanisms exist for dating many of them. For other 'undated editions', such as many of those issued by the Peter Pauper Press, the number and variety of printings likewise argues for popularity.[34]

But it is not only the number and variety of printings that are of moment. One has also to be alive to the size of editions. The great merit of the printing press, the ability at will to multiply copies, is variously employed by printers. Some, like the Four Seas Company (latterly, Branden), issued copies of *A Shropshire Lad* in the tens of thousands. But then, too, there were those, like Frederic Prokosch, whose editions of individual poems are so small as to raise the question of their printers' purpose in issuing texts. It is only on occasion that statistics of production survive, and it is rarely possible to establish that they are reliable. Further, there are additional factors which complicate the question involving the dates of binding, the manner of distribution, the fate of the edition or impression – whether the edition was sold out, remaindered, pulped, lost to fire or flood.[35]

For other American editions, information is scantier and, as has been implied, likely to be even more complex: for many years, *A Shropshire Lad* was not copyright in the United States, and the result was any number of 'piracies', though the term is misleading. But sorting out these reprints, authorized and unauthorized, is no easy matter. When a certain Housman collector acquired a copy of Haldeman–Julius's 'Little Blue Book No. 306', *A Shropshire Lad*, he pencilled onto the title page '1st issue | Republished 1931 | The extraordinarily | rare 1920 edition' (now in a private collection). Nothing could be farther from the truth. There are at least four distinct forms of this impression. The first, and earliest, belongs to the 'Ten Cent Pocket Series'; the second carries, on the verso of the title leaf, 'Copyright, 1931 | Haldeman–Julius Company'; the third is identical with the second, save that the date has been removed, though no effort has been made to centre the text of the first line; and the fourth, and latest, has no copyright notice at all with 'HALDEMAN–JULIUS COMPANY' instead of 'HALDEMAN–JULIUS PUBLICATIONS' on the title page. The collector's copy belongs to the third group.[36]

Meanwhile, in England, the Harrap edition, illustrated by Agnes Miller Parker, appeared in 1940, 1942, 1953 (reset), 1954, 1957, 1960, 1962, 1965, 1969, 1972, 1974, 1977 (twice), 1980, 1984 and 1985. It was reissued in 1996.

The size of the Four Seas printings, the varying dates of the

Blaisdell illustrated editions, the size and approximate datings of the Haldeman–Julius printings, the variety of Peter Pauper Press issues and the number of Harrap reprints do not merely exhibit the continuing popularity of *A Shropshire Lad* among ordinary readers. They show that, even when the price of the first edition was in decline and the critics were hostile, Housman found readers in the thousands: that, in short, he remained a popular poet.

Notes

For kindnesses and courtesies, I am grateful to the late Seymour Adelman, Audrey S. Arellanes, Benjamin Watson (University of San Francisco), Adolfo Caso (Branden Publishing Company, Boston), Eugene DeGruson (Pittsburg State University, Kansas), John Dooley (Bryn Mawr College, Pennsylvania), the late G. B. A. Fletcher, Patricia A. Gazin, Rinard Z. Hart, Sue A. Kaplan (UCLA), the late Geoffrey Keynes, Kt, Mark Samuels Lasner, Charles Mohr, Stephen Tabor (William Andrews Clark Library, Los Angeles), Donald Tinker, Clark B. Wikle Jr and Julia Wikle.

Among booksellers and auction house representatives, I am beholden to David Block (The Book Block, Cos Cob, Connecticut), David J. Bromer (Bromer Booksellers, Boston, Massachusetts), Brian Courter (Swann Galleries, New York), Muir Dawson (Dawson's Book Shop, Los Angeles), David J. Holmes (David J. Holmes, Autographs, Philadelphia), George Houlé (Houlé Books and Autographs, Los Angeles), the late Samuel W. Katz (Los Angles), James A. Lorson (Lorson's Books & Prints, Fullerton, California), Nicholas Poole-Wilson (Bernard Quaritch Ltd, London), Barbara Rootenberg (B & L Rootenberg, Rare Books, Sherman Oaks, California), Nancy Rupert (Heritage Bookshop & Bindery, Los Angeles), Franklin V. Spellman (Krown & Spellman, Beverly Hills), Linda Tucker (Black Sun Books, New York), Ben Weinstein (Heritage Bookshop and Bindery, Los Angeles), and the late Jacob Israel Zeitlin. For discussion and criticism I am especially indebted to my former colleague at Zeitlin & Ver Brugge, Jeff Weber (Jeff Weber Rare Books, Glendale, California).

Finally, I am obliged to The Bodleian Library, Oxford; The British Library, London; Bryn Mawr College, Bryn Mawr, Pennsylvania; Case Western Reserve University, Cleveland, Ohio; Colby College, Waterville, Maine; Harvard University, Cambridge, Massachusetts; The Library of Congress, Washington, DC; The Lilly Library, Indiana University, Bloomington; Loyola Marymount University, Los Angeles; Pittsburg State University, Kansas; Princeton University, New Jersey; St John's College, Oxford; Trinity College, Cambridge; University Library, Cambridge; University of California, Berkeley; University of California, Los Angeles (Interlibrary Loan; Special Collections); University of Illinois, Urbana-Champaign; University of San Francisco; University of Virginia, Charlottesville; and Yale University, New Haven, Connecticut.

1. The book was of course not originally titled *A Shropshire Lad.* The earlier version, called *Poems by Terence Hearsay,* consisted of 66 poems, commencing with *ASL* III and concluding with *ASL* LXII. See Naiditch, *Problems in the Life and Writings of A. E. Housman* (Beverly Hills, CA: Krown & Spellman, 1995) (henceforth, *PLW/AEH*) pp. 92–3. For confirmation of Carter and Sparrow's ordering of the labels, see *PLW/AEH*, pp. 113–16. The so-called Label C and, in all probability, the missing Label D *et similia* have no bibliographical authority. The copy with Label C had been entirely rebound: see ibid., pp. 116–17. One copy of Lane's edition carries Label A.

2. L. Housman, *A. E. H.* (London: Jonathan Cape, 1937) p. 81; cf. ibid., p. 180. See also Richards, *Housman: 1897–1936,* (London: OUP, Humphrey Milford, 1941) p. 16 n. 1: 'it is . . . likely that his final six copies were what are known in the trade as "overs" – for the paper for a book never gives exactly the number ordered. There are always a few copies in excess, and unless an undertaking to sell only a certain number has been given these "overs" can properly be disposed of in the ordinary manner': 'always' should of course be 'often': both the University College London and the Los Angeles printings of Housman's light verse are scarcer than their imprints allow.

3. Galen is omitted by T. F. Dibdin, *An Introduction to the Knowledge of Rare and Valuable Editions of the Greek and Latin Classics* (London, 1804, edn 2 and 1827, edn 4) and by J. W. Moss, *A Manual of Classical Bibliography* (London, 1825).

   In the late eighteenth century, an ordinary copy of the *editio princeps* of Galen, published by the heirs of Aldus in 1525, could be obtained for prices ranging from 10s.6d. to £1.9s. As late as the early twentieth century, copies sold for £8 and $105. The last set to come on the market brought over $50 000. See *Bibliotheca Pinelliana,* London, 2 March 1789, no. 6574 (£1.6s.); *A Catalogue of a Select and Valuable Collection of Ancient and Modern Books, containing the Libraries of the Late Rev. Philip Lloyd, D. D . . ., and many other valuable collections lately purchased* (London: Thomas Payne, 1792), p. 44 no. 1265 (21s.); *A Catalogue of the Valuable Library of Russell Plumtree, M. D.* (London: Leigh & Sotheby, 20 March 1794, no. 488) (10s.6d.). It would be easy to multiply examples. For sales from 1882 to 1902, see *Auction Prices of Books,* ed. Luther S. Livingston 2, New York, 1905, p. 201. The last set to come onto the market was sold through Zeitlin & Ver Brugge Booksellers (private information).

   That the Galen was an Aldine may add to the surprise, for Aldines were being collected by the end of the seventeenth century: the earliest collector, excluding Grolier, may have been the Baron de Hohendorf, who appears to have grouped his holdings by publisher (cf. *Bibliotheca Hohendorfiana,* La Haye, 1720, e.g. pp. 215–24: 'Editiones Aldinae in Octavo'). See also Naiditch, 'Aldines in England from Henry VIII to Elizabeth I', *Classical Bulletin* 68 (1992) 91–3.

4. For reasons for Housman's fall from popularity, see *PLW/AEH* p. 214; Naiditch, '"The Slashing Style that All Know and Few Applaud": the Invective of A. E. Housman', *Aspects of Nineteenth*

Century British Classical Scholarship, ed. H. D. Jocelyn (Liverpool, 1996) p. 140; and Randy Lynn Meyer, *A. E. Housman and the Critics*, Dissertation, University of Toledo (Ohio), 1994 (summarized *DAI-A*55108), Feb. 1995, p. 2407 [CD-ROM].

See too Timothy Steele, *Missing Measures: Modern Poetry and the Revolt against Meter* (Fayetteville/London: University of Arkansas Press, 1990). Since 1990, a change may have taken place: see Humphrey Clucas, *Through Time and Place to Roam: Essays on A. E. Housman* (University of Salzburg, 1995) p. 2: '[Housman] did not move with the times; *Last Poems*, famously, was published in the same year as *The Waste Land*. Yet that jibe does not have quite the force it once did. The whole modernist movement – Eliot, Pound, David Jones – increasingly looks like a dried-up backwater; the main stream has run quietly on through the likes of Hardy, Housman, Edward Thomas . . . poets who use traditional forms and traditional means of discourse.'

5. See Fritz de Marez Oyens and Paul Needham, *The Estelle Doheny Collection Part I* (New York: Christie, Manson & Woods, 1987) no. 1, pp. 23–6 (census: no. 18 has been broken up); the price is reported, for example, in *American Book Prices Current* 94, 1988, 313. For the size of the original edition: Aeneas Silvius, who saw the work on sale at Frankfurt in October 1454, reports that it consisted either of 158 or 180 copies (P. Needham, *Papers of the Bibliographical Society of America* 79, 1985, 308–10, brought to my attention by Sue A. Kaplan).

The rarity of the Gutenberg Bible is enhanced because all save one of the known copies are now in institutional collections. (Individual leaves, which can fetch, for example, £8500, of course turn up on the market almost every year.) For *A. E. H. W. W.*, see W. White, *A. E. Housman: a Bibliography* (Godalming: St Paul's Bibliographies, 1982) no. 17. Of the dozen copies of the edition, six are known to survive. Four are in institutional collections (Lilly; Princeton; St John's College, Sparrow Collection; and University of Virginia, Charlottesville). The fifth is in a private collection, probably to be donated to an institution; the sixth was on the market and, I am told, may have been acquired by an institution (*Zeitlin & Ver Brugge* cat. 265, 1982, no. 56 = *Black Sun Books* cat. 79, 1988, no. 448 ($225)).

6. Nicolas Barker has called the observation, that rare books in very fine condition are likely to increase in price where ordinary copies may not increase, 'Livingstone's Law' ('American Book Prices Current 1895–1995', *American Book Prices Current* 100, 1995, xiv).

7. Seymour Adelman, *Help from Heaven* (New Castle, Del.: Oak Knoll (Bird and Bull Press), 1984) (scroll). The New York dealer was Lew D. Feldman of the eponymous House of El Dieff (cf. 'Prices and Buyers' Names', *Sotheby & Co.*, 8–9 July 1968). The collection belonged to Housman's great-nephew Robert E. Symons (cf. *Housman Society Journal* 9, 1983, 21–2).

For book collecting, see, for example, John Carter, *Taste and Technique in Book Collecting*, 1970 (London: Private Libraries Association, 1977);

for auctions, for example, Frank Hermann, *Sotheby's: Portrait of an Auction House* (London: Chatto & Windus, 1980), Arthur Freeman and Janet Eng Freeman, *Anatomy of an Auction* (London: The Book Collector, 1990), and *Property of a Gentlemen: the Formation, Organisation and Dispersal of the Private Library 1620–1920*, eds Robin Myers and Michael Harris (Winchester: St Paul's Bibliographies, 1991); and, less well known, Charles F. Heartman, *Twenty-Five Years in the Auction Business and What Now?* (privately printed, 1938), and Drif Field, *Not 84 Charing Cross Road* (London: Drif Field Guides, 1994) (cf. Paul Minet, *Antiquarian Book Monthly Review*, July 1994, 30: I am grateful to Charles Mohr for bringing Field and the late Samuel W. Katz for bringing Minet to my attention).

The modern book trade is less well served by historians and writers: see, for example, Andrew Block, *A Short History of the Principal London Antiquarian Booksellers and Book-Auctioneers* (London: D. Archer, 1993); A. L. P. Norrington, *Blackwell's 1879–1979: the History of a Family Firm* (Oxford: Blackwell, 1983); Madeleine B. Stern, *Antiquarian Bookselling in the United States: a History from the Origins to the 1940s* (Westport, Conn.: Greenwood Press, 1985).

8. Jackson's copy, Trinity College, Cambridge C13.74. (For Housman and Jackson, see Naiditch, *A. E. Housman at University College, London: the Election of 1892* (Leiden: E.J. Brill, 1988 (henceforth, *AEH/UCL*)) pp. 165–72, and *PLW/AEH*, p. 221. Bynner's copy, Harvard University, Houghton Library, *EC9.H8176s. 1896(B): his bookplate, which possibly lends itself to precise dating, reads 'HAL | WITTER | BYNNER | HIS BOOK | COURAGE | L'AMI | LE DIABLE | EST MORT'. (See *Thirty Housman Letters to Witter Bynner*, ed. T. B. Haber (New York: Alfred A. Knopf, 1957); *The Works of Witter Bynner: Selected Letters*, ed. J. Kraft (New York: Farrar, Straus, Giroux, 1981). Keynes's copy is now in the University Library, Cambridge, Keynes Collection. (For his collection, see *Bibliotheca Bibliographici*, London: Trianon Press, 1964.)

9. For the first, see *Hodgson*, 26 November 1919, no. 719 (purchased by the American bookseller James F. Drake). For the second, see Grant Richards to Housman, 20 September 1920, recording a sale by Henderson, the 'Red' bookseller in Charing Cross Road (University of Illinois, Urbana-Champaign, Grant Richards Letterbooks, 30.317; also available in microfilm by Chadwyck-Healey). For the third, see *Hodgson* 1 March 1923, no. 538 (purchased by Maggs Brothers). On occasion, here and elsewhere in this article, I derive my information on auctions from *American Book Prices Current, Book-Prices Current* or *Book Prices Current*, and have not had occasion to examine the auction catalogue itself.

10. It is impossible to identify the first Housman collector with certainty. An enthusiast began to write to Housman as early as March 1897 (see L. Housman, *A. E. H.* (London: Jonathan Cape, 1937) p. 136. Sir Geoffrey Keynes told me that he began to collect Housman in 1906 (*per litt.* 1 May 1982; for Keynes, see, for example, his autobiography, *The Gates of Memory*, Oxford: Clarendon Press, 1981). John Quinn

affirms that '[m]ost of the books were secured by me as they were issued or published and that accounts for their good condition' (*Complete Catalogue of the Library of John Quinn sold by Auction in Five Parts* (New York: The Anderson Galleries, 1924) p. [v]). It is certainly possible that Quinn had purchased the first British edition not long after its publication, for copies reached the United States this early (see *PLW/AEH*, p. 97 n. 1). By the time of his sale Quinn owned the *Shropshire Lad* both of 1896 and 1897; the first volume of Manilius; and the first edition of *Last Poems* (*ibid.*, p. 420 nos 4266–9); for Quinn, see, most conveniently, Donald C. Dickinson, *Dictionary of American Book Collectors* (New York: Greenwood Press, 1986) pp. 264–5, with list of sources for his life.

11. *James F. Drake* cat. 166, *c.* 1924, nos 163, 284, 60; *Bernard Quaritch* cat. 421, 1928, nos 435, 138, 244, 392. I anticipate an objection by noting that the resurgence of interest in Melville had just begun: see David A. Randall, *Dukedom Large Enough* (New York: Random House, 1969) pp. 206–7.

12. *Anderson Galleries*, 12–13 January 1925, no. 226a; *Drake* cat. 172, November 1925, no. 178; *Sotheby*, 21 June 1926, no. 423; *American Art Association*, 14–16 February 1927, no. 635; Quaritch (Yale University, Beinecke Library, Ip H816 896); *Drake* cat. 200, 1928, no. 200; *Quaritch* cat. 421, November 1928, no. 435.

With regard only to special copies, Laurence Housman boasted that by 'artful incitement [he] drove the second-hand book market to increase its bids for certain "unopened" copies of *A Shropshire Lad . . .* from five pounds to fifty pounds, and finally (for a signed copy) seventy pounds' (*The Unexpected Years*, Indianapolis: Bobbs-Merrill, 1936, p. 221 = London: Jonathan Cape, 1936, p. 262, albeit with minor changes). The prices are questionable: in an unpublished letter, Laurence starts it at £12 and ends it at £65 (LH to unknown, 3 July 1934: Yale University, Beinecke Library). So also Housman himself puts the highpoint at £80 (*Letters*, p. 327). Laurence's allusions to one of his brother's letters suggests that the highpoint occurred in 1925 (*Letters*, p. 232). Neither Laurence nor Housman makes reference to Mrs Prescott's copy (notes 23–4 below).

13. *This Book-Collecting Game* (Boston: Little, Brown, 1928) pp. 38–9.

14. *Anderson Galleries*, 7–10 January 1929, no. 691. M. J. Bruccoli, *The Fortunes of Mitchell Kennerley, Bookman* (San Diego/New York: Harcourt Brace Jovanovich, 1986) p. 199. In 1930, Housman referred in passing to a bookseller who offered £120 for a signed (presentation?) copy (*Letters*, p. 292).

The decline in prices pleased Housman. 'One good result of the present financial stringency is that the absurd prices which used to be paid for the first edition of *A Shropshire Lad* are now abating' (1932: *Letters*, p. 318). See also, for example, *Letters*, p. 327.

15. Information derived from *American Book Prices Current, Book Prices Current, Book-Prices Current, Bookman's Price Index* and my own files.

16. See *PLW/AEH*, pp. 114–15. There is also a copy, once owned by Mary Brettell Housman, inscribed 'From A. E. H.' (Loyola Marymount

University, Los Angeles, Chi 821 H842 sh-1896). See also *AEH/UCL*, pp. 132 n. 43–22.

17. *American Art Association/Anderson Galleries*, 9–10 December 1936, no. 428; *Parke-Bernet*, 29–30 November 1961, no. 315; *Sotheby*, New York, 16–17 May 1984, no. 462. For Mrs Wise's given name, see A. Burnett in *PLW/AEH*, p. 12 n. 2 and Robin Shaw, *Housman's Places* (Bromsgrove: The Housman Society, 1995) p. 93.

18. *Charles Hamilton*, auction 4, 21 May 1964, no. 93. For the price, see *American Book Prices Current* 70, 358. Cf. J. Carter, *Book Collector* 11, Spring 1962, 84. (For Maycock, see *PLW/AEH*, pp. 19–21 and [Leo Dolenski and John Dooley] *The Name and Nature of A. E. Housman*, Bryn Mawr College Library, Pierpoint Morgan Library, New York: 1986, pp. 29–31.)

19. Stonehill to William White, 14 May 1942: University of Virginia, Charlottesville, 10743/11 (1936–47). For a copy of *A Shropshire Lad* lacking the front endpaper, see *BAR* 31, p. 449 (*Hodgson*, 27 June 1934, no. 820).

20. *Sotheby's*, New York, 10 May 1984, no. 629; *Christie's*, New York, 6 February 1981, no. 163. Cf. J. Carter, *Book Collector* 14, 1965, 216–17; *Book Block* cat. 25, 1993, no. 24; *David J. Holmes* cat. 46, 1994, no. 49. A copy with a presentation slip reading 'With the compliments of the Author' was offered for sale in 1951 for £75. Apparently, this is the only known example of the slip: *P. H. Muir for Elkin Mathews* cat. 123, October 1951, no. 24; now, Princeton University ExC3790.28.385.12 = J. Harlin O'Connell Collection.

21. Cf. *American Book Prices Current*; see also Van Allen Bradley, *The Book Collector's Handbook of Values* (New York: Putnam, 1978³, *s.u.*); Allen Ahearn and Patricia Ahearn, *Collected Books: the Guide to Values* (New York: Putnam, 1991) *s.u.*

22. See Robert W. Stallman, 'Annotated Bibliography of A. E. Housman: a Critical Study', *Publications of the Modern Language Association of America* 60 (1945) 463–502; Abdul-Wahid Lúlúa, *A. E. Housman: Critical Reputation, 1896–1962*, Dissertation [Case] Western Reserve University, 1962; Christopher Ricks, *A. E. Housman, a Collection of Critical Essays* (Englewood Cliffs, NJ: Prentice-Hall, 1968); Ghussan R. Greene, *The Public Reception of A. E. Housman's Poetry in England and America*, Dissertation, University of South Carolina, 1978 (not seen); G. R. Greene, 'Housman since 1936 – Popular Responses and Professional Revaluations in America', *Housman Society Journal* 12 (1986) 30–46; Philip Gardner, *A. E. Housman: the Critical Heritage* (London/New York: Routledge, 1992); Randy Lynn Meyer, *A. E. Housman and the Critics*, Dissertation, University of Toledo (Ohio), 1994. The chief scholars to go beyond the 'critical heritage' are William White and Tom Burns Haber.

23. For examples, see *PLW/AEH*, pp. 212–13.

24. Graves, *A. E. Housman: the Scholar-Poet* (London: Routledge & Kegan Paul, 1979) (= Oxford, 1981) pp. 119, 279 n. 37. T. A. Hoagwood regards this as established fact: 'Sales grew; especially after the 1906 edition,' *A. E. Housman Revisited* (New York: Twayne, 1995) p. 23. Cf. Richards,

Housman 1897–1936 (London, 1941) pp. 33–4: 'My son Charles, when he was with me in my publishing business in about 1922, pleased Housman by getting out a chart, a graph, showing the sales month by month and year by year, from, I think, 1905. Housman, however, tucked it away in so safe a place that he could never find it again. The rising figures gave him pleasure, but they suggested no great popularity.' Richards was not sufficiently careful as a publisher and consequently has a reputation for unethical behaviour, at least sometimes deserved. For his relations with Housman, see J. D. Tunnicliffe and M. Buncombe, 'A. E. Housman and the Failure of Grant Richards Limited in 1926', *HSJ* 11 (1985) 101–6. Other examples of Richards's culpability in his dealings with authors could be supplied.

25. Library of Congress, Grant Richards Papers box 6. It is to be noted that, until 1922/23, Housman did not seek royalties. In consequence, he would have had no means for easily recognizing the imposture, save his belief that the 'boom' began with the war.

26. Of the 1915 issue, two copies survive in the William White Collection, University of Virginia, Charlottesville; two more in a private collection in Kansas; and a fifth in a private collection in California. Of the 1916 issue, I remark *G. F. Sims* cat. 14, *c.* 1951, no. 138 (inscribed to Martin Secker), now in the Adelman Collection, Bryn Mawr College, R.B.R. PR 4809.H15 A7 1916. The second is in a private collection in Kansas.

27. I have had occasions to examine several large collections of *A Shropshire Lad*: the collections of Seymour Adelman and Houston Martin, the latter incorporated in the Adelman Collection at Bryn Mawr; the Carl J. Weber Collection at Colby College, Waterville, Maine; the William White Collection at the University of Virginia, Charlottesville; three private collections in California and one in Kansas. In addition I have seen any number of smaller collections, for example at the Lilly Library and the University of San Francisco. The White Collection includes over 180 copies of *A Shropshire Lad*; some of the others, one hundred or more.

28. Lilly Library, Indiana University, Bloomington, Housman Mss 3 box 2 folder 6.

29. British Library, Add. Ms. 44923 f. 3r.

30. H. to Seymour Adelman, 30 December 1933: L. Housman, *A. E. H.* (London: Jonathan Cape, 1937) = *Letters*, p. 350.

31. The issues of Illustrated Editions are numerous, and appear in different formats, but the publisher's custom of including his address enables its issues to be distinguished: this firm was at 100 Fifth Avenue in 1932 (*Publishers' Weekly* 123, 21 January 1933, 229); 104 Fifth Avenue, 1933 – *c.* 1939 (*PW* 125, 1934, 252; *PW* 137, 1940, 243); and 220 Fourth Avenue by 1940 (*PW* 139, 1941, 254).

32. W. White, *A. E. Housman: a Bibliography* (Godalming: St Paul's Bibliographies, 1982) p. 10 n. 2.

33. For the first relevant appearance in the publishers' directory of Arden Book Company, see *PW* 131, 1937, 230 with White's copy (*c.* 1944); for Hartsdale House, see *PW* 151, 1947, 457; for Halcyon House (earlier

listed with Blue Ribbon Books in New York and, from 1941, in Garden City), see *PW* 153, 1948, 336 with White's copy (1951).

34. *Recalling Peter: the Life and Times of Peter Beilenson and his Peter Pauper Press* (New York: The Typophiles, 1964) is of no help in resolving most of the problems associated with this press.

35. According to the copyright notice of the 1989 issue (International Pocket Library, Division of Branden), the six printings total 42 000 copies. Mr Adolfo Caso of Branden kindly informs me that, around 1994, 10 000 more copies were printed (*per tel.* 11 December 1995). The earliest belongs to 1919 or, possibly, 1918. In the first impression, the copyright notice is dated 1918 and the introduction by William Stanley Braithwaite is dated March 1918. But, in the Library of Congress Copyright Office, Braithwaite's introduction was entered on 1 November 1919, and the book itself was stamped 17 November 1919 (Library of Congress PR 4809.H15 A7 1918 copy 2). And, in the second impression, the first is assigned to November 1919, the date of the introduction being deleted. The third impression dates to 1931.

For Prokosch, see Nicolas Barker, *The Butterfly Books* (London: Bertram Rota, 1987). In 1982, after his imposture was discovered by Arthur Freeman and established by Barker, Prokosch produced texts consisting nominally of five copies each: for example 'Loveliest of Trees' (Grasse: Prometheus Press, 1982) (Bodleian Library, Oxford, Ms. Eng. e 23/3). He did not, however, limit himself to poems from *A Shropshire Lad*. I am grateful to James E. Lorson of Lorson's Books and Prints, Fullerton, and George Houlé of Houlé Rare Books and Autographs, Los Angeles, for kindly permitting me to examine the Housman pamphlets in their sets of the Prometheus Press.

36. My reconstruction of the sequence differs from the publisher's records. Mr Eugene DeGruson of the Haldeman–Julius Collection, Pittsburg State University, Kansas, tells me that these records show that the first printing was advertised in Haldeman–Julius's *Appeal to Reason*, 2 September 1922, p. 1; that this printing appeared in three issues of 10 000 each; that the second edition, carrying the copyright notice of 1931, consisted of 5000 copies; and that the second edition was reprinted in 1947 in 10 000 copies (*per tel.* 22 November 1995). (Haldeman–Julius did not often publish verse: even so, he affirmed that, from 1915, he sold 114 000 copies of Wilde's *Ballad of Reading Gaol*; from 1919, 152 000 copies of Poe's *Raven* etc.; from 1920, 83 000 copies of Shakespeare's *Sonnets* (*My Second 25 Years*, Girard (1949), pp. 112, 114, 111). Of works whose printings approximate that of *A Shropshire Lad*, one may note Shakespeare's *Measure for Measure*, 40 000; Ibsen's *The Wild Duck*, 43 000; and Josh Billings' *Humourous Epigrams*, 40 000 (ibid., pp. 111, 113, 117).

With regard to the problem in hand, the difficulties are threefold and, at present, have not been resolved. First, there are at least four versions of the work, not three. Secondly, Housman's copy (University of San Francisco, Special Collections PR 4809.H15 A7 1931), lacking any copyright notice, was purchased after his death at Blackwell's: in this form, one would otherwise have assigned it to 1947 or afterwards. Thirdly, the true first 'Little Blue Book No. 306' seems to be very scarce: I have seen only two copies of this edition and, judging from filled or broken numbers – see page numbers 5, 7, 49 and 51 – neither is likely to be the first issue (White Collection: University of Virginia, Charlottesville, PR 4809.H15A7 1923d; UCLA Special Collections coll. 627 box 4, the latter with additional defects). Of course, there will be others; and, as with the second impression of Gow's memoir, now that the matter has been given publicity copies will likely enough begin to surface.

It is interesting that Haldeman–Julius anticipated by nearly three weeks the announcement of *Last Poems* in the *Times Literary Supplement* for 21 September 1922 (Grant Richards, *Housman 1897–1936*, London: Humphrey Milford, 1941, p. 199).

I owe my knowledge of Eugene DeGruson's address to Richard Colles Johnson and G. Thomas Tanselle, 'The Haldeman–Julius "Little Blue Books" as a Bibliographical Problem', *The Papers of the Bibliographical Society of America* 64 (1970) 29 n.*, my first efforts to reach him having failed.

11

A. E. Housman's Use of Biblical Narrative

Carol Efrati

It is a fact well known to everyone interested in the poetry of A. E. Housman that he was accustomed to take a phrase or verse from the Bible and, by slightly altering the text or the context, twist the biblical verse to his own use. Davis P. Harding and Vincent Friemarck are but two who have published studies of this technique.[1]

However, it was not only isolated excerpts which were used in this way by Housman. In a few – a very few – poems, he did precisely the same thing for complete narratives, thrice from the Old Testament and twice from the New. In each case, his treatment throws a new light on an old story as well as providing a new vantage point from which to view the poet and his work.

Housman's familiarity with the Bible can hardly be overstated. He came from a clerical family (both of his grandfathers were Anglican ministers) in which reading from the Scriptures was part of the daily routine, as attendance at church was part of the weekly routine. In general, however, all levels of Victorian society were far more steeped in the Bible than is the usual case today. One need only refer to Hardy's rustics, who habitually quote from all parts of it, to demonstrate that the habit of applying biblical quotations to the events of daily life, as well as the propensity for debating the significance of various passages, was pervasive in Victoria's England. Housman could depend upon a reader immediately identifying biblical phrases and allusions as a modern poet cannot, and such biblical allusions and references were natural to him. He handled them with ease, and this same ease he brought to the treatment of several biblical stories.

When there was an element of coercion, Housman's advocacy was engaged on the side of the coerced, with whom he identified himself, the person subject to rules, both secular and religious, about which he had not been consulted in advance and to which he might give lip service but not heart's obedience. Three of the poems to be discussed examine this question in a pure form as they concern acquiescence in the commandments of God only. Man's rules do not enter the matter. There are several Old Testament stories which centre on the keeping – or breaking – of orders from the Deity. The first, of course, is the story of Adam and Eve.

Adam is the original sinner, but Housman does not deal with the transgression itself. Rather, he is interested in one reason for it: discontent. This is one of the very few poems which seems to have escaped critical attention.

> When Adam walked in Eden young,
>   Happy, 'tis writ, was he,
> While high the fruit of knowledge hung
>   Unbitten on the tree.
>
> Happy was he the livelong day;
>   I doubt 'tis written wrong:
> The heart of man, for all they say,
>   Was never happy long.
>
> And now my feet are tired of rest,
>   And here they will not stay,
> And the soul fevers in my breast
>   And aches to be away.

$(AP \text{ III})^2$

Since it was God Who created Adam and determined his nature, Adam's discontent is of the same origin as himself. God must have intended it to be part of his nature when making him.

It is on this basis that Housman questions the biblical account of life in pre-lapsarian Eden, for Adam, being the prototypical man, must have found, as all men do, that happiness is at best temporary. It was not the eating of the fruit of the forbidden tree which caused him to lose his primordial bliss; rather it was the lack of the potential for continuing contentment in primordial bliss which caused him to eat of the fruit. Housman here uses the word 'doubt' in its older meaning of 'suspect' which clarifies the meaning considerably.

In the third verse, Housman both puts himself in place of Adam and sees Adam's restlessness reflected in himself, for the 'he' of the first two verses becomes 'my' in these last lines. Adam, it is suggested, was discontented with Paradise itself, just as post-lapsarian man is discontented with his condition, and this modern discontent is only a reflection or continuation of Adam's, the natural state of all mankind. After having lived long enough in the world, there is a need to pass on to something else. The 'I' persona, whom I read as Housman, is ready 'now' to die, to quit his body and the world and 'to be away' as, he implies, Adam was ready to leave Eden.

This implication obviously stands the biblical account on its head, reversing the tenor, the motives and the entire 'moral' of the story. And that is precisely what Housman was accustomed to do with such material.

Those scriptural stories from the Old Testament which Housman used as a basis for his poetry, like this prototypical one of Adam, deal with breaking divine edicts – and the consequences of such transgression. Such is the story of Lot's wife – and Lot himself.

> Half-way, for one commandment broken,
>   The woman made her endless halt,
> And she to-day, a glistering token,
>   Stands in the wilderness of salt.
> Behind, the vats of judgment brewing
>   Thundered, and thick the brimstone snowed;
> He to the hill of his undoing
>   Pursued his road.

> (*MP* XXXV)

Here is a poem which is all too easy to read, or to misread. Raymond Mortimer considered it only 'a witty epigram on Noah [*sic*], who fled the sinful cities of the plain only to fall, on a mountain, into incest'.[3] It is not easy to understand how a serious critic could confuse Noah with Lot, Sodom and Gomorrah with the antediluvian world, and (presumably) Mt Ararat in Turkey with the Negev in Israel. Dismissing the Noahide confusion, there-fore, as due to carelessness about the context, in this case the source material, let us consider only Lot and his wife, the subjects of this poem, which is indeed perhaps 'a witty epigram' but is a great many other things as well.

The text is clear, but to understand its full resonance one needs to hold in mind not merely the bare bones of the story and the post-pillar-of-salt events, but also its personal significance *for Housman.* It is as well to begin with a sketch of the Scriptural events.

Lot's wife, well away from Sodom in the direction of safety, broke a single commandment, looked back and was turned into a pillar of salt on the shore of the Dead Sea, rather an extreme punishment for wanting a last, farewell, glimpse of her home which was in the process of being destroyed. One of the points made is thus that it is the fact of transgression rather than the importance or rationality of the law being transgressed which provokes the penalty.

Following her transformation, Lot continued towards his own destiny, which involved becoming drunk, committing incest with his daughters, and through them fathering the race of Moab (the translation of the Hebrew word is 'from the father') from which later was to arise Ruth and through her King David. Did Housman know Hebrew? I have found no hard evidence that he did, but there are at least two indications that he was to some degree at least acquainted with the language. The choice of Housman in 1896 to chair the Public Lecture ('The Faust of the Talmud') given by the Chief Rabbi, Hermann Adler, on Goethe's *Faust* and Elisha ben Abuya, an apostate in the reign of the Emperor Hadrian,[4] may be taken to indicate that he was known to have some familiarity with the Talmud and thus with one of the languages in which it was written. In addition, he certainly knew something of the principles of Hebrew versification, at least 'the interrogation being of course in Hebrew poetry tantamount to the strongest affirmation',[5] which again seems to point to a knowledge of the language. And his use of the phrase 'of course' indicates that he assumed this was common knowledge. He may well have assumed that the derivation of the word 'Moab' was equally generally known and thus part of the equipment his readers would bring to the understanding of his poem.

I wish to discuss this biblically based poem, as well as the others taken up in this paper, without entering into unrelated biblical exegesis. However, this story in its entirety indicates that without the sins of the Sodomites, Lot's wife, and Lot himself, the Psalmist

could never have been born. They may thus be analogous typo-
logically to 'the fortunate fall' and therefore part of the Deity's
master plan for human history.

The first thing to note, however, is that Lot is not identified
by name (although the details make his identity patent despite
Mortimer's confusion). Lot is simply 'He', universalized into Everyman; equally, Lot's wife is 'the woman', universalized into
Everywoman. The broken commandment is likewise unspecified;
it is the paradigmatic Law of God, the type of Everylaw, that
'He may keep that will and can' but 'Not I' (*LP* XII), nor Lot's
wife. Housman's identification with the transgressor is quite clear.

It can, of course, be argued that none of these, neither Lot, his
wife nor the sin, need be specific, as Housman could depend on
the reader (although he did not himself choose to publish this
poem) to make the necessary identifications. But it can also be
argued that the exact identities are immaterial as the theme is
punishment for a single transgression and is relevant to many
other incidents. The story of Samson could have served equally
well to demonstrate the extreme consequences of breaking one
commandment. Thus, the importance lies not in who broke what
law, but rather in the fact that a law was broken, and in the
inevitability of the punishment for such a transgression of a prohibition which may seem minor, even unreasonable or illogical.

Most biblical prohibitions concern man's relationships with his
society, and especially with his fellow men. Here the prohibition
concerns only the relationship between man, or woman, and God,
and that relationship is one of total dominance on the one side
and unquestioning obedience on the other. The penalty for refusing
this obedience is extreme, not 'jail and gallows and hell-fire' (*LP*
XII) but metamorphosis into a mineral form. It is not only society
that wrests individuals to its will; it is God Himself.

Let it be noted, however, that 'He' broke no commandment,
and yet it is to 'his undoing' that he proceeds. Here there are
many ways of reading the undertext. Both her breaking and his
keeping of the law lead to 'undoing'. Since one is doomed (or
saved) whether one obeys or not, it does not much matter which
one does. This is pure (or impure) antinomianism and as such
applicable only to avowed Christians who argue that the possession of 'grace' exempts them from moral laws. Since the subjects
of the poem are not Christians, and since Housman himself rejected
the foundation of Christianity (as we shall shortly see), it seems

to me that the term is not applicable to this poem or to its author. In any case, this reading is not the one which seems best.

The poem also may be read thus: her breaking of the commandment, thereby removing herself from his side, leads directly to his downfall as well (the nature of which is again not specified although it could be assumed to be generally known), thus making 'the woman' doubly responsible, both for her own undoing and for his. This makes Lot's wife an anti-type of Eve, as Lot is of Adam, and by her role as Everywoman (as Lot is Everyman), makes her guilty of his fall, a reading which I believe Housman would have scornfully rejected as simplistic. However one reads it, his 'undoing' is clearly not the result of his own actions but of another's. He is guiltless, yet he too is punished, unless there is an implication that he should have stayed with her rather than proceeding on his way. I consider all of these readings equally unsatisfactory and untenable, though the first marginally less so.

There is another way of reading the poem which seems far more satisfactory. The woman halts eternally because she has looked back. The man proceeds to disaster because he does not look back. Paralysis results from an exclusive focus on the past, what is behind in time rather than (or in addition to) space, and calamity results from the refusal to contemplate the past at all. As Professor Flieger has remarked, 'to look back with regret, like Lot's wife, is to risk losing the capacity and the will to go forward',[6] to which I would add that to go into the future without first assimilating the past is to risk losing the wisdom and experience to choose one's path wisely. In this reading, the undertext implies that 'the woman' was so tied to the past that she could not go forward, whereas the man, turning his back upon the past, could only go blindly towards his doom. To be tethered to history and to ignore it are equally good formulae for destruction.

The term 'undoing' can be read in different ways. The textual reference is to a hill where 'He' will meet disaster. But 'undoing' means 'disrobing' as well as 'disaster'. This implies the exposure of Lot's nakedness, undisguised by any clothing (costume), which of course refers directly back to the biblical nature of 'his undoing' in which the one consists of the other. In the biblical story, outlined above, the aftermath of Lot's wife's transformation is his seduction by his daughters who, thinking that they and their father are the last surviving human beings, have made him drunk for that purpose with the hope (fulfilled) of bearing children to continue the race. And the result of this seduction is the birth of the people of Moab, the people from whom sprang Ruth the great-grandmother of King David. The whole matter is thus ambiguous and ambivalent.

The ambiguity, and the ambivalence, are both reflected in a letter Housman wrote to Grant Richards:

> To include me in an anthology of the Nineties would be just as technically correct, and just as essentially inappropriate, as to include Lot in a book on Sodomites; in saying which I am not saying a word against sodomy, nor implying that intoxication and incest are in any way preferable.[7]

In this letter, although not in the poem, the nature of the 'undoing' is specified – intoxication and incest – and these 'sins' are placed in the same category as sodomy, the practices of the men of Sodom. This is, parenthetically, the closest Housman ever came to a public affirmation of his own 'sinfulness', and by the jocular tone of the reference, he implicitly denies its applicability to himself, indicating no more than an academic interest in the matter. As we know, however, his interest was very far from academic.

What the poem seems to be implying is that Lot's own actions were at least as sinful as those of the destroyed Sodomites, or alternatively as non-sinful. 'His' susceptibility to drink and sexual temptation place him on the same level as them. This susceptibility is Lot's basic nature, and it is this which is revealed on 'the hill of his undoing' where the mask of his propriety is removed. And one's basic nature can only be ascribed to one Entity: 'the God that made him' (*AP* XVIII).

The consequences of transgression extend not only to 'He' and 'the woman', but to the earth in general, for Sodom here is not even identified as a city. The focus is once more on the punishment, and here the brimstone which 'snowed' and the woman 'in the wilderness of salt' are linked by the common characteristic of snow and salt: their white colour. White, however, is the traditional colour of purity and innocence. The text is turned on its head by the use of colour symbolism, and the undertext by this means subtly absolves both 'the woman' and the city of guilt. If they are white, they, like 'He', are punished gratuitously. The undertext thus implies that God's justice is fundamentally flawed and unjust. If this be blasphemy, so be it.

From whatever direction we approach the lyric, we end with the same conclusion. Housman has implicitly charged a black-and-white tale of sin and punishment with a host of shades of grey; he has raised questions about both the sin and the punishment, about their relationship to each other and about their righteousness. He has replaced stark clarity with blurred ambiguity.

The next lyric presents a textual problem. In the standard editions, it consists of seven stanzas. However, in Housman's note-books, there is an additional stanza. Whether this is in fact part of the poem to be considered or is a separate poem fortuitously placed there cannot now be determined. When Laurence Housman prepared his brother's manuscript poems for publication, he included it as part of this work. In the Jonathan Cape edition of the *Collected Poems*, the first one-volume edition of the four separate books of poetry, and the edition on which all later editions are based, it was deleted without any real explanation by the editor John Carter (Norman Marlow believes correctly) as being in fact an independent quatrain.

Carter says, 'Closer examination made it clear that this stanza . . . does not belong to this poem.'[8] However, he does not give any account of the 'closer examination' and I have been unable to discover his rationale. The verse is not included in any edition of *More Poems* after that edited by Laurence Housman, whose opinion, he perhaps having discussed the notebook material with his brother and certainly having more familiarity with his brother's mental and associational habits than any later editor could have, should not have been so lightly disregarded. I am not so sure as Carter and Marlow, and I am here replacing it, on grounds that I hope to make clear.

> When Israel out of Egypt came
>   Safe in the sea they trod;
> By day in cloud, by night in flame,
>   Went on before them God.
>
> He brought them with a stretched out hand
>   Dry-footed through the foam,
> Past sword and famine, rock and sand,
>   Lust and rebellion, home.

I never over Horeb heard
   The blast of Advent blow;
No fire-faced prophet brought me word
   Which way behoved me go.

Ascended is the cloudy flame,
   The mount of thunder dumb;
The tokens that to Israel came,
   To me they have not come.

I see the country far away
   Where I shall never stand;
The heart goes where no footstep may
   Into the promised land.

The realm I look upon and die
   Another man will own;
He shall attain the heaven that I
   Perish and have not known.

But I will go where they are hid
   That never were begot,
To my inheritance amid
   The nation that is not

(MP II)

[Where mixed with me the sandstorms drift,
   And nerve and heart and brain
Are ashes for the air to lift
   And lightly shower again.][9]

Structurally, the poem can be divided into a two-verse prologue (the account of the Exodus) and a series of reflections by
the narrator about the personal significance of these events. The
text of the 'prologue' is a straightforward, if highly condensed,
account of the Exodus, the details suggesting and referring to
specific incidents in the biblical account.

'Sword' refers to external opposition (both Pharaoh's armies
and the forces of Amalek). 'Famine, rock and sand' suggest natural
obstacles (the paucity of food and water countered by the springs
issuing from the rocks, quails and manna).

'Rebellion' suggests both internal tribal unrest (the sons of Korah, Aaron and Miriam, and Aaron's sons) and Moses' own breaking of God's command, for Numbers XX.viii–xii tells that God instructed Moses to 'speak ye unto the rock . . . and it shall give forth his water' but what Moses in fact did was to coerce the rock rather than address it: 'And Moses lifted up his hand, and with his rod he smote the rock twice.' The punishment for this is the heart of the story as Housman interprets it: 'And the Lord spake unto Moses . . . Because ye believed me not . . ., therefore ye shall not bring this congregation into the land which I have given them'[10] – 'given them' but not given you. Moses cannot even hope to enter the land of the promise – although others will – and this ban provides the emotional cord linking the prophet to the poet, as we shall see.

'Lust' suggests the forbidden, pagan worship of the golden calf, associated with fertility rituals of the most obvious type. Thus, although apparently passed over in silence, the incident of the golden calf is implicit in the reference, and every single event of the Exodus is touched upon.

It is noteworthy that the manuscript[11] shows an open choice between 'rebellion' and 'idolatry'. The former can and does refer to several separate incidents not otherwise indicated; the latter can refer only to the incident of the golden calf, already present at least peripherally in the ambience of 'lust'. I suspect this was Laurence Housman's reason for opting in favour of 'rebellion', and I suspect that this would also have been Housman's final choice.

The events are not arranged chronologically but rather in a logical sequence moving inward: the active enemy, the passive opposition of nature, tribal unrest, and individual defiance and transgression.

It is with the gradual shift from the historico-biblical context of the 'prologue' to the personal focus of the main body of the poem that undertextual problems arise. The historical frame does not cut off abruptly but gradually gives way in verses 3 and 4 to the personal application. Mount Sinai/Horeb is specified as the central locale of these two verses, with the blowing of the shofar and the giving of Torah ('the way'), after which the manifestations of God (the pillars of cloud and of fire and the thunder) vanish from the material world. Thus, God's 'tokens' vanish from the sight of 'Israel', but they have never been manifested to the narrator at all. He was not at Sinai.

In these two verses, the isolated, individual 'I' compares his state with that of the collective, communally tribal 'Israel' which still affirms each year at the Passover seder that every member of the tribe is to regard himself as having been personally present at Sinai. It is at least possible that Housman was aware of this ceremonial.

With verse 5, the locale shifts from Mount Sinai to Mount Nevo, as the focus shifts from the collective, 'Israel', to the individual, Moses, who then modulates into 'I', the poet-persona. It was Moses who looked upon a land of promise for which his heart yearned but which, forbidden to him because of his disobedience to God's express command, was promised to his successor. It was from Mount Nevo that, dying, he looked upon 'the realm', and there that he died.

Mount Nevo is the traditional site, now in Jordan, of these events, but one should note that the Hebrew word for 'mountain peak' is 'pisgah'. The spot would be designated in Hebrew as (transliterated) 'Pisgat Nevo', in English 'Nevo Peak', or usually simply 'Mount Pisgah' ('mountain peak'). So there are two 'Mount Pisgahs' involved. The first is the top of Nevo from which Moses looked upon his promised land to the west. The second is Housman's 'Mount Pisgah', the field above his home in Fockbury, from which as a child he was accustomed to look at his own promised land, Shropshire, his 'land of lost content' (*ASL* XL). This was the spot referred to in *LP* XXXIX ('And I would climb the beacon / That looked to Wales away'). The two vantage points are merged in verse 5, as the biblical promised land is implicitly conflated with Shropshire, and the prophet modulates into the poet.

It is with the dying Moses that the narrator identifies himself, permitted to look upon, but forbidden to touch, the land of Canaan. In these two verses, then, we hear the voice of the dying Moses filtered through another consciousness.

It is necessary to turn to biography to understand why Housman saw in Moses an echo of himself. Like the prophet, he had glimpsed a 'promised land' which was forbidden to him by God's decree. Moses Jackson, the man he loved passionately, was as forbidden to him as Canaan was to Moses, and he, like Moses, had to content himself with the sight of what he most desired without, because of the Divine edict, being permitted to possess it. A close and enduring friendship was all that was possible. Like Moses, he too was permitted only to gaze longingly at what he was forbidden by God to possess, not in his case the physical macrocosm of the land from which he was forever divided by death but the metaphoric microcosm of his friend, beloved, longed for, forbidden by 'The laws of God, the laws of man' (*LP* XII), from whom he was forever divided by life. In this identification with the biblical Moses, Housman united himself poetically with that Moses' modern namesake.

Only after this does the focus narrow to the narrator and concentrate exclusively on him as he contemplates his own death. Unlike that of the biblical figure, his inheritance is not the living nation but 'the nation that is not', the unbegotten, the dead, the non-existent. Here, the questionable added verse both strengthens this identification of the poet/narrator with Moses and clarifies it. The non-existence he evokes consists of the dissolution of all that is essentially human ('nerve and heart and brain') and the absorption of the residue into the natural world of sand and ash, a sterile dry world of dust.

The very terms 'sand' and 'ash' recall the burnt-out fire and the desert setting of the 'prologue', providing a rounded and satisfying structural frame for the text. This added verse cannot but refer the reader back to the scenes of the Biblical events of the 'prologue'.

Note also that in addition to the death of the narrator in a desert setting, which recalls that of Moses, the residue is in the form of 'ashes'. Housman's intention, which was carried out, was that his body be cremated, literally turned into 'ashes for the air to lift', and this completes the identification process of poet, prophet and persona.

It is now appropriate to turn to the manuscript text of the poem, one of the earliest Housman ever wrote, the fourth entry in the first notebook of his poetry, dated no later than 1887, the second and third sheets in the manuscript collection now at the Library of Congress in Washington DC.

The first manuscript page shows three groups of verses. The first two verses are marked '[2–A]' and are followed by a blank space the requisite size for an additional verse. Then we find verses 6 and 7, marked '[2–B]' and the small space between them is marked '> <', indicating that another verse insertion between them is being contemplated. Then we find a second blank space the same size as the first blank. This is followed by the debatable verse, marked '[2–C]'.

On the following sheet we find a blank space, followed by the fifth verse, marked '[3–A]'. Then there is another verse-sized blank, followed by verses 4 and 3, in that order, marked '[2–B]'. The notations in brackets seem to indicate the order of the verses as originally projected by Housman. The debatable verse is clearly part of this tentative poetic structure. Nor can I discern any indication at all that it does not belong with the other verses on these two sheets, all of which were ultimately integrated to create the poem as we have it.

As the foregoing makes clear, my own inclination is to agree with Laurence Housman and Philip Gardner, who calls it the 'last, and perhaps most beautiful, stanza', and adds that its removal has resulted in 'a poem which . . . ends abruptly where it once ended perfectly'.[12] I would only add that it seems to me that structurally, linguistically, figuratively and psychologically, as well as in terms of the manuscript evidence, it not only fits the poem but is essential to it. I am therefore in complete disagreement with Carter, Marlow and all the editors after Laurence Housman who have excised this verse. I believe it is indeed the eighth verse of the poem and an integral part of it.

Other problems are raised by this poem. The promised land is usually implicitly identified by critics as the Christian heaven which another will enter even if the narrator will not. This is true as far as it goes, but it misses several points, for this is not a Christian poem, and to read it as such is to misread it. In part it is a very personal poem, and in part a very Jewish one. What it is not in any way is Christian.

The reading as a personal poem has been largely explored above. It need only be added that in this reading the denial of the Promised Land to the persona is a reference to his friend's marriage (giving 'ownership' of the land to 'another man') and departure from England. The gender of the legitimate 'owner' is of course appropriately shifted, as in many other poems. This gave that which he most desired (his 'promised land') to another and denied him even the consolation of almost daily contact, exiling him psychologically.

It has already been suggested that Housman had at least some knowledge of Hebrew. It seems that he was also both interested in and knowledgeable about Judaism,[13] and this poem is, in some ways, a very Jewish poem in more than its subject. The poem can be read simply (or not so simply) as a poem of exile and abandonment, of the yearning for what is attainable only in the imagination but in all logic never in reality. On one level, this is a poem about the essence of exile.

Tom Burns Haber connects this poem to Housman's despair at his mother's death and consequent sense that God, 'the guide and salvation of others', had abandoned him, denying him both guidance and sustenance 'in the time of his greatest need'.[14] This may or may not have entered into the emotional stratum on which the poem draws, but there is another, and perhaps more appropriate, source for the imagery: the Bible itself – and the Rabbinic commentary upon it.

The 'cloudy flame' has vanished, and the 'mount of thunder' is silent; God has withdrawn His direct presence from the world, becoming the hidden God of Rabbinic commentary, the absent God of the Bible in which Housman was well versed. This concept is made explicit in Deuteronomy XXXI. xvii–xviii ('I will forsake them, and I will hide my face from them . . . And I will surely hide my face') and xlv ('thou art a God that hideth thyself'). The age of miracles is over, and man has been left to make his own way as best he can without manifest guidance, immediate, divine guidance. This is the generation that has neither heard the prophet nor seen the tokens.

Housman may have identified himself not only with the prophet but with the people of Israel as a whole, condemned to a long exile from that for which they yearned. This suggests that the animating spirit of this poem is Jewish and that what we find is not so much a denial of the Christian concept of the Resurrection (which Housman did indeed reject in poem after poem) as the acceptance of this very Jewish concept universalized. Another man, an orthodox Christian, may perhaps attain to a Christian heaven, but not the poet who sees his 'inheritance amid / The nation that is not', that is to say the nation that is not a nation, that is in eternal exile, the people of Israel, dispersed, scorned, apparently abandoned by God, as Housman felt that he had been abandoned both by God and by Moses Jackson ('He would not stay for me to stand and gaze', *AP* VII) who are thus in a sense conflated – Moses, the 'man of God', is united on one side with Moses, Housman's personal God, and on the other side with the forsaken poet himself. In some way, Housman seems to have felt spiritually linked to the people who stood at the time as a paradigm of dispossession.

If reading the above lyric with an eye on its personal and Jewish themes yields a very different undertext from that deriving from a solid middle-class, conventionally Victorian, Christian reading, this is hardly to be wondered at given its theme. Again, we should note that Housman never published these verses since they were perhaps both too personal and too explicitly non-Christian. When dealing with specifically Christian material, as in the following poems, Housman is even more iconoclastic, and a great deal more careful to provide a mask for the undertext – so careful, indeed, that it is possible to miss the presence of the undertext entirely. For the next poem is a denial of the very basis of Christianity itself, not the Resurrection but the Incarnation.

THE CARPENTER'S SON

'Here the hangman stops his cart:
Now the best of friends must part.
Fare you well, for ill fare I:
Live, lads, and I will die.

'Oh, at home had I but stayed
'Prenticed to my father's trade,
Had I stuck to plane and adze,
I had not been lost, my lads.

'Then I might have built perhaps
Gallows-trees for other chaps,
Never dangled on my own,
Had I but left ill alone.

'Now, you see, they hang me high,
And the people passing by
Stop to shake their fists and curse;
So 'tis come from ill to worse.

'Here hang I, and right and left
Two poor fellows hang for theft:
All the same's the luck we prove,
Though the midmost hangs for love.

'Comrades all, that stand and gaze,
Walk henceforth in other ways;
See my neck and save your own:
Comrades all, leave ill alone.

'Make some day a decent end,
Shrewder fellows than your friend.
Fare you well, for ill fare I:
Live, lads, and I will die.'

(*ASL* XLVII)

This poem, from *A Shropshire Lad*, was published by Housman himself, who took great care to disguise its true subject, as noted above. The title, ambiguous as it is, does not clearly indicate that this is a treatment of the Crucifixion. Like so many other of his titles, it is equivocal. The text is also deliberately misleading, opening the way to more than one possible (and erroneous) interpretation. The hyphenated 'gallows-tree' collapses the Victorian gallows into the Cross (the 'Tree'). 'Dangled' and 'hung' are also ambiguous, equally applicable to both modes of execution.

'Love', with its multiplicity of possible meanings, is the most ambiguous word of all. As Keith Jebb has noted, the 'ill' that the speaker could not 'leave alone' 'seems to have been love [but] what that love is we are not told'.[15] There has for long been an underground tradition that Christ was homosexual, but this is such a shocking notion that when it was presented only a few years ago in San Francisco it all but caused riots. Nevertheless, this idea may just possibly lie at the heart of the poem.

A. F. Allison considered this poem 'ridiculous in character and situation'.[16] C. B. Tinker thought it a 'horrible burlesque of the Crucifixion'.[17] It is, of course, neither 'ridiculous' nor a 'burlesque'. Marlow noted the 'ironic twist' given to the familiar phrase 'Leave well enough alone' which results in paradox,[18] but remained silent on the nature of that paradox. Nesca Robb found a 'startling reminiscence of Calvary' but was more interested in the general moral.[19]

S. G. Andrews proceeded to twist the poem almost as its author was accustomed to twisting the Bible itself. He pointed out, most truly, that allusion usually functions to familiarize the unfamiliar but thought that here the 'key motifs and details which parallel the story of Christ', that he is a carpenter's son executed between two thieves 'for love', serve rather to defamiliarize the familiar. So far, so good. He then proceeded to misread entirely, stating that whereas Christ 'died for love' of all mankind, the eponymous hero here 'had committed some crime of passion [with no double meaning to the word "passion" at all]', thus shifting the nature of the parallel. Let us pause to note that nothing *in the text* suggests the nature of the 'love' for which the gallows is the penalty. Andrews continued, the 'repeated allusions to Christ do not help us to understand the carpenter's son or his fate. Instead, they encourage us to transfer the speech . . . to the mouth of Christ and to search for a sense in which that speech might apply to him [*sic*]'. He concluded that the poem suggests the need to learn a philosophical acceptance of evil and suffering, an idea 'developed by means of an unusual use of allusion' which, instead of clarifying the carpenter's son, 'reinterprets the significance of the Crucifixion' by suggesting that the lesson is the futility of warring with evil and that practical, realistic, 'shrewder' folk will 'learn to accept it as an inevitable condition in an imperfect universe'.[20]

The common error in all these readings is to separate the titular character from Christ, thus reducing the poem to allusion, parallel or 'burlesque'. In fact, here we do not have a parallel suggested by allusion, much less a 'burlesque'. Here we have a treatment of the Crucifixion itself. The titular character is not like Christ nor reminiscent of Christ; he *is* Christ. Haber, who understood this point, called the poem 'an affront to orthodoxy'[21] which of course it is, for as W. L. Phelps noted, the point of view is detached 'not only from conventional religious belief but from conventional reverence',[22] a judgment which, if non-specific, has the virtue of being to the point. Of course the approach is not conventionally pious, and Phelps at least seems to have understood what the poem was about without becoming distracted by its theological implications concerning the nature of evil.

The most nearly satisfactory reading, neatly balancing the text and the undertext, is, not surprisingly, that of Robert Graves. In his admirable essay, he calls this what it is: 'an apocryphal account of the Crucifixion' with daring, if not blasphemous, implications. By calling the Cross a 'gallows-tree' and the disciples 'lads' instead of 'brethren' or 'children', Housman sufficiently obscured the identification to produce 'the intended irony of the poem which is strewn with the plainest scriptural allusions'.[23] One of these plain scriptural references Housman uses to provide what Eugene D. Le Mire calls the crowning irony: his entreaty to men '*not* to follow Him'.[24] Housman's typical turning of biblical motifs on their heads is nowhere better illustrated.

But even Robert Graves, perceptive as he is, missed what I see as the main thrust of the text. There are only two ways of regarding

Christ: either he was a carpenter's son, Joshua Ben Joseph of Nazareth, or he was the son of God, the Messiah. If the latter, then in tampering with evil He indeed 'stuck' to His Father's 'trade'. But that 'trade' is specified by 'plane and adze' as carpentry rather than Godship. He indeed must be, then, what he is called in the title: the [mortal] carpenter's son and not God's. These lines only make sense as a denial of Christ's divinity. In denying the Sonship of Jesus, we have an account of the Crucifixion which also denies its theological import, making it a common execution.

To return to Jebb: 'Housman's Christ will not rise from the dead.'[25] The divine Christ is replaced by the human Joshua; the entire text is an affirmation of his merely human status, a human status emphasized by the condemned man's own words. As a man suffering human 'justice', he is as appropriate an object of sympathy as anyone incarcerated in Portland or being hung in Shrewsbury jail. This is the carefully camouflaged undertext, and carefully camouflaged it had to be to escape even greater condemnation as the most outrageous blasphemy (at least from the Christian point of view). If in '1887' man was perhaps raised to Christhood, here Christ is lowered, or perhaps restored, to mere manhood, and there is no 'perhaps' about it. He is not 'The Carpenter's Son' but only the carpenter's son.

Let us also not forget that, recognizing the executed felon as Christ, we are dealing with the same entity whose 'laws' were responsible for the persecution of Oscar Wilde and, potentially at least, of Housman himself had his masquerade been less successful. The carpenter's son's (whether capitalized or not) attempts to combat evil loosed additional evil on the world, and as in some sense the author of persecution, it is poetic justice that he was himself persecuted. Here, from a Christian point of view, is the ultimate combination of blasphemies, all neatly enclosed in one package and so heavily masked by its wrappings that, although it makes the Christian reader distinctly uneasy, its essence, being unthinkable, is unrecognizable.

Housman returned to the subject of Christ in another poem at which we shall now look.

EASTER HYMN

If in that Syrian garden, ages slain,
You sleep, and know not you are dead in vain,

Nor even in dreams behold how dark and bright
Ascends in smoke and fire by day and night
The hate you died to quench and could but fan,
Sleep well and see no morning, son of man.

But if, the grave rent and the stone rolled by,
At the right hand of majesty on high
You sit, and sitting so remember yet
Your tears, your agony and bloody sweat,
Your cross and passion and the life you gave,
Bow hither out of heaven and see and save.

(*MP* I)

Here there is again the exploration of the two possibilities and their implications in a balanced structure in which the positive first verse (here, startlingly, the denial of Christ's divinity) is set against its negative counterpart (even more startlingly, the divinity of Christ). This results in a poem 'poised midway between acceptance and rejection of the Resurrection'.[26] Having looked at Housman's treatment of the Incarnation, we should be quite prepared for the inevitable result of his consideration of the Resurrection. A poem that at first was 'poised midway' between the possible alternatives has, by the end, made up its mind, and it reaches – inevitably – the same conclusion as 'The Carpenter's Son'.

The 'hate' that 'dark and bright / Ascends in smoke and fire by day and night' and which Jesus 'died to quench and could but fan' evokes both the pillars of smoke and fire of 'When Israel out of Egypt came' (the 'tokens' of Divine guidance) and the religious persecutions and burnings at the stake with which history is all too full. Thus, religious persecution *becomes* the still-present 'token' of God's presence in the world.

But the poem says that 'you died to quench' this 'hate'. With what religious persecution was Jesus' life – and death – connected? It was the persecution by the pagan Romans of the Jews, and the rumblings of revolt in Judea against the attempts of Rome to delegitimize Judaism, a revolt which burst out in literal flame less than a century later with the rebellion of Rabbi Akiva and General Bar Kochba against the Imperium and the burning of Jerusalem in 72 AD. This would indicate that Jesus was attempting to 'quench' the flame of revolt against Rome, and what a pretty kettle of both religious and historical fish this provides!

That Jesus' ministry did in fact 'fan' the flames of religious hatred and persecution, not only against the Jews but between opposing Christian sects, is, on the other hand, obvious from even the most cursory reading of history. His death was, indeed, 'in vain'.

The first verse, then, considers Christ as an idealistic and well-meaning (if singularly ineffective) man but no more, while the second considers that He actually was more. Each verse begins with 'If', if 'You' were only a 'son of man' and if 'You' were the Saviour being the controlling conditions, and each verse examines the logical results of its own 'if'.

In the first verse, the 'if' postulates an endless dreamless sleep, Housman's usual description of death, which denies not only Jesus' own resurrection but his promise of eternal life in heaven to all believers. His death is ascribed to his attempts to substitute love for hate, attempts which only resulted in an accretion of hate, in the 'smoke and fire' of religious persecution. In this sense, he 'dies for love' as in the preceding poem, but creates only further hate.

If, continues the second verse, Jesus was indeed the Messiah and is now ensconced at God's right hand in heaven, and if, and this second understood 'if' is not to be ignored, so ensconced, He has not completely forgotten the persecution which He underwent in life and how that life ended, if these two postulates are true, then the time has certainly arrived when He should return to earth ('Bow hither out of heaven'), look on the results of His first ministry ('and see'), and undo the harm He has done ('and save').

The title of the poem suggests not only the Crucifixion which is commemorated at Easter, but the promise of the Resurrection, the very subject of the 'if'. And it is a hymn, a prayer. But there is no response. The prayer is unanswered. There is no salvation for the world, which continues to run 'ruinward' (*MP* XLIII). The balance of the evidence of man's own experience tilts inexorably in favour of the conclusion of the first verse.

All that Jesus can do is lie in death like everyone else, and as a man the poet can wish for him the finest benison, endless sleep. As the Messiah, He must instead be indicted for forgetting His own experiences, responsibilities and promises, and the poet herein pens the indictment, combining it with a final plea for Divine intervention, a plea that is answered only by silence. The kindest possible conclusion, then, is that he is indeed the carpenter's son, but not The Carpenter's Son.

The foregoing examination of those poems in which Housman directly handled a biblical theme suggests that he indeed identified himself with those who were in some way the victims of Divine Justice as well as with those who were the victims of human 'justice' and that, in fact, he saw little difference between 'the laws of God' and 'the laws of man', which were equally unjust. His sympathies were always on the side of the 'Culprit'.

It further suggests that Housman's vaunted atheism was in fact religious faith turned inside out. He knew what he was rejecting: not only the Christian faith in which he had been raised but also Judaism. He did not reject religion without giving it every chance, and it is impossible not to feel, for example at the conclusion of the last poem discussed, that the author hoped to the very end that he had been wrong, that there was indeed a God – and a Saviour – but that this hope, like so many in his life, was doomed to disappointment.

Finally, it is clear that the same techniques which Housman used in handling individual verses and allusions could be – and were – applied to complete narratives, although far more carefully disguised. The paradoxical result (which I suspect Housman would have grimly relished) is that although his use of individual references has been analysed by more than one outraged critic, his treatment of full narratives has largely been accepted at face value, or misinterpreted, or twisted, or else ignored – until now.

Notes

1. Davis P. Harding, 'A Note on Housman's Use of the Bible', *MLN* LXV (March 1950) 205–7, and Vincent Friemarck, 'Further Notes on Housman's Use of the Bible', *MLN* LXVII (December 1952) 548–50.
2. The standard abbreviations – *ASL, LP, MP* and *AP* – are used throughout. The texts are those of *A. E. Housman: Collected Poems and Selected Prose*, ed. Christopher Ricks (London: Allen Lane, The Penguin Press, 1988).
3. Raymond Mortimer, 'Housman Relics', *The New Statesman and Nation* XII (24 October 1936) 631 and 634.
4. P. G. Naiditch, *A. E. Housman at University College, London: The Election of 1892* (Leiden: E. J. Brill, 1988) p. 150.
5. A. E. Housman, 'Horatiana [I]', in *The Classical Papers of A. E. Housman*, 3 vols, eds J. Diggle and F. R. D. Goodyear (Cambridge: Cambridge University Press, 1972) vol. I, pp. 1–8.
6. Verlyn Flieger, *Splintered Light: Logos and Language in Tolkien's World*

(Grand Rapids, Mich.: Wm. [*sic*] Eerdmans, 1983) p. 155.

7. A. E. Housman, Letter to Grant Richards, 9 October 1928, *The Letters of A. E. Housman,* ed. Henry Maas (London: Rubert Hart-Davis, 1971) p. 271.

8. *The Collected Poems of A. E. Housman,* ed. John Carter (London: Jonathan Cape, 1939), 'Note on the Text,' p. 248. For Norman Marlow's acquiescence, see his *A. E. Housman: Scholar and Poet* (London: Routledge & Kegan Paul, 1958) p. 125.

9. A. E. Housman, *More Poems,* ed. Laurence Housman (New York: Alfred A. Knopf, 1936) p. 7.

10. This and other quotations from the Bible are taken from the Authorized King James version.

11. A. E. Housman, the Manuscript Remnants now in the Library of Congress, Washington DC, Item A-2, sheet 2.

12. Philip Gardner (ed.), *A. E. Housman: The Critical Heritage* (London: Routledge, 1992) p. 38 and p. 54 n. 88.

13. Laurence Housman reports his brother as saying that '[t]he Hebrews had a higher code of morals than the Egyptians, and did not allow themselves to be perverted from non-belief in a future life by Egyptian superstition. The Sadducees represented the orthodox religion . . .: the Pharisees were the modernists' (*My Brother, A. E. Housman* (New York: Charles Scribner's Sons, 1938 pp. 114–15), a comment which could only have been made by someone who had investigated the tenets of Judaism and considered them in the context of ancient belief systems, and which also, incidentally, shows more knowledge of the politico-religious situation in Judaea at the time of Christ than would have been common.

14. Tom Burns Haber, *A. E. Housman* (Boston: Twayne, 1967) p. 31.

15. Keith Jebb, *A. E. Housman* (Bridgend, Mid Glamorgan: Seren Books, 1992) p. 82.

16. A. F. Allison, 'The Poetry of A. E. Housman', *RES* 19 (1943) 276–84.

17. C. B. Tinker, 'Housman's Poetry', *Yale Review* XXV (Autumn, 1935) 84–95.

18. Marlow, op. cit., pp. 147–8.

19. Nesca A. Robb, *Four in Exile* (Port Washington, NY: Kennikat Press, 1948) p. 21.

20. S. G. Andrews, no title, *Explicator* (October 1960), reprinted in *Explicator Cyclopedia,* vol. I, 174–5.

21. Tom Burns Haber, 'The Spirit of the Perverse in A. E. H.', *The South Atlantic Quarterly* XL (1941) 368–78.

22. William Lyon Phelps, *The Advance of English Poetry in the 20th Century* (New York: Dodd, Mead, 1918) pp. 68–9.

23. Robert Graves, 'The Carpenter's Son', *On English Poetry* (London: William Heinemann, 1922) pp. 31–3.

24. Eugene D. Le Mire, 'The Irony and Ethics of *A Shropshire Lad', University of Windsor Review* I (Spring, 1965) 109–27.

25. Jebb, op. cit.

26. Haber, op. cit., p. 120.

12

The Spirit of *Haiku* and A. E. Housman

Takeshi Obata

If one may start with a short account of the characteristics of traditional Japanese verse, the following views of Anthony Thwaite are appropriate:

> ... its gentle melancholy;.... the sad lessons of transience which nature teaches us, the quiet pleasures of solitude ...
>
> *(Japanese Verse:* Penguin, p. xxxviii)

In addition to the above-mentioned characteristics, he also refers to its 'tough stoicism' and 'humorous, deflationary, sharp-eyed little poems of *senryu'*, which is written in the same 17-syllable form as the *haiku*. Some of these characteristics may be shared by every nation loving poetry in all ages. I venture to say, however, that there are some similarities between the English and the Japanese in their liking for emotion in poetry, though I know that I consciously disregard great differences in poetical forms and traditions between the two peoples.

It is true that there has been interaction between them. Concerning the influence of English poetry upon Japanese poets in the modern age, it is often said that, before and after 1910, some Japanese poets were deeply influenced by the Pre-Raphaelites: Ariake Kambara (1876–1952) was an ardent admirer of D. G. Rossetti. And some young lovers of poetry in those days were fond of reading in translation the poems of Robert Herrick, Thomas Gray and other lyric poets. They were surely charmed with lyricism expressed at once briefly and deeply in short poems. On the other hand, it is a well-known fact that *haiku* attracted the interest of poets associated with the Imagist Movement.

Among many lyrical poets, I think A. E. Housman must be

one of those whose poetry bears some similarity to *haiku*. *A Shropshire Lad* was first and favourably reviewed by Professor Tokuboku Hirata (1873–1943) in the August 1916 issue of *Eigo Seinen* (vol. VIII, no. 9). He praised the poet for the refined style of his poetry, referring to its indescribable pathos and freshness with a ballad-like simplicity and lightness of tone. (See *The Housman Journal,* vol. 8, 1982, pp. 29–35.) What Professor Hirata wrote about the characteristics of Housman's poetry might be partly related to the views which Anthony Thwaite expressed concerning traditional Japanese verse.

It is time to draw attention to some rough resemblances between A. E. Housman's poems and *haiku* or *senryu*. By giving several instances where there seem to be similar qualities of poetical emotion, and by indicating that Housman's poems might well be accepted in the pagan tradition of Japanese verse in defiance of the deep gap in culture, I should like to suggest, though it may be nothing new to say, that poetic image and imagination delicately respond to one another beyond time and space.

First of all, though, R. H. Blyth's views on *waka* and *haiku*. According to James Kirkup's brief account of Blyth, he was an Essexman, born on 3 December 1898. 'He read widely in English Literature' in London University and 'in 1924 he left England to ... take up a post as assistant professor at Keijo University' (now Seoul). 'He became interested in Japanese Culture and Zen Buddhism in particular. After the war, he began teaching at Gakushuin and, at the same time, he became private tutor to the Crown Prince, now Emperor Akihito' (*The Genius of Haiku,* p. 1). He published a considerable number of books on *zen* and *haiku*. He briefly summarizes the points of *haiku* as follows:

> *Haiku* are [sic] ordinary things in ordinary words. Further, *haiku* is both more physical and more spiritual ... More physical in that it goes back to the sensation; more spiritual in eschewing beauty and morality and thought.
>
> (*The Genius of Haiku*, pp. 78–9)

We may naturally compare the well-known sentence in *The Name and Nature of Poetry* by A. E. Housman: 'Poetry indeed seems to me more physical than intellectual.'

Haiku has its 'season word' (kigo) 'or expression hinting at the time of the year appropriate to the context ... Many kigo are self-explanatory' (*Japanese Verse*, p. lxvii) and this 'kigo', if it is effectively used, easily conveys a common poetic emotion to readers and calls forth a sympathetic response in them. Intelligence and understanding by the readers are not necessarily demanded.

With regard to Housman's words and themes in his poetry, it may be helpful to quote Professor Norman Page's views: 'it looks as though Housman has the uncanny power of creating out of banal materials literary effects that are powerful, even unforgettable' (*Housman Society Journal*, vol. 17, 1991, p. 35). And also with regard to Housman's lyric topoi, Professor John Bayley tells us that 'they leave intact the solitude of the poet's own experiences but make them appear to be common to all . . .' (*Housman's Poems*, Clarendon Press, 1992, p. 110). In both the best *haiku* and in Housman's poems, 'banal materials' and 'topoi' easily penetrate into readers' minds and evoke their sympathy.

Basho (1644–94), who made efforts to establish the way *haiku* (and *haikai*) were to take, advocated that 'poetry was to be brought back to daily life', and expressed his views as follows:

> The poet should 'mingle with the herd yet preserve a noble mind'; he should 'beautify plain speech'; he should always retain his sympathy with frailty, and feel for the *sabi* – patinated loneliness and desolation – in nature; . . .
>
> (*Japanese Verse*, p. lxvi)

One may perhaps say that the attitude towards the poetry of Basho and Housman is quite similar, apart from the spirit of *sabi*.

Issa (1763–1827), one of the great names in the history of *haiku*, 'brought *haiku* down to the level of the common man':

> His diction was much more that of the street and his personal miseries awakened in him a deep compassion for other living beings which he uses to satirize man's heartlessness: . . .
>
> (*Japanese Verse*, p. lxvii)

When we remember the monosyllabic brief expressions in Housman's poems, his feelings for young soldiers or country lads and his ironic views on fatalism, surely it can be seen that there is something in common between Housman and the *haiku* poets.

There are so many *haiku* poets in a sense; most Japanese, both young and old alike, could squeeze out something of *haiku*, whether it is good or poor. And there are several schools in the *haiku* world which were separately developed. The spirit of *haiku*, however, is considered to be ultimately traced back to Zen. Accordingly, it may not be too much to say that *haiku* poets seem to have shown basic resemblances in poetical ideas, as compared with the English poets, though of course every poet has his or her own poetic characteristics.

I proceed to take up some examples of poetic ideas and emotions in *haiku* poems which remind one of some of A. E. Housman's poems.

In the following *haiku* by Shiki, there is apparently no poetical thought except the scene of ants parading in the height of summer:

Summer sky / clear after rain – / Ants on parade.

(*Zen Poetry,* Penguin, p. 129)

The response from the reader will naturally depend on what he feels, but I am reminded of the image of young soldiers marching without thinking of their duties or destiny:

On the idle hill of summer,
    Sleepy with the flow of streams,
Far I hear the steady drummer
    Drumming like a noise in dreams.
                        . . .
    Soldiers marching, all to die.

(*ASL* XXXV)

The following is Kyorai's (1651–1740) *haiku:*

Even in my town / now, I sleep / like a traveller.

(*Zen Poetry*, p. 117)

This poem tells us about the fact of his sleep, but what the poet reveals to us, keeping sorrow under control, seems to be not only a temporary sleep in this unsettled world but also the uncertainty of life. The situation in the following poem, although more complicated, seems similar:

> He hears: no more remembered
>   In fields where I was known,
> Here I lie down in London
>   And turn to rest alone.

(*ASL* LII)

The word 'turn' suggests that 'I' cannot fall asleep easily. His sleep in London is temporary 'like a traveller', and his spirit wanders 'far in a western brookland' (*ASL* LII). And even in his home town, his quiet sleep cannot be assured. His dreams do not give him peaceful repose, but leave him alone to wander like a ghost:

> My dreams are of a field afar
>   And blood and smoke and shot.
> There in their graves my comrades are,
>   In my grave I am not.

(*MP* XXXIX)

The poetic quintessence of the above poem is comparable with the following *haiku* by Basho.

Sick on a journey / over parched fields / dreams wander on.

(*Zen Poetry*, p. 92)

Housman's pessimistic fatalism (though I do not think it represents the whole of Housman's outlook) may be seen in the following:

> Now through the friendless world we fare
>   And sigh upon the road.

(*ASL* XXXVIII)

> Therefore, since the world has still
> Much good, but much less good than ill . . .

(*ASL* LXII)

His idea of this world may be compared to the *haiku* by Issa (1763–1827):

> Never forget: / we walk on hell, / gazing at flowers.

> (*Zen Poetry,* p. 108)

The flowers we are gazing at are the ones of sorrow that give us trivial joy in this ruthless world:

> But here and there will flower / The solitary stars

> (*ASL* LXIII)

Again, two poems from Issa:

> When plum / blooms – / a freeze in hell.

> (*Zen Poetry,* p. 104)

> Dew spreads / the seeds of hell / are sown.

> (*Zen Poetry,* p. 111)

These *haiku* seem to respond secretly to Housman's views of life and the world, though there is also apparent the irresistible urge to seize the moment in his case:

> 'Tis spring; come out to ramble
> The hilly brakes around,
> For under thorn and bramble
> About the hollow ground
> The primroses are found.

> (*ASL* XXIX)

We may also remember the well-known poem, 'Loveliest of trees, the cherry now / Is hung with bloom along the bough' (*ASL* II).

One of the characteristics of Housman's poetry often referred to is his humour. I cannot easily tell 'humour' from 'joke' or 'comic spirit', but if it is allowed to use both of them in the way of

rough definition, the following views on Housman's humour by
Professor John Bayley and Professor Norman Page are noteworthy:

> . . . most of his poems – and the best ones – contain jokes of
> one sort or another, as well as buried humour, but jokes are
> serious and meaningful things to him.
>
> (*Housman Society Journal,* vol. 17, 1991, p. 29)

> . . . . Housman's verse in this category surely displays a critical
> approach to life and literature: by detecting absurdities hidden
> just below the surface, he explodes pretentiousness and pomposity.
>
> (*Ibid,* p. 12)

With regard to comic or humorous verses, we also have *senryu,*
which shares the same origin with *haiku* and

> . . . freed from the restrictions on *haiku*, such as season words, . . .
> most often employ a colloquial style and satirize human emo-
> tions and failings.
>
> (*Japanese Verse,* p. xxv)

Blyth tells us very briefly and properly about the humour of *senryu:*

> 'Humour' means joyful, unsentimental pathos that arises from
> the paradox inherent in the nature of things. Poetry and humour
> are thus very close; we may say that they are two different
> aspects of the same thing. Poetry is *satori,* it is seeing all things
> as good. Humour is laughing at all things; in Buddhist parlance,
> seeing that 'all things are empty in their self-nature', and rejoicing
> in this truth.
>
> (*The Genius of Haiku,* p. 121)

When we can take an objective but emotional view of all things
in this world, we may realize that 'they are all empty, without
self, without absolute existence' (*Zen Poetry,* p. 30). Such an attitude towards release from self-centredness may bring us a sense
of humour, through which we may calmly accept our whole being,
and even 'the iniquity of heaven', as nothing.

Isn't there something relevant to the spirit of *senryu* in the nature
of A. E. Housman's poetry? The following *senryu* was quoted by
Blyth as 'a particularly fine example of tragedy and humour united':

He hanged himself / At Ueno, / Facing the Yoshiwara.

(*Ibid*, p. 122)

'Yoshiwara' was a notorious area of brothels located near Ueno Station where, in the old days, many people from the poor districts of Tohoku gathered and dispersed. The man committed suicide at Ueno for 'some wretched prostitute', who may have been sold for her poor family and whom the man had loved. Blyth regards the suicide as a 'kind of parody':

[The parody] also disinfects the scene of all falsity, eternal love, and other sentimentality. We see a human being stripped bare of all but his painful life and solitary death. There is also another element, seen in the place, Ueno, of exhibitionism, a quality of which the greatest men are not free.

(*Ibid.*, p. 123)

This *senryu* makes an impression of ironical nonsense and vainness rather than of individual tragedy, and also reminds us of *ASL* XVI:

> The nettle nods, the wind blows over,
> The man, he does not move,
> The lover of the grave, the lover
> That hanged himself for love.

Professor Bayley indicates that 'this image does not represent the individual tragedy' (*Housman's Poems*, p. 187). And also, as Professor Norman Page properly suggests, 'nonsense beneath the surface' (*Housman Society Journal*, vol. 17) is disclosed. After all, both the *senryu* and Housman's poem represent nothingness caused by the sad consequences, vanity and emptiness of our doings and, eventually, tragicomedy.

Some of the pain and agony we suffer result from thinking:

> Think no more; 'tis only thinking
> Lay lads underground

(*ASL* XLIX)

And if they think, they fasten
Their hands upon their hearts

(LP X)

Shinkichi Takahashi (1901–) writes in his 'Flight of the sparrow'
as follows:

What's Zen? 'Thought,' say masters,
'makes a fool.' How free the brainless
sparrow. Chirrup – before the first 'chi',
a billion years . . .

(Zen Poetry, p. 134)

Human beings, however, cannot easily escape from thinking and
eventually from suffering, which I think A. E. Housman accepted whole-
heartedly. Some of his poems are permeated with his deep and generous
compassion for the weak, though they seem to be blunt and curt.

But dead or living, drunk or dry,
Soldier, I wish you well.

(ASL XXII)

The following *haiku* is by Buson:

I go; / Thou stayest: / Two autumns.

Again Blyth's remark concerning the above poem:

. . . the whole of life is given here, our meetings, our partings,
the world of nature we each live in, different yet the same.
(The Genius of Haiku, p. 110)

Blyth also gives another good example from Buson which
'expresses (by not expressing) that faint feeling of sympathy and
respect we have for man in his struggle with heat and weight
and loneliness and poverty':

The travelling pedlars, / Passing each other /
On the summer moor.

What Blyth saw in Buson's *haiku* must also be related to a sense
of humanity felt in some of Housman's poems, though Housman's
sympathy seems to be directed mostly towards country lads or
unknown soldiers.

One of the main reasons why Housman's poems irresistibly
captivate some Japanese may be explained by what I have hither-
to remarked on *haiku*; some of his poems bear a resemblance to
the characteristics of *haiku* and to some aspects of *senryu*.

Such a similarity to *haiku*, however, may explain why Housman's
poetry escaped modern Japanese poets' notice and had little influence upon them. Some young poets pursued the traditional form
of poems so as to promote a quite new trend, and others objected
to and parted from the traditional verse so as to develop an absolutely new style in poetry. In either case, they must have felt it
difficult in their experiments to realize their ideas with the old style
unchanged or to wipe away the old traces which had penetrated
into the depth of their minds and from which they tried to escape.
Accordingly, though there were some signs and traces in Housman's
poems which reminded them of some Japanese poetic emotions,
his poetry may have made little appeal to those young poets and
to the scholars who were interested in the new tendencies of English poetry. If intellectual novelty had been one of the typical aspects
of Housman's poems, there might have been a greater acceptance
of his poetry among the rising generation in the modern age.
The lyrical emotion of Housman's poems, as seen also in some
traditional Japanese verse, was apparently too similar in its characteristic to penetrate deep into the poetic mind in Japan, though it is
clear that a few scholars took great interest in A. E. Housman's poetry.

Select Bibliography

EDITIONS

Burnett, Archie (ed.), *The Poems of A. E. Housman* (Oxford: Clarendon Press, 1997).

Carter, John (ed.), *The Collected Poems* (London: Jonathan Cape, 1939, etc.).

Carter, John (ed.), *A. E. Housman: Selected Prose* (Cambridge: Cambridge University Press, 1961, corr. repr. 1962).

Diggle, J. and Goodyear, F. D. R. (eds), *The Classical Papers of A. E. Housman*, 3 vols (Cambridge: Cambridge University Press, 1972).

Haber, Tom Burns (ed.), *The Manuscript Poems of A. E. Housman* (London: Oxford University Press, 1955).

Maas, Henry (ed.), *The Letters of A. E. Housman* (London: Rupert Hart-Davis, 1971).

Ricks, Christopher (ed.), *A. E. Housman: Collected Poems and Selected Prose* (London: Allen Lane, The Penguin Press, 1988).

BIBLIOGRAPHICAL AND BIOGRAPHICAL

Alfred Edward Housman: Recollections (Bromsgrove School for the Housman Memorial Fund, 1936). Contains material by Katharine Symons (sister), A. W. Pollard, Laurence Housman, R. W. Chambers, Alan Ker, A. S. F. Gow and John Sparrow.

Carter, John and Sparrow, John (eds), *A. E. Housman: A Bibliography*, 2nd edn, revised by William White (St Paul's Bibliographies, Foxbury Meadow, Godalming, Surrey, 1982).

Gow, A. S. F., *A. E. Housman: A Sketch* (Cambridge: Cambridge University Press, 1936).

Graves, Richard Perceval, *A. E. Housman: The Scholar-Poet* (London and Henley: Routledge & Kegan Paul, 1979).

Housman, Laurence, *A. E. H.* (London: Jonathan Cape, 1937).

Marlow, Norman, *A. E. Housman: Scholar and Poet* (London: Routledge & Kegan Paul, 1958).

Naiditch, P. G., *Problems in the Life and Writings of A. E. Housman* (Beverley Hills: Krown & Spellman, 1995).

Page, Norman, *A. E. Housman: a Critical Biography* (Macmillan, 1983, repr. 1996).

Pugh, John, *Bromsgrove and the Housmans* (Bromsgrove, Worcestershire: The Housman Society, 1974).

Richards, Grant, *Housman: 1897–1936* (London: OUP Humphrey Milford, 1941).

Withers, Percy, *A Buried Life: Personal Recollections of A. E. Housman* (London: Jonathan Cape, 1940).

CRITICAL

Bayley, John, *Housman's Poems* (Oxford: Clarendon Press, 1995).
Gardner, Philip (ed.), *A. E. Housman: The Critical Heritage* (London: Routledge, 1992),
Jebb, Keith, *A. E. Housman* (Bridgend: Seren Books, 1992).
Leggett, B. J., *Housman's Land of Lost Content: A Critical Study of 'A Shropshire Lad'* (Knoxville: University of Tennessee, 1970).
Christopher Ricks (ed.), *A. E. Housman: A Collection of Critical Essays* (Englewood Cliffs, NJ: Prentice-Hall, 1968).

There are numerous essays of bibliographical, biographical and critical interest in the annual volumes of the *Housman Society Journal* from 1974 onwards.

During 1996, the Housman Society were responsible for the publication of *Housman's Places*, by Robin Shaw, *Unkind to Unicorns*, a selection of the light verse edited by Roy Birch, and *The Westerly Wanderer*, a short life by Jeremy Bourne.

Index